BERNARD HARE

Bernard Hare was born in 1958 into a Leeds mining family. He was educated at grammar school and gained a BA in applied Social Studies at Hatfield Polytechnic, after which he became a social worker in London. But following the miners' strike of 1984 he dropped out of the system and returned to Leeds, and has since worked variously as a mechanic, community worker and removal man. He now writes, plays chess, and works in community arts – he has edited *Reflections*, a collection of pieces by the creative writing class at East Leeds Family Learning Centre, and *Flatlands*, an anthology of writing and a CD of music put together by the Flatlands Community Arts Group, which he co-founded.

'A cross between a grim fairytale and a reflective, brazen anecdote. Hare's honesty about himself and his motives, and the detail of the blasted lives on this Leeds estate, are what makes it such a marvellous read.'
Alexander Masters, *Daily Mail*

'An astonishing account'
Anne Fine, Books of the Year, *Sunday Herald*

'Hare's prose is punchy, his anecdotes entertaining . . . But *Urban Grimshaw* is most memorable for its tenderness'
Toby Lichtig, *Observer*

'He writes with laconic self-deprecation, black humour and a humane, ever-present sense of railing against the system that failed Urban and his gang. The book is as exceptional as the bonds Hare formed.'
Tina Jackson, *Metro*

'As a record of contemporary Britain, it is searing . . . Hare is never sensationalist, sentimental, judgemental or self-regarding.'
Sheena Joughin, *Times Literary Supplement*

'Extraordinary for two reasons: it gives a voice to the voiceless, the illiterate underclass children failed by every adult in their lives since birth, from parents to social workers to government. And, to Hare's eternal credit, in parts it's deeply, darkly funny.'
Suzanne Harrington, *Irish Examiner*

'It reads like a novel – a gripping, vivid, deeply affecting piece of work'
Decca Aitkenhead, *New Statesman*

'Ultimately, this is an uplifting story, but the book brings out the failures of the criminal justice system in protecting these children.'
John Cooper, *The Times*

'A modern-day *Kes*'   Angela Barnes, *Yorkshire Evening Post*

'An eye-opening story that grips like a novel.'
Luke Richardson, *Books Quarterly*

BERNARD HARE
URBAN GRIMSHAW AND THE SHED CREW

SCEPTRE

First published in Great Britain in 2005 by Hodder and Stoughton
A division of Hodder Headline

This edition published in 2006

A Sceptre paperback

2

A CIP catalogue record for this title
is available from the British Library

ISBN 0 340 83735 7

Typeset in Sabon by Hewer Text UK Ltd, Edinburgh
Printed and bound by Clays Ltd, St Ives plc

Hodder Headline's policy is to use papers that are natural, renewable
and recyclable products and made from wood grown in sustainable
forests. The logging and manufacturing processes are expected to
conform to the environmental regulations of the country of origin.

Hodder and Stoughton Ltd
A division of Hodder Headline
338 Euston Road
London NW1 3BH

AUTHOR'S NOTE

I couldn't decide whether to dedicate this book to the kids of the Shed Crew (now all adults), to their kids, to my agent, or to Angela Pearce, an eighteen-year-old who was brutally murdered on our estate by a group of young people not unlike the Shed Crew. In the end, I decided to dedicate it to them all.

To the Shed Crew, because they have enriched my life in so many ways. They have forgiven me my foibles as I have forgiven them theirs – and that makes them family. It's like I've got a dozen kids. Those who were able to have contributed little poems and ditties, which they wrote at the time, and which I kept tucked away in an old shoebox. To protect identities I've changed all the names and some locations, but this a true story. These kids are real. They exist. They opened my eyes and they sobered me up, for which I am grateful.

To their kids – and at the last count there were fourteen – because I hope they get a better deal than their mums and dads, who we failed in so many ways. We can't really call ourselves a civilised society when children must lead lives of Dickensian squalor. Social exclusion is an interesting concept to those who don't suffer it, but a nightmare to those who do. Despite it, the Shed Crew have mostly turned into good parents because they didn't want their kids to go through what they did. Hopefully, their kids will look back and laugh at the grim times suffered by their parents as they sail into a twenty-first century full of freedom and opportunity – although I wouldn't bet on it.

To my agent, Maggie, because she has fostered this book

from beginning to end and believed in it even when I lost confidence. I've also had considerable help from Fergal Keane, editors Carole and Francesca, and the staff at Hodder and Stoughton. I can't mention everyone by name, but it's true to say that this book has been very much a team effort. My thanks to everyone who contributed their skills.

And I dedicate this book to the memory of Angela Pearce, because she shouldn't have died the way she did. It was wrong and there are no excuses. Her death made us take a long, hard look at ourselves. Her life was cut tragically short and she deserves to be remembered.

Having said all that, I hope the reader will enjoy meeting Urban Grimshaw and the Shed Crew just as much as I did. Please fasten your seatbelts.

Bernard Hare
November, 2004

GLOSSARY

Babylon	The Establishment and its agents.
Bolties	Bolt-croppers.
Bomb	The practice of wrapping noxious-tasting drugs in Rizla paper and swallowing.
Brown	Heroin.
Charver	Mate, pal, friend.
Chip	To leave, especially the scene of a crime.
Cushty	Sorted.
Dig	To inject drugs.
Dirty Digger	Intravenous drug user.
Dog-shelf	Floor.
Foil-face	Person who smokes heroin from tinfoil, a practice often called chasing the dragon.
Gouch	Dreamlike state induced by heroin use.
Grafting	Earning money for drugs by whatever means, mostly shoplifting, card fraud, blagging, street robbery, car crime, or prostitution.
Half-chat	Half-caste; person of mixed-race.
Jimmy's	St James's University Hospital, Leeds.
Joey	Person who does all the Joey work: going to the shops, making cups of tea, cooking, washing up, etc. Also, a Joey can be your own personal indentured slave or fag, either because they like the role, they are afraid of you, or they are too stupid to realise that you are taking them for a fool.
Kelly	Money.

Koompartoo	A fresh start.
Mispering	To go missing, to become a missing person.
Muppet	Fool, dupe, victim, target.
Mush	Outsider.
Nash	To run away.
Nosh	Blowjob, gobble, oral sex.
On top	The Babylon or its agents are upon us!
Pancrack	Dole office, DHSS.
Phet	Amphetamine, speed, whiz.
Rec	Recreation ground, communal land.
Scuffers	Police.
Slate	To put someone down verbally, to insult, deride or abuse.
Snailly	Nail varnish.
Tax	Stealing, demanding money with menaces.
Twocker	Joyrider or car thief, as in Taking Without Owner's Consent, written as TWOC on charge sheets.

PART ONE
A DAY IN THE LIFE OF THE SHED CREW

All one's inventions are true, you can be sure of that.
Poetry is as exact a science as geometry.
  Gustave Flaubert
  Letter to Louise Colet, 15 January 1853

Are you sitting comfortably?
Then I'll begin . . .

ONE
URBAN

We're the Shed Crew Posse of Lucifer Towers
and there's no one can beat our criminal powers.
There's Sparky, the twocker, and there's Urban, the thief,
and if anyone starts, Tyson sinks in the teeth.
There's Sam, who has friends, because he's a fluke,
the pathetic globule of parrot's puke.
There's Frank, the nonce, the sex offender,
but he can't help it because he's a bender.
There's an ugly fucking buah, called Trudi, the slag,
and we all hate her because she's a bag.
There's Greta, the junkie, the alcoholic –
only thing she's addicted to more is dick.
There's Skeeter and Kara and Pinky, who'll thump you,
and Simpkins and Molly and Pixie, who'll hump you,
and last but not least, there's Chop of the flat –
excuse his appearance, he's overly fat –
but, nevertheless, he's a kicking kinda guy,
and he'll always be a friend in our thieving fucking eyes.

Sparky
Chillin' on B-Wing,
HM Young Offenders' Institution, Doncatraz

Opposite the silver-grey façade of the Royal Armouries museum in Leeds, two large sewerage overflow pipes spill their filth and nastiness into the Aire and Calder Navigation. On that particular day, the left-hand pipe spewed a steady stream of sludge into the canal. The right-hand pipe was dry. Urban Grimshaw sat on the edge of the right-hand pipe, his feet dangling almost into the water. His brown Staff terrier, Tyson, lay quietly beside him, its head between its paws. Urban Grimshaw blew into a Kwik Save carrier-bag until it was fully inflated, then inhaled from the bag until it was empty again. He repeated this exercise several times, then stood up, extended his arms and declaimed forth unto the waters. He was twelve years old and four foot six, had jet-black hair, a slim build and a pallid, washed-out complexion. He wore blue tracksuit bottoms and a baggy orange T-shirt. The dark pipe framed him in a protective ring as he extended his arms. The glue-bag aside, I was reminded of Leonardo's *Vitruvian Man* drawing, where Everyman is measured out inside a circle.

'Urban!' I shouted. 'Urban! It's me!' But he couldn't hear me above the water.

Upstream by the railway station, the canal and the river join together and gently make their way through Leeds city centre as one. At the Royal Armouries, the two waterways divide once more into their separate courses. The water level drops a couple of metres, there are lock gates for canal traffic and a violent weir that accumulates flotsam and jetsam from the river. Had Urban Grimshaw slipped from his perch, the torrent would have carried him away downstream without a quarrel. I needed to get closer to him, so I carefully crossed the lock gates on to the man-made island between the lock and the weir.

'Urban! It's me!'

Tyson stood up and tilted his head, hearing me above the roar of the water. I didn't dare call to him. Tyson was loyal beyond reason, but as thick as ten short planks. If I called, he would probably jump into the river believing that to be the quickest line of approach. No doubt Urban would dive in to rescue him and both would be lost.

'Urban!'

He was only twenty metres away from me now, but there was still no response. He'd obviously been sniffing all afternoon. He was in the other dimension, Zombie Voodoo Land, talking in tongues to the water spirits. I could just about hear him above the roar of the water, yabbering on in his own personal sniffing language. 'Inshtak taki-naki, taki-naki!' he proclaimed. 'Nishtuk macrambo!' which translates loosely as, 'Go back, canal! Go back! It is not yet your time!'

My only hope was to get into the pipes, but the far riverbank didn't look promising. It was covered with thick brambles and thornbushes and fell steeply into the water. The slightest slip might prove fatal. Even if Urban had gone by that route, Tyson could never have made it. There had to be another way into the sewerage system, some easier means of access for workmen and children alike. The building site above the outfall pipes was the most likely point of entry, so I walked the long way round to it via Crown Point Bridge.

The site was a hive of industry: diggers and dumpers moving in all directions, men in yellow hats climbing up and down ladders, or walking on scaffolding calling to each other, generators and cement-mixers throbbing away in the background and a gigantic yellow crane swinging unimaginable loads across the sky. I strolled in as if I owned the place, donned a yellow hard-hat, which I found by a digger, and no one gave me a second glance. Trying to look like a legitimate surveyor, I rooted round the site searching for a means of access into the pipes. Towards the riverbank, I discovered an open manhole and clambered down it into the stinking sewer.

Urban Grimshaw was silhouetted in the light at the end of the tunnel. For a moment, I was in awe of him. There was something uniquely bizarre about the child, which I couldn't put my finger on.

Tyson paddled up towards me through the slime and filth. I

tickled his ears by way of a greeting while Urban's voice echoed eerily along the tunnel. 'I am the Great God Bokono, the Bringer of Fishcakes. Alert the alien scum-buckets to my presence, Macrambo Nectarian.'

Tyson and I splashed our way through fetid, stagnant pools of water towards him. Gently does it, I thought. One wrong move and he's gone. About twenty metres away from him, I slipped on a piece of excrement and landed flat on my back. Only the hard-hat saved my skull. Even then, I was stunned and winded. Tyson was fussing and barking and licking my face. His breath reeked like rat's puke.

Urban spun round. 'Who goes there? Meddlesome crepidarians.'

Soaking and shit-stained, I got to my feet. 'It's me, Urban. Chop.'

'Yellow-headed zamblasting fusticator!' he cried. 'Stignat vorton!' Then, without further warning, he threw his glue-bag towards me and dived head first into the river.

Fine, I thought. Lovely. Couldn't be better. This looks good. 'Yes, Your Honour, I was in the sewer at the time and the boy was intoxicated.'

I ran along the pipe to the water's edge. Urban Grimshaw was being carried off downstream by the current. He was bobbing along, waving at me. At least, he seemed to be waving, rather than appealing for help. I had no time to think. I removed my coat, the yellow hat, kicked off my shoes and followed him into the murky waters.

It was like jumping into freezing black treacle. The cold numbed me to the bone and for a moment I thought I would pass out from the shock. I sank to the bottom like a brick. The mud sucked tenaciously at my feet and I performed a bizarre, slow-motion underwater dance. As I tore one foot loose, the other sank deeper into the slurry on the bottom. Just when I thought it was time to stop dancing, the river itself tore me loose from the quagmire and tossed me along like a discarded aluminium beer barrel.

Urban was already a hundred metres away. Gasping for breath, I swam after him until he washed up between a barge and the dockside. I came up beside him, almost exhausted. For my benefit rather than his, we held on to the tyres hanging down from the barge and fought for breath. The shock had brought him back from Zombie Voodoo Land.

'You okay?' I asked, spitting filth and degradation from my mouth.

He coughed, spluttered and shook his head, but I got the impression that this meant 'Yes.'

'I came to say sorry,' I said.

He nodded. 'Me too. Sorry, Chop. I just needed a bit of a snifter.'

'It's all right. I take the occasional bracer myself.'

Urban and I had first met three months earlier in May '96. I knocked about with his mum, Greta, for a while. She was single, with six kids aged from six to sixteen, all but the eldest in care. She was living in a hostel and was down on her luck. She claimed that the kids had been unjustly snatched away from her by Social Services and she wasn't very happy about it. She told me a complete cock-and-bull story, but I wasn't as wise as I thought at the time and I agreed to help her. To hear her talk, you'd have thought that Social Services had kidnapped her kids and were using them as sex toys. She referred to all social workers as 'nonces'.

Greta was the only person I'd ever met who hated social workers more than I did. I'd trained and worked as a social worker in my younger days, but a minor criminal record had made it difficult for me to continue in that line of work. I still felt bitter about being excluded from the job I loved because of a couple of drunk-and-disorderly offences and an obstructing-the-police. I was a miner's son, brought up in the drink culture – getting drunk and carrying on with the police was part of my heritage. I hadn't realised it would cost me so dear. So I wasn't about to turn down a chance to get some small revenge on the politically correct powers-that-be that had ruined my life. Now this seems like wrong-thinking – today I would take more responsibility for my actions – but then it all made perfect sense, probably because my slight drink problem had developed into a slight drug problem.

Greta and I agreed that the two middle boys, Urban, twelve, and Frank, fourteen, would be the easiest to reclaim and we set to work. She took me to meet Urban under staff supervision at the Bulwell House children's home. There, I first became aware of him as another conscious being. He didn't say much but his busy eyes darted all around the room. You see a lot in someone's eyes, even without conversation. I felt like I knew him, like I'd seen him before – indeed, I had, a hundred times when I was a social worker. I liked him straight off, even though he presented himself as sulky and sullen. His attitude seemed justified, given his circumstances: he was in some kind of trouble and was being punished, which meant that he was under constant one-to-one supervision, wasn't allowed out and had to wear his pyjamas all day. When the member of staff asked to speak to Greta in private, Urban and I were left alone. The moment they were out of the room, Urban spoke his first words to me: 'You seem like a good bloke,' he said, 'so I'll give you some advice. Don't trust my mum. She'll destroy your life.'

There was a lot going on in those three simple sentences and I found it remarkable that a twelve-year-old was capable of constructing them. Had I heeded his advice, I might have walked away there and then. I didn't, perhaps because he reminded me of someone. Around 1980, I was working in a rough assessment centre in London. A thirteen-year-old kid from Middlesbrough came in one morning and he had a right broad Yorkshire accent, just like me. As the only two northerners in a world of southern namby-pambies, we naturally made a bond. I'd kept in touch with him ever since and watched him progress through the system. From care to detention centre to Borstal to prison; from petty criminal to hardened criminal to career criminal then dangerously deranged criminal, finally resulting in a long-term stretch for hacking off a taxi driver's hand after an argument over a few pounds. I thought maybe if I could help get this one home to his mum, I could stop him going down the same road. Greta had problems, but there was no real harm in her and just about anything was better than care.

Unfortunately, the plan didn't work out as originally devised. I tried to help Greta, but she was nuts. I arranged meetings with solicitors, doctors and social workers, but half the time she didn't turn up and I was left looking a fool. I'd track her down in the pub and end up getting smashed myself. Then we'd turn up half pissed at Social Services and it just didn't look good.

I let her stay at my flat for a while and we arranged home visits for Urban and Frank. Frank thanked me by stealing money from my wallet. I had left it on the side in my bedroom and the money disappeared while I was cooking. We had our meal and I was going to take them up to Temple Newsam for the afternoon, our local stately home and gardens. It's well worth a visit if you're in the area. In the end we didn't go, because while I was getting ready I noticed the money was missing. Immediately the finger was pointed at Frank.

'Give him it back, you stupid-looking tosser,' Greta told Frank. 'It's obvious you've nicked it.'

'Why is it obvious I've nicked it?' Frank protested. 'Urbie might have took it.'

'Because Urbie wouldn't take it, that's why. He likes him

more than he likes me and you. He's already asked me to leave off him cos he's all right. So that means you must've taken it, doesn't it, precious?'

'Well, I bet you took it, then, you silly fat slut.'

'I'll rip your fucking head off if you keep on, you bastard.'

And so on and so forth, as was their delightful way of conversing with one another.

The police soon became regular visitors to my flat. Urban and Frank hated the kids' homes and were habitual runaways. They seldom stayed more than a night at a time and only went back when the police got hold of them, then ran away again almost immediately. I had no idea where they stayed when they were on the run. The police, however, thought they were at my house and came banging on the door so regularly that my alarm clock was superfluous.

I was running a dodgy man-and-van service and took Urban to work with me on a number of occasions. He was out of school, so I thought it better he was with me than roaming the streets. I found him a willing and enthusiastic worker and good company on the longer journeys. We spent entire days together in my rickety old van and we became quite fond of each other. Frank, on the other hand, worked reluctantly and complained about the wages so I only took him a couple of times. I often asked Urban where he stayed when he ran away: I was worried he might be being exploited or abused. 'The only person who exploits me is you,' he said, so I upped his wages by 20p an hour. He was vague about his activities, but eventually I found out that he was staying in East End Park – 'Eastie' to the natives – with 'the Shed Crew'. I assumed they were older teenagers who shared a house. Whenever I asked too many questions, though, Urban always found a way to get off the subject. 'Look at those hills. Aren't they beautiful?'

Greta, meanwhile, knocked someone out in my lifts and I was getting dirty looks from the neighbours. But the day I took a load of computer tables to Liverpool was the last straw. On the way back I dropped Urban off in East End Park and returned home to find Greta naked in my living room with a bloke I'd never seen before. Any normal person would have killed them both, but I couldn't help thinking about Urban. Next morning, I went out and found Greta a house, also in East End Park; I paid the three-hundred-pound deposit out of my own pocket just to get rid of her. Houses were plentiful in the area because no one in their right mind wanted to live there. I moved her in and decided I'd done about as much as I could for her. In truth, I was sick of the whole crazy family. I had opened the Gates of Anarchy and was regretting it more by the day.

Then, one morning, Urban came knocking at my door as if nothing had happened. 'Any jobs today, Chop? I'm hungry.' I couldn't tell the poor kid all those things about his mother so I just said I wanted my old life back and I didn't want to see any of them ever again. He went ballistic on me, kicking the door and spitting, 'You're just the same as everyone else! A fucking piss-head, same as everyone else! I thought you were different, you piss-head bastard! Don't worry, you won't ever see me again, you fucking piss-head!'

By lunchtime, I had worked out what the fuss had been about. I'm not at my best first thing in the morning and can be insensitive. Ten fags and five cups of coffee later, my head had stopped spinning and I'd had a chance to think. Urban rated me. He rated me so highly that he was disappointed when I hadn't lived up to his expectations. In everything he said and did he was crying out for help, and he'd thought I was capable of answering the call. I'd let him down and he was angry. I got to thinking that no one had ever liked me that much before and what a cowardly, stinking piece of shit I was for sending him away. Maybe he even loved me, in which case I'd betrayed his love. I couldn't get any lower than that. It would probably cost me my business, my home, my reputation and my sanity, but I would help him if it killed me. I would get involved. I would do something. I didn't know what, but I'd start by going down to his regular haunt by the canal and apologising to him.

When we'd caught our breath, we clambered up on to the barge. Urban, lighter and nimbler, boarded first, then offered me his hand. I pulled myself up and we stood on the deck. We pointed at each other and laughed like schoolboys. When Urban laughed, you couldn't help but laugh with him.

'State of you,' he said.

'You can talk,' I said. 'You look like a drowned rat.'

Poor kid. His teeth were chattering and he had bright green nail varnish all over his face. Urban's routine was to shoplift several bottles of nail varnish, sniff them, sober up, shoplift more nail varnish, sniff them again, sober up again, ad infinitum. On a good day he might steal forty or fifty bottles. Each time he refilled his bag, a certain amount of spillage would be deposited around the mouthpiece, which would then be transferred to his lips, nose and cheeks until he looked like some monstrous, multicoloured gargoyle.

He shivered. Water dripped steadily from him on to the deck. 'Where's Tyson?'

We could hear a distant howl coming from the sewerage pipes. 'Come on,' I said. 'We'll go get him.'

A woman in a red coat with a child called over to us from the opposite bank, 'You all right? Need any help?'

'No, love, thanks. We're all right,' I told her. 'Just having a swim. Thanks all the same.' She waved and walked off towards the Armouries with the child.

Dripping and freezing, Urban and I made our way back to the building site. It was early afternoon and the sun was shining, but that only makes things worse when you've stepped fully clothed into a river. It was difficult to look nonchalant as we re-entered the site. Within a matter of yards an ageing construction worker challenged us: 'Is it raining shit now? You can't come in here.'

Urban rushed over and took the man's hand. 'My dog's trapped in the sewers, Mister, like on telly. Can you help us?' After a minutely timed pause, he added, 'Pleeeeeease.'

The guy was powerless, just as I always was. He took us across to the manhole and we heard Tyson's anguished wail from below. Urban rescued his dog and passed my coat and shoes up to me. I sat down on a pile of bricks and wrestled with my shoelaces. I'd already rejected the option of undoing them with my teeth. Cholera can be quite nasty, I've heard. Urban climbed up out of the hole and ruffled Tyson's back. The dog snapped playfully at his heels and the two ran excitedly around the site together, friends reunited.

The old man accompanied us to the gate to make sure we didn't nick anything. 'That your boy?' he asked. 'Shouldn't let him play in the sewers – there's germs. He might catch something. Why's his face green?'

What could I tell him? No, he's not my boy. He's the product of twenty years of Tory government. He's Mrs Thatcher's boy. I don't let him play in the sewers, he more or less lives down there. If he goes out on the streets, the police pick him up and take him to a children's home. He doesn't like children's homes because he gets nonced, beaten and bullied there. Germs are the least of his problems. A number of quaint, old-fashioned viruses have already infected him: Ignorance, Destitution, Addiction and Want, to name but four. His face is green because he's been sniffing nail varnish all day and communing with the High Lord Zombulglast. You may not be aware of it but there's a spaceship parked underneath the canal where the helicopter-people live. It's huge, like a zeppelin, and it's got big snarling teeth at the front, like an Alsatian.

They're having a war with the mole-people, in case you didn't know. Urban doesn't know which side to be on. He says the mole-people are quite nice. It's a worrying situation. The fighting could spill over.

'Yes, he's mine,' I said. 'Don't worry, I'll do everything I can to keep him out of the sewers in future. Thanks for your help. You're a good man.'

The three of us stood outside the building site – a man, a boy and a dog – not knowing quite what to do with ourselves. We were a ghastly sight. Urban was covered with nail varnish, I was covered with shit and we were both soaked to the skin. Tyson's jaws were covered with something black and gooey and he stank worse than we did. 'Well, Urban,' I said, 'where do we go from here?'

There was no way out for me now. A bond had formed between Urban and me and it no longer had anything to do with his mother. Maybe he saw me as the father he'd never had. Maybe I saw him as the son I'd never had. People surrounded us, but we were both alone in a great big horrible world. I knew then that I was into something I couldn't get out of. At least, not without tearing Urban to pieces in the process. I had little option but to go with the flow and see what happened.

'Best get cleaned up,' Urban said. 'We'll go to yours.'

'We'll catch pneumonia before we get there,' I said. My flat was a bus ride away and I certainly wasn't getting on a bus. 'We'll have to go to your mum's.' His mum was only up the road in East End Park.

Urban took my hand. 'Mum'll kill me. Can't we go to yours?' Then, after a minutely timed pause, '*Pleeeeeease.*'

I decided that if I was going to stick my nose into his affairs, I would have to be responsible about it. He was the child and I was the adult. I would have to make the decisions I thought were right, despite his pleas.

'No. You've got clean clothes at your mum's. We'll go there.'

'Can I stay at your house tonight, then?'

'If your mum says it's okay. Come on.'

Urban looked down at the pavement and mumbled something under his breath. I thought he said, 'Mum couldn't care less.'

TWO
ASHTRAYLAND

And did those feet in ancient time
Walk upon England's shit tips green?
And was the holy Lamb of God
In England's carbon monoxide seen?

And did the Countenance Divine
Shine forth upon our genetically modified hills?
And was Jerusalem cloned here
Among these dark Satanic Mills?

Bring me my Dig of burning gold:
Bring me my Viagra of desire:
Bring me my Foil: O clouds unfold!
Bring me my Milligrams of fire.

I shall not cease from Mental Flight,
Nor shall my Pork Sword sleep in my hand
Till we have trashed Jerusalem
In England's green and fucked-up Land.

(Based on a poem by someone else because I'm thick)
Skeeter
Fuck you

Urban and I walked along East Street, past the corrugated-metal façade of Howarth Timber. 'What's that say?' Urban said, pointing to a sign. He couldn't read or write, but his thirst for knowledge was insatiable. He loved having people read to him, like a blind man loves his guide dog.

' "DIY Store and Timber Yard. Open six days a week." '

'What's that?' he said, pointing to a billboard.

It was an advertisement for White Arrow Parcels. It showed a map of the British Isles with little lorries running all over it like lice. 'You know what that is, don't you?'

'A map,' he said.

'Yes, a map, but a map of what?'

'Don't know,' he said. 'Otherwise I wouldn't be asking.'

'But you've seen the maps in the van, haven't you?'

'Yeah, but, well, they don't mean anything, if you don't know what you're looking at.'

A horrible tightening began in my throat and travelled down to my stomach. I had to stop tears welling in my eyes. Geography was my favourite subject. I could draw you a rough map of just about anywhere in the world, tell you the capital city of every country, their mountain ranges, rivers, and a little about their history, economy, climate, vegetation and culture. Urban didn't recognise his own country when he saw it.

Like Urban, I had been brought up in inner-city Leeds, but in the sixties and seventies. I had a happy childhood and I got a good education. Even my brother, who had no academic interest whatsoever, got a tolerable education and a good apprenticeship in the printing industry. What had changed? Was it simply that education had been more important to us back then? Just as enlightenment is seen as the only way to break the endless cycle of death and rebirth, so we saw education as the only way to break the endless cycle of poverty and exploitation. If you tried to bunk school, a neighbour would most likely grab you by the ear and drag you down there, almost in passing, on her way to work. The whole community took an interest in the education of its children – and we were a community. My mum and dad liked a drink, so my brother and I were often left to our own devices, but it was a simple matter to nip down to the pub in the event of an emergency, or if we needed money for pop and crisps. Our nan was at the top of the street and an auntie lived just down the road. Support was never far away.

But things had changed dramatically since those halcyon days. Our communities had been decimated. Most Eastie people blamed Thatcher and traced the problems back to the miners' strike of 1984. My own family had been torn apart in the strike, my father humiliated and turned into a living ghost, my faith in the nation destroyed. Add to this the destruction of virtually all the heavy industry in the city between the sixties and eighties and you had a recipe for disaster. As more and more people became unemployed, disenchanted and angry, survival took precedence over abstract concepts like community and education. Ultimately it became every man for himself, which left children like Urban standing on street corners with nobody giving a damn about them.

I could have remained aloof from it all. I was earning good money in London when the strike kicked off. I worked through it and sent money home to my dad, who wasn't getting any strike pay or benefits. I also joined a miners' support group to raise money for the National Union of Mineworkers. We invited strikers to give us talks and went into pubs shaking buckets at people. In some London pubs you could fill the bucket, in others you had to wipe the spit from your face with a towel, and there was no way of telling which was which until you got inside. It wasn't the strike that got to me (there had been other strikes in '72 and '74) – I could never quite come to terms with being spat at by my fellow countrymen. As the miners marched back to work, defeated but defiant, I was winding up my affairs in the big smoke. For me, London had lost its charm.

I had kicked out at a system I saw as manipulative and corrupt, thereby causing my own social exclusion and my slow descent into the underclass. Back home, I bought an Escort van and set up as a mechanic. In the motor trade, it's compulsory to do something crooked every day and I soon added further offences to my collection. It's also compulsory to get drunk every night after work and I was soon back in the heart of the drink culture that had raised me. A lawsuit for accidentally setting a customer's car on fire and a drink-driving ban finally put paid to my ill-fated venture into the world of wheels.

I was on my arse and had little choice but to go back into some form of social work. The leader-in-charge couldn't believe her luck when I applied for a low paid job as a community development worker in a local community centre. She was suspicious about why someone with my qualifications and experience would want to work in such a backwater, but eventually she took a chance. I worked there happily for several years, until it closed in 1990 in a round of spending cuts and I was back on my arse.

So I was used to the life of shit that we were leading, but Urban's ignorance shocked even me. Yet his intelligence and good nature were evident, despite his handicaps. Consciousness is built with words and language, which Urban possessed in abundance even if he couldn't write them down. I decided that henceforth I would be loyal to Urban Grimshaw and Urban Grimshaw alone. If the country ever wanted my loyalty back, they would have to make Urban Grimshaw king. Meanwhile, I would start another country, a kingdom of the mind, with its own laws, religion and culture.

I wasn't even sure that Urban knew the name of the country in which he lived.

'Leeds,' he said. 'We live in Leeds.'

'No, that's our town,' I told him. 'Lots of towns together make a country. What's the name of our country, our nation?'

He furrowed his brow. Thought long and hard. 'Ashtray-land, is it?'

Ashtrayland. How very apt. That would be the name of our country within a country, our nation within a nation. Ashtray-land Forever. *In God We Trust.* I resolved to start writing the constitution at the first possible opportunity.

Meanwhile, we walked on. Outside Batty's Brushworks we came upon a circular street hoarding, like those you see in Paris, covered with a multi-coloured riot of posters. One showed a young girl with rockets taking off from her hair.

'What's that say?' Urban requested.

'"Uplifting Funky House, Every Friday at the Majestyk, Leeds."' He looked puzzled. 'It's like a nightclub, rave type of thing,' I explained.

Another poster was fluorescent-pink and covered with spirals. 'What's that say?'

'"Futurewormhole@thefruitcupboard, ten till late."'

'What's that mean?'

'I don't like to think about it.'

'But what's it mean?'

'I don't know,' I insisted. 'I don't know everything. Get off my case.'

'Make something up, then.'

'Okay. It means get smashed enough and one day you'll disappear up your own arsehole and then there'll be nothing to worry about. How does that grab you?'

'By the bollocks,' he said. 'By the fucking bollocks.'

One of the things I liked about Urban Grimshaw was his manner of speaking. At twelve years old, he talked like a little old man. It was possible to have an adult conversation with him. His sense of humour was subtle and profound. He was wise beyond his years. He had an air of Socrates about him, always asking questions and thereby exposing your stupidity when you didn't know the answer. A touch of Dalí too. He said the most bizarre and ridiculous things, especially when he was sniffing, which made you soon come to a full understanding of the true principles of surrealism. There was just something very peculiar about him. He wasn't your normal twelve-year-old. He had known such hardship, suffered so much and matured so early that he was like a grown-up in a child's body. He was twelve, going on thirty-seven. Oddly enough, I was thirty-seven at the time, going on twelve. Maybe that was why we got on so well.

When I examine my motives, I can see that I wasn't entirely answering Urban's needs. I was also answering my own. At the time I told myself that I had taken him on because I needed an assistant. In some parts of Leeds, you couldn't leave a van unattended for two seconds without something being stolen off the back. I needed a second pair of eyes as well as a second pair of hands. Even then the question must be asked, why choose a twelve-year-old for the job?

Probably because my own emotional development had been arrested at that age. I was one of only three kids from our junior school who passed the eleven-plus exam. My proud parents decided it was probably worth the extra money for uniforms and equipment and packed me off to grammar school. From day one, I knew that my life had changed dramatically for the worse. In junior school, it hadn't taken much to excel: it was a small school in a poor area. Then I was dropped among the brainiest kids from all over the city. From being a big fish in a small pond, the opposite was suddenly the case. I was relegated to mediocrity through no fault of my own. Worse, when I got home all my old mates were on my case because I was a stuck-up little shit who went to grammar school. They'd all failed the eleven-plus and were happily making new lives for themselves at the local comprehensive. I was suddenly an outsider in my own community.

Thank God for Judo. Just when things looked like they couldn't get any worse, I made a new friend. Like me, Judo was a little scruffier than the other kids, a little more watchful and a little more disrespectful towards the teachers. Like me, he didn't quite fit in. Both alone in a strange new world, we agreed to team up. Our motto: *United we stand, divided we fall*. We became the best of friends, friends like you can only be when you're twelve years old, when you were previously alone and when all the world was against you. We were inseparable. The teachers called us 'the terrible twins'. We were at that lurid age when strange hairs were sprouting on our bodies, and girls, previously seen as weaker, stupider versions of boys, invaded our dreams like phantoms in the night. We took our first birds to the flicks, went on our first camping expeditions, committed our first criminal offences, stood in the Boys' Pen at Elland Road, and generally took the piss out of the world together. Then, one morning he didn't turn up for school. My form master called me up to his desk and informed me unceremoniously that Judo had been run over and killed the night before. He knew how close we were and he was terribly sorry to have to be the one to break it to me. After that day, my dad says, I was never the same again. The normally long, slow change from happy-go-lucky child to moody, brooding adolescent happened for me overnight. I went into a shell and missed out on a good deal of my youth because of it.

Walking on, we cut through Saxton Gardens, an array of five East-German-style flat blocks staggering raggedly up the Old Bank Hill. I had an auntie who lived there when I was Urban's age. The flats were nice back then and stayed nice into the eighties. They were a combination of dark red brick, with cream-painted windows and railings. Multi-coloured, metal-faced balconies completed the picture. Now the cream paint had turned off-yellow and was peeling away from the windows and railings. The balconies were brown with rust. Many of the flats were boarded up. Litter dotted the whole estate.

Beside the off-licence at the top of the estate we passed through a narrow ginnel and climbed past trees, long grass and blackberry bushes up the Old Bank Hill towards Mount St Mary's church. This patch of land was a hidden oasis, a modern ruin. Bits of brick wall, never quite demolished, stuck out amid the greenery. It was a magical, forgotten place, a secret garden full of birdsong and wonder. As if by magic, Urban and Tyson disappeared into the bushes.

I found them at the stone circle half-way up the hill. This was a sleepy, shaded hollow, which had been tarmacked and landscaped. Bottles, cans, wrappers and broken glass were scattered liberally around the area. A Yorkshire-stone wall encircled a bed of trampled shrubs, broken saplings and thornbushes with pink flowers. Urban and Tyson were standing in the middle of it. Urban smiled cockily, as if he owned the place. Tyson raised a leg and left his scent.

You got a good view from the stone circle. A broken, rotted bench looked out across the city. I plopped down on it to give my weary legs a rest and gazed out on the dark satanic mills along the river, now converted into offices, the fuck-you glass tower of the Royal Armouries, the Victorian order of the Corn Exchange dome and the parish church spire, the kinky new yuppie townhouses by the canal where the nonces lived, the municipal pride of the town-hall and civic-hall clocks, the gleaming white phallus of the university, and the modern office-block monstrosities. This was the image, the soundbite, the idea that Leeds City Council tried to convey to the world: a busy, modern, thriving hub of commerce and industry. To the east, you saw the truth: endless slab-like tower blocks where people eked out an existence dependent upon drugs, television and their Giro to get them through the week. Between the tower blocks, there were legions of back-to-back terraced houses, with the occasional church spire or chimney sticking up to break the monotony. A bleak, ugly termite mound on the landscape.

Urban produced three bright-red Metro temporary bus stops from the bushes and threw them into a pile in the middle of the circle. The resultant piece he called *Bokono At Work*. I congratulated him on his eye. A masterly creation. Fit for our own Tate Modern, if we'd had one. 'Come on,' I said. 'Let's make some tracks.'

Climbing the decrepit old staircase at the top of the hill, we were confronted by the imposing Gothic façade of Mount St Mary's church, monumental in aspect. It was built in Victorian times when they liked to put the fear of God into you. Now the mighty stone was blackened and eaten away by acid rain, the doorways were boarded up, and the magnificent leaded windows were peppered with a thousand jagged holes from stones, bricks and airgun pellets. A sign on the vaulted front door said, 'Keep Out, Private, Danger' – a warning, a threat and a promise. Urban lobbed a couple of extra stones through a window, adding his own signature to the composition.

At the apex of the gable, high above, the figure of Christ looked down on us from a cross. Everywhere else in Leeds, there was a background chorus of traffic noise. Here, in this neglected little alcove, the silence was absolute. I was saddened that such a noble building had been allowed to fall into ruin. Behind the church was Mount St Mary's Roman Catholic School. If no one cared about the church, what message were they sending out to the kids? Had we lost faith as well as hope? And, if so, where did that leave charity?

We passed through a narrow ginnel overhung with cherry trees and emerged into Richmond Hill Close, a street of bright new brick-built federation houses with gardens and garages. It wasn't a posh street – you could tell that from the cars, mainly Escorts, Astras, Nissans and suchlike – but it was tidy, decent, clean and respectable. How it should be. How it used to be.

We crossed Upper Accommodation Road and climbed over a low brick wall into the grounds of the hostel. This was where the homeless, manless families lived. Technically, we men weren't allowed to visit because we're all potential rapists and nonces. Nevertheless, I'd been inside a time or two when Urban's mother lived there. I used to climb in through a back window, sneak upstairs to her room and chase the dragon all night with her. The hostel looked okay from the outside, but inside was a different story. The walls, doors and skirting-boards were painted in depressing colours. The furniture was cheap, plastic crap, torn and dishevelled. The beds had plastic mattress-covers, because all the kids were disturbed and wet the bed. Just for good measure, the majority of the women in there were smackheads, who shoplifted or prostituted themselves to pay for their gear. On the positive side, if you got in and remained undetected, you were guaranteed a toot and a shag.

We passed twenty metres of broken-down fencing, which gave kids from the hostel easy access to the busy railway line, crossed over the bridge and entered Eastie proper. East End Park has clearly defined borders: York Road, a six-lane urban motorway to the north; Ivy Street bypass to the east; the park itself to the south; and the railway cutting to the west. If you didn't live in this small area, you weren't an Eastie Boy or Girl. Within this quarter-mile-square area, there were several off-licences, two working-men's clubs, a pub, a primary school, a doctor's, a dentist's, a bookie's, row upon row of two-up-two-down terraces and, for those with aspirations, the odd street of through-terraces with small gardens front or back. Estimated population: four or five thousand, mainly white, unemployed inhabitants.

The top of East Park Drive was the best place to get a true feel for East End Park. The geometry was astounding. The arrow-straight road ran off into the distance towards its vanishing point. Row upon row of red-brick gable-ends receded into the breach, getting smaller and smaller, and fainter and fainter, as they went. Telegraph poles stuck out of the pavement at random locations, their wires zigzagging crazily along. The Tarmac was a glistening river of glass from countless broken bottles and innumerable broken windscreens from untold stolen cars. There were blackened, melted patches dotted along the road, where twock cars had been burnt to a cinder. 'B.D. & J.B. Off-licence and Grocers' was immediately to my right. It had wire-mesh netting over the windows, and four small bollards defended the door against prospective ram-raid attempts. All round the entrance little spots of chewing-gum were trodden into the pavement. Next door, John's Fish and Chip Shop was closed. When they were frying, the smell of warm fish and chips drifted all the way down the Drive. Even though it was closed, there was still the vague whiff of vinegar and salty newspaper in the air. From above came the incessant chirrup of birdsong. Pigeons, sparrows, gulls and crows roosted on the gutters and the telegraph wires, arguing over territory and calling to their mates.

Soon we were at Greta's. Glensdale Terrace was much the same as any other street in East End Park. It started at the bottom near the railway wall, crossed East Park Drive half-way along its course, made its way up a slight incline and was suddenly curtailed by East Park View at the top. I knew it well, because I had lived there from birth until I was sixteen. Mum didn't like it, but we stayed there while my nan was alive. When she died, we moved to the other side of the estate where the houses were slightly bigger and better. Mum had cancer-of-the-everything and only lived another couple of years. Dad was still kicking and lived up the top end in the Berthas. I would have to be careful. The jungle tom-toms could still reach him and I didn't want him knowing too much of my business. He was the only man alive who could tear me off a strip with impunity.

My dad is one of the old school, with old-fashioned ways. A good socialist, he would have taken to Urban but would have disapproved of Greta. He would have seen her as a drunk, a druggie, a bad mother, and an all-round scarlet woman of the worst kind. Greta wasn't the sort of person you could take home to tea. Dad worried about what the neighbours said, and they wouldn't have said anything good about Greta. He was a product of the 'old' drink culture, *Coronation Street*-style, where everyone met up in the pub and drinking indoors was a no-no. The traditional drink culture had since developed into a drink *and* drug culture, where imbibing indoors was not only cheaper but a necessity because the drug component of our activities was illegal. Greta and I belonged to this new generation, and the pater, in his mid-sixties, had singularly failed to move with the times.

The old shop on the corner of the Drive and Glensdale Terrace had been freshly torched, which was a shame because I had many fond memories of it. I used to go there for my sweets when I was a kid. You could go to the shops on your own in those days without fear of the nonces getting you. (No Internet back then.) They had a Lucky Dip tub and old Mr Walker who owned the place always gave you an extra Black Jack, Refresher or Penny McGowan in your packet, or a Milky Way if you were lucky. The truly remarkable thing was that they had a cigarette machine on the wall outside, and they used to leave it there overnight. Nowadays, it would last about seven seconds. As a matter of fact, I'd rag it off the wall myself before the smackheads got to it. The fag machine was gone, but the sign was still above the door: 'YOUR LOCAL *Best Buy* GENERAL STORE. Prop: H Walker, Esq.'. The sign's light-blue paint had been fading even in the sixties. Now it was blackened, charred and burnt by the ravages of time. It had survived the Blitz, only to be decimated by a firestorm of social exclusion and neglect. Like many a man's mind in the Faustian depths of Ashtrayland, the shop's door and windows had been boarded up with thick metal sheeting – 'Eastie Curtains' – which was completely painted over, top to bottom, with graffiti. The result was reminiscent of the work of Jackson Pollock, the crap American artist, in that it was impossible to pick out any single message or tag amid the chaos.

'Historically, politically, philosophically, architecturally, artistically and anthropologically, Mr Walker's shop is of immense cultural significance,' I mused.

Urban screwed his face up. 'Eh?'

'This shop,' I said. 'It's like a work of art.'

He said, 'It's not *like* a work of art. It *is* a work of art. I did it.'

'You can't have done all that,' I said. 'I recognise many different hands at work. Different styles, different ideas regarding texture, form and composition.'

'No,' he said. 'Stupid. I mean I burned the fucker down. I put a petrol bomb through the window.'

I looked at him there, four foot six in his dirty Nike trainers. It was hard to believe that he and children like him were responsible for the destruction all around us but that was about the size of it. This was what our so-called leaders failed to understand. You can't let children go hungry, uncared-for and uneducated without one day reaping the whirlwind.

This was Urban's territory now so I followed him up the street. I was feeling uncomfortable. Nowadays I only ventured into Eastie to see my dad and never came down this end of the estate at all. I could feel the houses pressing in on me. Even though everything was the same, everything had changed. The pavements were the same, but now they seemed scruffier, the hopscotch marks replaced by dog shit and broken glass. The right angles where the pavement met the wall were the same, but now weeds and nettles were growing out of them. The houses were the same, but every fourth one was boarded up, and every second one had thick metal bars or grilles across its windows. The air used to be filled with the sound of women, in pinnies, nattering and chatting. Now the street was deserted and all you could hear was rave music blaring from a house at the top. The Tarmac had a ribbon of a slightly different hue running down its middle, where the cable services had been installed. The guttering, roofs and chimneys looked dangerously unstable.

Three fresh-faced girls, Urban's age, or a little older, came out of a house and skipped down the street towards us.

'Hello, Urban.'

'Hello, Urban.'

'Hello, Urban.'

Urban put on a spurt of speed to get past them and the girls fell about laughing and giggling. The tallest, a blonde of twelve or thirteen, wearing a yellow summer dress and dazzling white ankle socks, called after him, 'Urban! Amy wants to know if you'll go out with her. Will you go out with Amy, Urban? Urban, who's your friend? Kelly says she wants to go out with him.'

I was embarrassed to hear such a comment from the child, especially as I knew her slightly. I couldn't remember her name, but her dad was a mate of my brother's and I'd seen her in the pub with him.

'No, I don't,' Kelly protested. 'Shut up, Molly! I'd rather go out wi' Tyson.' Tyson, taking full advantage of the situation, ambled over to Kelly and got his ears a good tickling.

The third girl, presumably Amy, shouted, 'I love you, Urban, even if you are a little knobhead.'

Urban ignored them pointedly until they disappeared round the corner into the Drive. 'Silly sluts,' he mumbled, as Tyson and I caught him up. With real sadness in his voice, he said, 'Do you know what they do? They hang about in the midden yards all night, sniffing, drinking, shagging and dishing out blowjobs. Last week, they had a National Blow-job Day and everyone on the patch got a nosh. I think that's sad, me.'

The houses in Glensdale Terrace came in blocks of four, with midden yards between each, which was where the dustbins were kept, for want of gardens. When I was a very small child, there were outside toilets in them and most people were in and out of the yards on a daily basis, so they were always kept well swept and spotlessly scrubbed. I popped my head into the first one we passed, just to see how they were progressing in this, the modern age. The high brick walls were topped with vicious-looking razor wire, a new addition since my time. The toilets were now demolished, of course, leaving a clear area roughly ten metres square for the dustbins. Un-fortunately, there were none in evidence. It looked as if people were throwing rubbish directly into the yard, no longer bothering with dustbins or black bags. It was a foot deep in raw, untreated refuse. Piled on top of the rubbish was a charred and burnt settee, a yellow car bonnet, several used condoms, countless glue-bags and lighter-gas canisters, and dozens of empty blue plastic bottles, the hallmark of White Lightning or 'Quite Frightening' cider, as we called it. At seven or eight per cent alcohol by volume, it was much stronger than normal beer. You could buy a litre for the price of a loaf so it was by far the favourite tipple of children and young people in the ten-to-fifteen age group. Wriggling and writhing in the centre of the yard was a flesh-tingling pile of rotten carpet, which was almost certainly alive. I got a mental picture of the three young girls, pissed or glued-up to the eyeballs, swallowing spunk and being fucked up against the walls by the older boys. The thought was enough to rot my soul. East End Park was rapidly becoming a disaster zone.

When we were half-way up the street, a silver BMW 320i careered round the corner. Anyone in their right mind would have slowed to fifty, knocked it down to second and only then applied the handbrake, thereby achieving the perfect hand-brake-turn. This crank almost went into a lamp-post. As the car wheel-spun to get going again, a horrid, high-pitched whine pierced the quiet of the street and clouds of dust and grit were thrown into the air. The car accelerated madly down the street, skidded to a halt beside us and the driver threw open the passenger door. 'Get in, Urban!'

'Can't,' Urban said. 'I've got to—'

'Get in, knobhead. I haven't got all day.' The driver looked about fifteen, bold, cheeky, ginger, lightly freckled, a menace to himself and society. He was well-built, but his face was thin and gaunt. His sensitive, intelligent eyes somehow didn't belong in that head, which somehow didn't belong on those shoulders. He wore a bottle green sweatshirt and a brown and white baseball cap advertising the Sox – whoever they might be. He was the perfect All American Boy. I was a skinhead at his age, English through and through.

The sound of a siren could be heard in the distance, getting closer and closer, and louder and louder, until a T5 came screaming round the corner. 'Got to go,' said the boy, pressing on the accelerator. 'Watch me leave these poor, hopeless gloits. I'll pick you up laters, Urb. Meet at the Slip around nine and we'll go round the shed.' With the passenger door flapping and the T5 in hot pursuit, the car sped off down the street and hurtled across the Drive.

'Sparky,' Urban informed me. 'Shed Crew,' he added, as if that fully explained the matter.

Urban spoke a lot about his friends in the Shed Crew, but it had never occurred to me that their name meant exactly what it said. 'Go round the shed?' I said. 'There really is a shed?'

'Course,' he said. 'Where do you think I've been staying?'

'Well, I thought you stayed with your mum most of the time, or with friends.'

'The odd night,' he said, 'but I prefer the shed. It's shit at Mum's and the scuffers come looking for me there. They don't know about the shed so it's safe.'

'Urban,' I said, 'you don't have to hide from the police, you know. The police won't hurt you. I know they're arseholes, but they wouldn't do anything to a kid.'

'Chop,' he said, 'I do have to hide from the police. The police will hurt me. You don't know nothing.'

What could I say? In his spare time, he obviously inhabited some secret world that I knew nothing about. I was intrigued. 'I'd like to meet the Shed Crew,' I said.

'You will,' he said. 'Sooner than you think.'

Finally, we stood before the door of number seventy-three. The loud rave music I'd heard at the bottom of the street emanated from within. If you looked closely, you could see the door reverberating from the din. The handle rattled away to itself like a smackhead. The three empty milk bottles on the doorstep tinkled lightly against each other like distant wind chimes.

Urban wore a look of utter disdain. He gritted his teeth, took a deep breath and pushed the door handle downwards. 'Here we are, then,' he said bitterly. 'Home sweet home.'

THREE
ZOMBIE VOODOO LAND

Have you ever seen things that aren't really there?
Like giraffes with green and purple hair,
Or live mannequins, or cardboard streets,
Or little people with massive feet?

I've seen things you'd never believe,
Butane gas made my eyes deceive,
It took me away to a different place
Where things were pretty, all dressed in lace.

I've seen statues move and come to life,
I've been chased through a maze by a carving knife,
I've fallen from trees, floated through time,
I've watched my own hands shimmer and shine.

I've travelled right through to Heaven's station
On my holiday of hallucination.
Quite fantastic, but to my shame,
It made a good job of destroying my brain.

Kara MacNamara
Doing a nash from reality

In the living room, a scene of utter bedlam confronted us, like something out of Doré's *London*. Greta led a chaotic lifestyle and it showed in every fibre of the carpet, but it was the atmosphere that most disturbed me. The music was deafening and drilled straight through your brain. The air was so thick with smoke that I thought perhaps there'd been a fire. The sickly-sweet smell of cider pervaded the whole room, and a half-dozen glassy-eyed kids lazed about the place in various stages of intoxication.

The room was smaller than I remembered it from when I moved Greta in, approximately five metres by five, and sparsely furnished. A red three-seater settee lounged in the centre of the room, populated by three teenagers: two boys aged around fourteen and between them a girl, maybe a year younger. I knew the boy on the left – he was Frank Grimshaw, Urban's older brother.

I also recognised the girl. Her name was Trudi and I'd met her once before at the hostel. Greta and I had arranged one of our brown sessions, where we got loads of brown and got smashed out of our faces, but when I arrived Trudi was sitting there watching television. Greta introduced her as her 'adopted' daughter. Greta and I went to one of the other units and got smashed with Spacey Tracy, her mate. Greta got so out of it that I had to carry her back to her room and put her to bed. Young Trudi was still watching television, but had changed into her nightclothes. She obviously rated herself in her little nightdress and ankle socks and tried it on blatantly with me. She looked like some starving, emaciated, anorexic supermodel and I wasn't tempted in the least. I preferred something with a bit more meat.

I think we forged a mutual respect that night. I gained hers by not noncing her up, even though it was offered on a plate. She gained mine by being a complicated character I couldn't quite figure out. Everything she said was either ironic or tongue-in-cheek – advanced stuff for a thirteen-year-old. She was aware of her sexuality and projected it outwards, like a ventriloquist throws his voice. She came from a big, rambling family that was scattered all over Leeds, and had a confusing array of dads and step-dads. Somewhere along the line, she had run away from her family and adopted Greta as her stand-in mum.

A wooden coffee-table crowded with spliff-making paraphernalia stood between the settee and the fire. Three Pot Noodle containers filled with cider also took up table space, leaving rings of urine-coloured liquid in their wake. The table quite upset me. I wanted to sweep everything into the bin and wipe it down with a disinfected cloth. There were alcoves on either side of the chimney-breast, each furnished with a low, pine-effect shelf. Two small children in baseball caps, a boy and a girl of ten or eleven, sat in the left-hand alcove, while the other provided a home for the pounding stereo system. A wicker wastepaper basket lay on its side nearby, spewing its contents over the carpet like an erupting volcano. At the back of the room, against the wall, stood a dirty old sideboard, which would have looked good if it had been sanded down and given a fresh coat of varnish. Behind it, in the far corner of the room, the stairway door stood open. A slim, ginger-haired girl of about fourteen sat on the bottom stair drinking from a can of Tennent's Super. She wore the blue uniform of Mount St Mary's School. The walls of the room were papered in seventies kitsch: brown concentric squares on a garish orange background. The matching brown curtains were three-quarters closed, allowing only a thin shaft of light to pierce the gloom. This ray of hope lit up the swirling clouds of smoke so that they looked like fields of stardust floating in space. The carpet was threadbare and desperately needed Hoovering. There were no pictures on the walls, no ornaments, no television, no phone, no lampshade, no books.

Frank Grimshaw was rolling a joint. He licked it, stuck it together with a final flourish, screwed the end into a point, lit it, inhaled deeply, exhaled and, finally, turned to his brother. 'Where've you been then, you little knobhead?'

'Fuck off, spastic,' Urban replied. 'Where's Mum?'

'Shops, and you better get all that shit off your face before she gets back or you're dead.'

Urban, aware of this, went into the kitchen. I watched him pour scouring powder on to his hands, wet them under the tap and bring them up to his face. A section of broken mirror with sharp, jagged edges stood behind the taps. Urban examined himself and began to work at the bright-green nail varnish. Some of the more stubborn stains proved resistant to his endeavours, so he poured more scouring powder on to a tea-towel and redoubled his efforts. Soon his face was as clean as a freshly scrubbed toilet.

Back in the living room, we found Frank necking with Trudi. Is it true that opposites attract? He had longish, girlish, straw-coloured hair, a spotty complexion and was five kilos overweight. She had shortish, boyish, earth-coloured hair, a fresh complexion and was five kilos underweight. All the other kids were watching them expectantly, as if something important was about to happen.

Frank was the only one who approached my size, so I said, 'Frank, can you lend me a T-shirt and a pair of trackie-bottoms, mate? We're a bit wet.'

'Suppose so,' he said. 'You owe me, though. I didn't want to mention it, but you stink like shit. Urbie, get him some clobber, you little puff.'

Evidently frustrated because Frank was ignoring her by talking to us, Trudi turned impatiently towards the boy to her right. He took a preparatory mouthful of cider and sportingly allowed her to stick her tongue into his mouth.

'Away, Chop,' Urban said, moving towards the stairway door in the corner. 'Move, Kara,' he said, to the girl who was sitting there. I gave her a non-committal nod and a smile as I passed.

'Going upstairs with your bum-chum, Urbie?' she called

after us. The frightening thing is that had I been a paedophile going upstairs with Urban I don't think anyone would have challenged me. The only question in Frank's mind would have been how much to charge.

At the top of the stairs, we reached a small landing. Before us was the master bedroom. To the left a staircase gave access to the attic and to the right a bathroom. Urban went in and emerged rubbing his hair with a towel. 'You don't want none of Frank's stinky stuff. You'll catch scabies. I'll get you some of Mum's stuff.'

We entered the master bedroom. The double bed was the only item of furniture in the room, still precisely positioned where I had left it when I moved them in. Even the floorboards were bare. Liberally scattered across and around it was an imaginative selection of makeup, clothing, fag packets, magazines, cups, photographs, letters, ashtrays, beer cans and further evidence of dope-use. My discerning eye even picked out a discarded hypodermic needle. Tracey Emin has since immortalised the scene with her wonderfully evocative *My Bed*. A quilt-cover pinned over the window was the only concession towards privacy, decency and civility.

This kind of living was not considered a discomfort in Ashtrayland. A bed was for sleeping and shagging in and anything else was beside the point. Fancy blankets and quilts, elaborate bedsteads and the latest high-tech headboards were, frankly, superfluous. Not all societies in the history of the world have been able to make material possessions and comfort their priority. In Ashtrayland, materialism was not only irrelevant but could be a burden. You might have to do a moonlight flit at a moment's notice. Therefore, needs must, you travelled light.

The alcoves in the bedroom were piled a foot deep with neatly folded clothes. Urban rummaged about in them and threw me a T-shirt and a pair of jeans. 'Stick them on. My stuff's upstairs.' He went up to the attic, while I stripped off, dried myself and changed into his mother's clothing. I wasn't sure what to do with my own soggy clothes, but eventually I decided to throw them in the bath in the hope that Greta would wash them for me. I discovered that it was already full of dirty clothes so there was hardly any room for mine. I threw them in anyway and squelched everything down a bit. Bits of shit floated off my jeans, but there was little I could do about it. I scooped up what I could and put it down the toilet. My hands were left covered in a thin film of nastiness, which I washed off in the sink. There was no shampoo in evidence, or hot water, so I washed the canal-excrement out of my hair as best I could with cold water and soap.

Urban came back downstairs gleaming like a pin. He picked up his South Park toothbrush, squirted a pea-sized dollop of toothpaste on to it and slammed it into his mouth. He wore stonewashed Levi's, a checked lumberjack shirt with a button-down collar, Nike trainers and a Sox baseball cap, the very picture of American cultural imperialism.

Scrubbing doggedly at his teeth, he said, 'Stigglo cadie tushtay aglow plane tomig?'

'Speak English,' I said, rubbing my hair. 'You're not at the canal now, you know.'

He took the toothbrush out of his mouth. 'Still okay to stay at yours tonight? There's a smackhead in my room.'

I thought I'd misheard him. 'What did you say?'

'There's a smackhead crashed out on my bed.'

'What kind of smackhead?'

'The kind you don't want in your bedroom. See why I prefer the shed?'

Before I could say any more, the door creaked open and the ten-year-old boy from downstairs sidled into the room. He had blond hair, a bronze face and wore his Nike baseball cap turned back to front. 'All right, Urb? What's up?'

'All right, Sam? What you hanging around with them lot for?'

'Just having a weed. Nowt else to do. Where've you been?'

'Canal.'

'Snaygiffaygin?' he inquired in pig Latin, which meant, 'Sniffing?' Presumably he spoke in pig Latin so that I wouldn't pick up the meaning of the question, not realising that I'd been with Urban half the afternoon, or that my generation had invented this particular dialect some thirty years ago and that I therefore spoke it fluently.

'Snaygiffaygin laigike aygif baygastaygard,' I informed him.

The boy completely ignored me. Keeping his eyes firmly on Urban, he said, 'Who's that?'

Urban cupped his hands under the tap and filled his mouth with water. 'Choprrgh,' he attempted, then gargled extensively and spat into the sink.

'Choprrgh? Choprrgh who?'

'Just Chop.'

'Where from?'

'Round here.'

'Dirty digger?'

'Nope.'

'Foil-face?'

'Nope.'

'Pisspotical?'

'Nope.'

'Kiddy-fiddler?'

'Nope.'

'Fence?'

'Nope.'

'Pusher?'

'Nope.'

'Joey?'

'Nope.'

'What, then?'

I didn't fit into any of their stereotypes. 'Don't know, but he's sorted.'

The boy looked at me with new respect. 'Sorted' was even better than 'all right' in his vocabulary. He offered me his hand and his eyes. 'Samuel,' he said. 'Pleased to meet you, Mr Chop.'

Urban and Sam had fantastic eyes – all guile and innocence – like sparklers. I don't know what happened to me in the years between childhood and middle age, but somewhere along the line the light had gone out of mine. At some indefinite point in time, they had simply clouded over. No conscious decision was made. It just happened. Life defeated me.

Back downstairs, the music blared on. As I pushed past the ginger-haired girl, she gave me what I can only describe as an old-fashioned look: part suspicion, part contempt, part innuendo, but mostly puzzlement. Who are you? What are you doing here? What do you want? Ignoring her, I squeezed into the alcove with Sam and the baseball-capped little girl. By threatening to call in the mental-health department, I got them to turn down the music.

Urban stood behind the settee and called Tyson over. The dog jumped up at him enthusiastically. Out of spite, Urban patted the settee at the back of Frank's head, encouraging Tyson to jump up and down there.

Frank was quick to bite: 'Fuck off, Urbie, or I'll smash your fucking head in.'

'Yeah, he fucking will,' his girlfriend concurred.

'Shut up, Trudi. I'm talking,' Frank said, perhaps sensing some threat to his manhood in Trudi's assertive behaviour.

'Well, I'm talking as well, aren't I?' Trudi responded. 'You're not the only one allowed to talk, you know.'

'I know, but I'm actually talking now so shut the fuck up.'

'You shut the fuck up, you knobhead.'

Frank stood up. 'Know what? You do my fucking box in, you do.'

Trudi stood up too. Putting her hands on her hips and shaking her locks, she looked him right in the eye. 'Know what? You do my fucking box in you do so what you gunner do about it, you fucking noncing bastard? Eh? Want to make something of it? Eh?'

Frank pushed her back on to the settee. 'Shurrup trying to impersonate me mam, you silly slut. It's not funny.'

Everyone in the room was laughing, including me: Trudi's impersonation had been spot on, perfectly capturing Greta's actions, tone and manner. I wanted to applaud, but wasn't sure of the etiquette. I didn't want to make a blunder, which might cause the kids to be suspicious of me. I knew that I was in the middle of an alien culture – like being on holiday – and I didn't want to miss a second of it. I'd known many groups of kids, but always in a structured environment, always as a social worker, always having to be the one in control. I'd never been able just to sit back and let things happen. I saw an opportunity to observe something unique. Urban had taken me under his wing, which meant that I was 'all right'. No social worker, sociologist, reporter, writer, psychologist or anthropologist would ever have a better opportunity to view an unknown culture from within. I felt a bit like Little Big Man must have felt at the Battle of the Little Bighorn.

Sam pointed to the table. 'All right to make a spliff, Frank, mate?'

Frank nodded.

Sam knelt down before the table, pulled out a King Size Rizla and started putting a joint together. 'Good gear this, Frank.'

'That's about all he can do is smoke spliff,' Trudi said. 'He's not much use in the trouser department, if you follow my drift.'

Exasperated, Frank said, 'I've told you to shut up, haven't I?'

'So what? Who gives a fuck what you've told me to do?'

While Trudi and Frank were arguing, I saw Sam bite off a chunk of dope and pass it to the baseball-capped little girl. Swiftly, she pulled out the elasticated waistband of her trackie-bottoms and popped it into her knickers. She glanced at me and put an index finger to her lips. She might almost have been telling me to keep quiet because her imaginary baby was asleep in its imaginary cot and she didn't want anyone imaginary to disturb it. Long blonde hair, big blue eyes, butter wouldn't melt in her mouth. You know the type.

The girl on the stairs saw the manoeuvre too, but said nothing. Her hair was tied back in a frizzy ponytail. She sported the orange complexion common to all ginners, with the matching freckled face. She wore gold earrings, gold necklaces and a gold ring on every finger, all of which matched and enhanced her warm ginger glow. Only the blue beer can and the blue school uniform seemed out of place. She called over to me from her sentry post at the bottom of the stairs, 'Here, mate, what's your name again?'

'Chop,' I told her.

'Do you work, Chop?' she enquired, taking a long, thought-ful pull from her can of beer. 'Do you work, Chop? Do you work in a sweaty sock shop, Chop? Hickory dickory dock, Chop, the mouse ran up the clock.' She raised her eyebrows, as if she had said something profound. I liked the way she played with words, even if she didn't make any sense. She struck me as a budding writer or poet. I smiled back and meticulously didn't say a word.

Urban rescued me from the strained silence. 'She's nuts,' he said. 'We call her and Molly "the Strangers to Logic".'

The ginger-haired girl looked at me again, this time making

her eyeballs go cross-eyed. 'They don't appreciate my talents,' she said. 'Fucking Philistines.'

I couldn't remember what Urban had called her so I asked her her name.

'Kara MacNamara,' she said. 'Don't wear it out, mush.'

Sam came over with the joint and squashed himself in between the baseball-capped little girl and me. 'Want a blowback, Pixie?' She nodded, whereupon he turned the joint round and put the lit end into his mouth. He brought his lips up to hers and blew a steady stream of smoke out of the roach end of the joint and into her mouth. She swallowed and let her head slump back against the wall, contented. Then he turned to me. 'Want one, Mr Chop?'

'No, thanks,' I said. My lungs were already shot from too many blowbacks and hot-knives in the past. 'You're best off just smoking it normally,' I informed him. 'Much less damaging.'

'Who cares?' he said, offhandedly passing me the spliff, intimating by his tone and manner that I should smoke it exactly as I pleased and he would do the same.

'No one cares about us,' croaked Pixie. 'All the grown-ups are out of it. We're on our own.' I learned that she and Sam were best friends. She didn't come from Eastie, but was living on the estate with an uncle because her own mother was in jail 'for the duration'. Almost as an aside, she added, 'That's if you can call it living.'

Urban had mentioned a girl called Pixie. We were on our way to Huddersfield and I remembered him talking about her because he said he felt sorry for her. I had him down as Worst-off-Kid-in-the-World and I was surprised that he should feel sorry for someone else. He told me she was staying out nights and shagging boys and it wasn't right, because she was only ten. Her family were so fucked up with drugs that they didn't even know what day it was, never mind what Pixie was up to.

Such a beautiful child, leading such a horrid existence – I didn't know what to say to her. 'Never mind,' I said pathetically. 'It all works out in the end.' She shook her head and closed her eyes.

I now knew the name of everybody in the room, except for the lad sitting at the far end of the settee. I squeezed my way between Trudi and the table – Trudi pretended to trip me up as I passed – and offered him the spliff. He had medium-length fair hair in a basin-cut, his fringe continuing all the way round his head just above the ears. His face was pale, paler even than Urban's, as white as paint. Short, with only a slight frame, he somehow managed to appear strong and robust. Overall, he looked more like a farmhand than a city boy. With distrustful eyes he weighed me up for several seconds, eventually accepting the spliff without a word. I offered him my hand. 'Chop. Nice to meet you. What's your name?' He ignored me, got up, went into the kitchen and came back swigging out of a plastic carton of milk. Using his left hand for balance, he hopped up on to the sideboard and sat there sullenly surveying the room, keeping his thoughts to himself.

'Here, Chop,' Kara called, above the music. 'Damaged goods, mate. That's Skeeter. Don't waste your time. Don't turn your back on him neither. He'll stab you soon as look at you.' The boy gave Kara a nod of approval, as if she had just given him a glowing character reference.

'Still waters run deep,' Urban added, and moved as far from Skeeter as was possible in such a small room to sit in the alcove with the juniors. Dutifully Tyson strolled over, placed himself between Skeeter and his master and thereby grew in my estimation.

I was left with little option but to sit on the settee next to Trudi. 'Chop,' she said. 'That's a funny name. Where'd you get your name from, Chop?'

'It's a nickname,' I told her. 'My dad was a miner and you always got a nickname in the pits.'

'How come?'

'Don't know, really. You had your formal name that the Government and the bosses knew. Then you had your nickname that only your friends and family knew. It was your secret name. Only you could decide who to tell it to.' She looked at me, gormless. 'Don't you have a nickname?'

'Yeah, *Slut*,' Frank interrupted.

'Shut up, knobhead,' Trudi protested. 'I'm trying to talk to the nice man.'

Frank said, 'Yeah, you'll be trying to suck his cock in about three seconds flat, knowing you.'

'Well, there's no point trying to suck yours, is there? Might as well chew a soggy dishcloth. A small one.'

Acutely embarrassed, I looked for something to do. Down the side of the cushion, I noticed a tin of lighter gas. I picked it up and put it on the table. 'Do you do much gas, Chop?' Trudi enquired.

'No, I've got a petrol lighter,' I said. 'A Zippo.'

Everyone fell about laughing and there were various comments about my naïvety. 'No,' she said. 'Come here, I'll show you.' She took the canister in both hands and inserted the red adaptor between her teeth. Then she pushed the can, spraying pure butane into her mouth.

I tried to grab it from her. 'What are you doing? That's deadly fucking poison. It'll kill you stone dead.'

Deftly she defended the can with her right hand and continued to apply it to her mouth with the left. After ten or twelve seconds, she was sated. Eyes glazed, she passed it to me. 'Spongooliferous dandelions,' she confided, throwing an arm round my shoulders and trying to kiss me. I planted my hand in her face and held her off at a safe distance.

'Warning! Bio-hazard!' Kara called, from the back of the room.

'Try a blast,' Frank said. 'You and her look like you'd make a good team.'

'Better not,' I said. I didn't want to die suddenly and unexpectedly. I removed Trudi's arm from my shoulders and put the can back on the table, whereupon Sam shot over like a retriever and took it to the alcove. He took a blast, then Pixie, then Urban.

'Speech!' Kara shouted, when Urban had the can. Everyone joined in, chanting, 'Speech! Speech! Speech! Speech! Speech!'

Urban, eyes spinning, stood up and took a bow. 'Assembled Infidel! Assure the alien serpula, my gnu is as good as your parrot. Parasitic slap-worms trample my turtle. Never before have dovecotes and dachshunds hawked at my trumpet. Never again will carpets and Syria combine. I give you my word.' He bowed and sat down.

When the can was empty, Urban threw it to Tyson, who chewed at it enthusiastically, eventually making a hole and providing the last blast for himself. The dog howled in appreciation and everyone laughed at his animal stupidity.

I was feeling increasingly uncomfortable. I thought I'd seen everything – but a gas-sniffing dog? These kids were out of control and were doing anything they pleased. No moral values, no self-control, no sense of worth. Only the younger children seemed to realise that anything was wrong. The older ones were brain-dead by the look of them.

No wonder. Of the seven kids in the room, it looked like Kara was the only one still in school. The summer holidays had recently ended, but only she was in uniform. I knew that Urban had simply stopped going to school when he was seven. Frank had been expelled at ten. No one had ever chased either of them up. When I asked Sam which school he went to, he raised his eyebrows, astonished by my stupidity. 'School?' he said. 'No, no, no, we don't go to school. Where've you been?'

'You're being socially excluded,' I told him. 'You should go in and kick off until somebody listens to you.'

He shook his head again. 'No, no, no, Mr Chop. That's how I got booted out in the first place. And I don't know what you mean by overly exuded. I might be overly exuded, but at least I'm not a fat cunt like you.'

These kids were too far gone. They were never going to fit into normal schools. We needed special schools with an alternative curriculum. I assumed Kara had survived in education because her intelligence was evidently above the average, but I discovered that she spent most of her time bunking off in any case because school had nothing to offer her. She wasn't interested in listening to nuns telling her what to do when she had to come back and face the reality of East End Park, where survival was all that mattered.

Similarly, the majority had been through the care system. From my own experience, I knew that lack of beds, lack of properly trained staff, lack of will, lack of resources, a Kafka-esque, top-heavy bureaucracy, political correctness gone mad, a callous disregard for the United Nations Declaration of the Rights of the Child, and a complete loss of morale had contributed to the slow disintegration of child-care services. The care system was failing and alternative strategies were desperately needed. Health, justice, transport, housing, you name it – all failed. That was England towards the end of the twentieth century: a big, dirty, stinking failure. If it was a car, you'd scrap it.

I needed a spliff. Like Sam, I pointed to the table. 'Can I make one, Frank?'

'Yeah, go on,' Frank said. 'I'm going for a piss.' Instead of going upstairs as one might reasonably have expected, he simply went into the kitchen and pissed into the sink, all over the washing-up.

'You dirty fucking twat,' Urban said, in utter contempt, as Frank came back. 'You filthy, stinking bastard. I have to eat off them pots.'

'I'm warning you,' Frank cautioned, 'if you don't shut up, I'm gunner break your stupid neck.'

'Go on then, you mongy-faced bastard. Try it and watch how Tyson rips your throat out.'

Frank moved towards Urban. Tyson snarled and bared his teeth. Frank thought better of the idea. Instead, he went into the kitchen and returned with a plate of leftovers. 'Here, boy! Here, Tyson! Din-dins!' Tyson fell for it and bounced excitedly towards the proffered meal. Frank opened the front door and threw the plate into the street. Tyson flew out after it like a rocket. Then, businesslike, Frank went over to Urban and started punching him in the head. Hard.

After half a dozen man-size punches, I felt I had to intervene. I've an older brother so I know how it goes, but those punches were harder than I ever got and too many. I squeezed past Trudi's legs and grabbed Frank's arm, mid-punch. 'Whoa, Frank lad! That's enough!'

Unfortunately Frank's mood had changed. He spun round to face me. 'Who the fuck are you, like? Keep your fucking nose out.' From the corner of my eye, I saw Skeeter get down from the sideboard and move ominously towards me from the rear. Kara jumped up from her perch with alacrity, intercepted him and probably saved me from the heartbreak of a knife in the kidneys. She threw her arms round his shoulders, slapped a big, sloppy kiss on his lips, wrapped a leg round his hip and somehow pulled him down to the ground. 'Fuck me, baby!' she cried. 'Oh, fuck me, baby! Fuck me!' Frank and I were still eye-to-eye, but at the sight of this preposterous scene we both burst into laughter and the tension was broken. For reasons best known to herself, Trudi came up behind me and pushed me into Frank. Frank, attempting to retain his balance, wrapped his arms round me for safety and we plunged into the alcove. Like an out-of-control snowball, we collected Pixie, Sam and Urban on the way, ending up as a big pile of squirming bodies on the floor.

Greta chose just this moment to return to her charming abode.

FOUR
COMMANDER OF
THE NIGHT

I am Mistress Satanica,
Stealer of souls.
I live in darkness
And inhale the chaos around me.
I am Commander of the Night,
And you should be aware.
Don't look upon me too deeply:
What you see will scare.
My thoughts are my power,
The darkness my light,
I don't think you should be near tonight.

I revel in the pain I inflict,
The pain of today's society and broken dreams.
Your pain is my pain, as mine is yours.
You looked deep upon me, in me,
Do you think that was a mistake?
You tore open wounds that shouldn't be found,
Now I bleed upon you.
I told you not to be here tonight.

Spacey Tracy
9T6

Through the writhing pile of bodies, I saw her silhouetted in
the doorway. Hands on hips, she looked on aghast.

Unnervingly, she caught my eye, which was buried beneath numerous limbs and copious baseball caps at the time. She focused on me, as a snake zeros in on its prey. 'What the fucking hell is going on here?' she bawled. 'I said call round any time you like, not call round any time you like and nonce the fucking kids up!'

She stood there, eyes blazing. I forced myself up on to my hands and knees, displacing the bodies on top of me in the process. They tumbled off my back, one by one. 'Greta,' I said, 'I know what you're thinking, but I can explain.'

It was Greta's natural way to always see the worst in any given situation. Everyone was on the make, out to stitch her up, out to turn her over, pulling a blag, trying to get into her knickers or wanting to nonce the kids up. She did not discriminate. She saw the worst in everyone. She was already slightly drunk. She wobbled into the room, plopped her bagful of alcohol on the sideboard and glared unsteadily at Skeeter and Kara, who seemed to be performing a bizarre new form of foreplay on her carpet. 'Get up, you silly little perverts!' she commanded. Giggling, they got to their feet and brushed themselves down. 'Skeeter, you're seriously disturbed, lad. You need help. And, Kara, you're not all there, love. You need your head examining.'

Some secret sign must have passed between Skeeter and Kara. Playfully, but assertively, they each grabbed one of Greta's arms and in one swift movement catapulted her into the pile of bodies. Taken by surprise, I was knocked sideways by the impact and cracked my head against the wall. Skeeter and Kara quickly followed in and started tickling everyone. Not wishing to be left out, Trudi jumped on top for good measure. Seeing all this, Tyson rushed in through the open front door and sank his teeth into the crowd.

The situation was out of control. I had hundreds of kilograms on top of me, I was flat on my face and I was at the bottom of the heap. I used every ounce of the strength in my body to try to push myself off the floor, but the burden was too heavy, and even as I heaved some of the dead weight off my back, it wriggled and writhed and came back at me from another direction. I was powerless and bemused. My eyes, it seemed, were the eyes that everyone wanted to poke, my guts the guts that everyone wanted to tickle, my hair the hair that everyone wanted to pull, and my arse the arse that everyone wanted to bite. I knew in that moment what it meant to be a member of the underclass.

I had first met Greta several months earlier. It was close to midnight, on a wet and windy night. My friend the Doctor and I were returning half-cut from the chess club, heading back to his flat for a few more games and a nightcap. I was secretary of the Burmantofts Chess Club, which met at the Spit and Slaver, a local working-men's club, every Wednesday evening. It's a thankless task trying to run a chess club in the middle of the drink culture. We spent more time boozing, arguing and taking the piss out of each other than we did playing chess – and we had a bitter rivalry with the darts and doms lot – but I loved the game and it was my attempt to keep the thinking arts alive in my little corner of the universe. My friend wasn't really a doctor. We called him the Doctor because he claimed to be a Doctor of English and he could quote Dr Johnson. We'd just reached his block when a woman came marching across the car park out of the blue. 'Oi, nonces!' she bellowed. 'Seen a book?'

I looked at the Doctor. The Doctor looked at me. My eyebrows were raised. His brow was furrowed. I was immediately enthralled. Where had she come from? She seemed to have materialised out of thin air. Where had she found the courage to accost two big, bolshy blokes in the early hours of the morning in what can only be described as a very rough neighbourhood? How had she reached the conclusion that we were nonces? What manner of book did she seek?

She was six foot tall, big for a woman in our part of the world, powerful and imposing. She had the presence. You knew she was there. She wore white trainers, beige jeans and a variation of the black bomber-jacket commonly favoured by the criminal classes. She sported an outgrown skinhead hair-cut, bird-style, with fringes at the forehead and the nape of the neck. A Borstal spot tattooed on her right cheek formally announced that she had been through the system. There was an odour about her, nothing offensive, just the absence of expensive soaps, toiletries and deodorants: a kind of carbolic fustiness, difficult to define, but which had probably been prevalent in the human race before the advent of the petro-chemical industry. She had the red complexion of a drinker and her eyes were too close together. Nice-looking, but scruffy, a little ragged round the edges, and she was obviously drunk, stoned, drugged up, or a combination of them all. Nevertheless, I was sucked into her sparkling green snake eyes. 'What's that you say, love?'

'Book, divvy! Seen a fucking book, or am I talking to a plank?' When I didn't answer, she tutted and started searching under the cars in the car park.

The Doctor knew trouble when he saw it. 'Coming in, or what?'

'Don't know,' I said. 'This looks too good to miss.'

He rubbed his magnetic fob against the security door, which opened with a click. 'Suit yourself,' he said, 'but use a condom. There's a lot of Aids about. I'll see you at the club next week.'

I did sort of fancy her. I won't deny it. She oozed a certain raw, untreated sexuality. She saw me looking at her. 'What you goggling at, devo?'

'Nothing.'

'Must be,' she said. 'No one goggles at nowt.' For no

obvious reason, she chose the next moment to wail at the sky at the top of her voice: 'I want me fucking X-File-faced book back, you bastard spanners!'

The good Doctor stopped in his tracks, came back, grabbed Greta's shoulder and slapped his hand over her mouth. Showing his true colours, he put his face up to hers and growled, 'Shut the fuck up, you stupid, ugly bitch.'

Like me, he had quickly calculated the degree of annoyance being caused to the neighbours. We were outside Lucifer Grange – sixteen storeys, a hundred flats, an average of 1.35 people per flat – which meant that approximately 135 people had simultaneously been woken up and were pulling back their curtains to see what all the commotion was about. The Doctor knew full well that the slightest complaint from any one of them would earn him a stern letter of rebuke from the council's antisocial-behaviour team.

Greta tore his hand loose from her mouth. 'Help!' she screamed. 'Rape! Nonces! Murderers! I'm getting raped by X-File, fucked-up-faced paedophiles! Call the fucking scuffers!'

'Forget it,' the Doctor said, letting her go. As always, he relied on Dr Johnson to summarise the situation: ' "The woman's a whore, and there's an end on't." ' He let himself into his block, allowing the heavy security door to slam firmly shut behind him. He left me standing in the car park with her, as if she were my problem and mine alone.

I had a Dr Johnson quote of my own: 'As I know more of mankind I expect less and less of them, and am ready now to call a man a *good man*, upon easier terms than I was formerly.'

Greta and I eyed each other up. We were both so alien to each other that I don't think either of us knew what to say. She broke the ice. 'What you hanging round with a prick like that for?'

'Good question,' I said. 'I'm not sure. I think it's because his Caro-Kann Defence is virtually impregnable. What sort of book have you lost?'

She scratched her head. Looked up and down the road. 'My Social Security book, dingy, what sort do you think? Do you think I'd be traipsing round in the pissing-down rain at midnight looking for *War and Fucking Peace?*'

I didn't know what else to do, so I invited her back to my place. 'I've got half a bottle of vodka in the fridge and a big pot of skunk. Care to join me for a nightcap?'

'Don't mind,' she said. 'Don't think you're noncing me up, though, cos you're not.'

'How old are you?' I enquired.

'Thirty-one,' she said.

'Well, how the fuck can I nonce you up if you're thirty-fucking-one?'

'Because I know what you nonces are like,' she said. 'You'll nonce anybody up and you don't even care how old they are.'

'Whatever,' I said, perplexed. 'Come on. I live two blocks up.'

So I took her home and I nonced her up.

Greta elbowed Kara in the face, tore Skeeter down to the ground by his hair, punched Frank in the mouth and finally freed herself from the mêlée. She kicked Tyson across the room and ragged the kids off the pile, one by one. 'Pack it in now!' she screamed. 'That's enough!' I was exposed, bruised, bleeding and battered. 'Look what you've done to poor old Chop, you silly little spastics. That's no way to treat a fucking guest.'

Urban gave me his hand, pulled me up and guided me to the settee. I sat down and tried to regain my composure. I had a grazed forehead, a busted nose and a savaged arse. My arse hurt most of all. I feared that Tyson had taken a rather large chunk out of it, but I didn't want to ask anyone to take a look in case Greta got the wrong end of the stick again. The coffee-table had been knocked across the room. All the rubbish that had previously stood on it was now scattered on the floor and the stench of spilt cider made me want to retch. Frank dived into it urgently, looking for his dope. 'Got it,' he said, picking it up and showing everyone. 'Found it.' He examined it carefully and came to the belated conclusion that it was smaller than it used to be. After some thought, he said, 'Here, who's been at my fucking weed?' I quite liked Frank. He was one of life's losers, like me.

Kara and I knew the guilty parties but were never called to testify. Greta took control of the situation. 'Frank, get in that fucking kitchen and do the washing-up. I bet you've been pissing in the sink again, you filthy little bastard. Urban, upstairs and tidy my room. Chop's wearing my clothes, which means you've been in there rooting about again. If there's one crease out of place, I'm gunner smash your fucking head in. Kara, Hoover up in here. Trudi, dust, tidy and empty the rubbish. Skeeter, Sam and Pixie, get that dirty fucking smack-head out of Urban's room and dump him in the midden yard. Chop, pour me a drink.'

To my surprise, everyone did exactly as they were told. They were well enough acquainted with Greta's moods to know that it wasn't a good time to argue with her. Later, when she'd had a few more, would be a safer bet. Frank went into the kitchen, ran the taps and started in on the washing-up. Urban went upstairs. Kara plugged in the Hoover and started pushing it around the room. Trudi filled a carrier-bag with rubbish and dusted the surfaces with an old sock that she found in the kitchen. She winked at me a couple of times in passing, as if she and I were involved in some gigantic conspiracy. Skeeter, Sam and Pixie followed Urban upstairs and closed the door behind them. I retrieved a couple of Pot Noodle containers from the deck, used the sideboard as a bar and carried out my orders. With no specific task allocated to him, Tyson went outside and worried anyone who might be passing.

Greta and I sat on the settee and relaxed while the kids did all the Joey work. I wiped the blood from my nose with her T-shirt and rubbed my buttock. 'That fucking dog bit my arse,' I told her.

'Never mind,' she said, slurping cider from a Pot Noodle container. 'Dogs will be dogs. What can you do?'

With another wink, Trudi reassembled the table in front of me and, with an enigmatic smile, carefully put all the odds and sods back into place until they were untidy again.

'Dope, Frank!' Greta yelled. Frank came in sheepishly and put the dope on the table. 'Skin up, Chop,' she ordered. She obviously held shares or moral rights in the merchandise, so I skinned up.

As it was someone else's gear, I decided on a super-cone. Working on the arm of the settee, I stuck three King Size Rizlas together and tore at the paper until I had the perfect shape. I took a Regal from the cigarette packet, split it open and poured the tobacco on to my carefully shaped paper. Kara came past with the Hoover. 'Mind your feet.' I lifted my feet, added a double portion of dope just to piss Frank off and rolled the joint into shape. I roached it, lit it and sucked the smoke into my lungs. 'Ah, this is the life,' I said.

Upstairs, I heard a distant bang, bang, bang and a thud. Then, from behind the stairs door, I heard a louder and more localised bang, bang, bang, bang, bang and a thwock. Intrigued, I got up and opened the door. To my horror, an emaciated creature with blackened teeth plunged down the remaining couple of stairs and sprawled out comatose across the dog-shelf. He was a male of the species, probably in his twenties, barely alive. Skeeter, Sam, Pixie and Urban followed him down the stairs. The others leaped over him to get past, but Sam stood on his head and used him as a springboard.

Urban and Sam grabbed one leg, Skeeter and Pixie the other. With his head banging along to the insane beat of the rave music, they pulled him across the room and out into the street. Tyson went for the black-toothed apparition as soon as they got him outside. 'No, Tyson!' Urban cautioned. 'Nasty!'

I only found out later what had happened to the smackhead. In his sock drawer, Urban had a length of flex with a plug at one end and bare wires at the other. If he found anyone asleep in his room who he didn't like, his habit was to give them a quick 240 volts to let them know that they weren't particularly welcome.

From the doorway, I watched the kids drag the guy down the street, until they disappeared into the midden yard. Shaking my head, I went to sit next to Greta and handed her the spliff. 'Who's that, then?'

'Cod,' she said.

'Are you sure he's all right? Maybe we should call an ambulance.'

'Fuck him,' she said. 'What do I care?'

Urban Grimshaw was born on 5 November 1984 at Styal women's prison, Manchester. His mother was serving a nine-month sentence for 'hotels'. She was young and attractive at the time, the common-law wife of Bentham Stock. The hotel blag involved her using her considerable physical charms to pick up men, go back with them to their hotel rooms and begin foreplay. Bentham would then burst into the room, crying, 'That's my wife, you bastard!' He and Greta would then lay into the victim and steal all his money. They banked on their dupes being too embarrassed or humiliated to report the incident.

Their reign of terror soon came to an end, because they didn't change hotels regularly enough. They were brought to justice and punished by the long arm of the law. Bentham got three years, Greta nine months, the law never having advanced since the days of Mr Bumble the beadle: it was still an ass, still assuming that the husband is more responsible for wrong-doing than his wife. The nine months Greta served coincided almost exactly with Urban Grimshaw's gestation period. He spent this time warm and secure, cosseted in his mother's womb. It was the happiest time of his life.

Greta told me that she quite liked it too. For the first time since she could remember no men were trying to get their cocks up her minge, she got three square meals a day and no one was on her case. She was left alone by all and sundry because she was protected by the Code of the Underclass, which stated that pregnant women were temporarily ex-empted from the argy-bargy. No one beat her up, nonced her up or taxed her, a big improvement on her previous life. Urban Grimshaw slipped quietly into the world towards the end of her sentence. She said that as a baby he seldom cried, almost as though he sensed what a futile endeavour this would prove. At the time of his birth, he had two older siblings, Heidi, aged four, and Frank, aged two, both in the care of the local authority. Greta was all of nineteen. Bentham was twenty.

I knew Bentham, not to talk to but from a distance. He was well known as a hard-nut local knock-out case. I could hold my own in a punch-up, but Bentham was out of my division. He could have knocked me out as easily as I could have beaten him at chess. He was one of those blokes who wears a skinhead cut like he means it. Only little, but powerfully built. If he gave you a dirty look, it was time to be on your way.

Still, Bentham wasn't around when Greta got out, and she had a life to get on with. Greta wasn't the sort to hang around for years on end waiting for someone, so she went out one night and found herself an interim man. Others followed and she had three more kids: Rosie, James and Darryl. Then she met Kev, who didn't mind bringing up six kids who weren't his own, and finally settled into domestic bliss. Bentham got out of jail at some indeterminate point and went about his business as if Urban had never happened. He married another and had a big family. Greta didn't mind because she was all right with Kev. He wasn't violent, he brought money in and he was good with the kids. What more could any woman ask? She didn't ask where the money came from because, frankly, she didn't give a shit. They lived together for the next six or seven years. She had her nutty episodes and wandered off for a while, but Kev was forgiving and they always got back together. Love at first sight did not exist where Greta came from, but over the years she came to love and respect her little Kev. Heidi, on the other hand, the eldest girl, now approaching puberty, hated the slimy, two-faced, scum-sucking bastard with a vengeance.

Things reached crisis point the following year. The older kids were running wild, they weren't going to school and Heidi had made allegations about Kev. Greta, I suspect, had lost the plot and started drinking heavily and taking drugs before things came to a head, although she denies it to this day. Social Services had the kids on the at-risk register and no doubt the day came when they felt compelled to act. One day, they turned up in force and took the kids away.

For the children, it was out of the frying-pan and into the fire. Too hot to handle, they were split up and sent to different institutions. Heidi went to live with her grandmother, Frank and Urban were put in separate children's homes, Rosie and James were placed with foster-parents, and baby Darryl was sent to an institution for children with special needs. Greta went bananas for a while and that was about the state of play when I came into the equation.

I believe Social Services ought to have kept the kids together, no matter the cost or inconvenience to the taxpayer. If necessary, they should have opened a children's home especially for them. Kids aren't stupid. They know the score. Alone in care, they were badly bullied and abused. They knew instinctively that they should have been together and they went wild in protest. The younger three were easier to handle, but Frank and Urban trashed every children's home they were put in. At every opportunity, they went on the run – sometimes together, sometimes alone – and they looked for their mum, who had by now lost the house and gone mispering herself. As they saw it, anything was preferable to the children's homes. They slept rough if they had to, and among drunks, drug addicts, prostitutes and thieves when they could. Urban and Frank were seven and ten respectively.

It has taken me years to piece together everything that happened to the Grimshaw children in their formative years. I've learned bits here, bits there, and I don't claim to know everything or understand everything even now. I certainly didn't know half of it at the time. What I did know was that I wasn't prepared to put the blame on them. They were only children. Nor did I blame Greta, who was an obvious social inadequate if ever there was one. Where was the support, the guidance? The fabric of society was disintegrating around us.

The thing about Greta was that you couldn't help but drink and take drugs with her. She brought out the worst in you. Like Oscar Wilde, I could resist anything but temptation. If I was working or otherwise occupied I could lay off the beer and drugs for days or weeks on end, but if they were right there in front of me I was powerless – and with Greta they were always right there in front of me. I don't blame her for my behaviour: I got mashed because I liked to. I spent several weeks getting smashed out of my face with Greta before I even met any of her kids.

Maybe I needed a good woman to keep me on the straight and narrow, but if I had imagined Greta to be that woman I was soon disabused of the notion. Our physical relationship never took off: the spark wasn't there between us. There was no passion. I found it impossible to have any kind of relationship with her. The main problem was that she just wasn't monogamous. She shagged anyone she took a fancy to and didn't worry too much about the consequences. On one level I admired her for this, it was her body and she was free to do with it as she pleased, but it wasn't something I was willing to put up with from a partner. Another problem was that she was ever so slightly schizophrenic. I hadn't realised it when I first met her, but it got more and more obvious by the day. Had I been on the ball, I might have picked up on it at the hostel when her mate, Spacey Tracy, greeted her with, 'Hiya, Gret. Who are you today, then, love?' Finally, her behaviour swung from bizarre to erratic to violent in seconds. Drinking partners could look on amused from a distance, but sexual partners usually bore the brunt of it. If we kept it platonic, we got along. Besides which, she had lots of loose young mates with small brains but big tits who I wanted to get my hands on, and I had loads of ugly fat mates with small cocks but big wallets who she wanted to get her hands on. In effect, we were business partners.

I was starting to get drunk. The kids had drifted off, two by two, after finishing their tasks. Greta was in charge again and they no longer had a kids-only space. Sam and Pixie were the first to make their excuses. They had to be in by eight o'clock, they said, but I suspect they planned to consume their stolen merchandise. Frank and Skeeter left as soon as it was dark enough to go twocking. Trudi and Kara were bored and wanted to find some lads who might properly appreciate them. Urban and Tyson stayed behind, waiting for me.

'You're getting drunk, Chop. You said I could stay at yours tonight. Mum, Chop said I could go to work with him in the morning. Is that all right? Chop, you promised.' Urban wasn't going to let me chill out and relax. He considered his mother a bad influence on me. 'You promised . . .'

If nothing else, I was a man of my word. 'He's right, Gret. I did promise. Is it all right with you?'

'Sorted,' she said. 'No problem at all. I'll go out, if you lend us a tenner.'

Normally it's the babysitter who gets paid, but not in this case. I knew where she would go and I knew what the tenner would be spent on. She would go round to Gwyn Doyle's house, the same Gwyn Doyle who was better known as Foily Doily, an inveterate local smackhead. Greta made Urban wash his hands and face and put his coat on, and she made me brush my teeth. Rightly, she didn't want someone who reeked of cider looking after her kid. She gave Urban a kiss on the forehead and bade us farewell.

She was already tying her shoelaces as Urban and I left the house.

FIVE
A SEASON IN HELL

Prison boy wrote home one day,
   Found his true love gone away.
When he asked the reason why,
   She answered him with this reply:
If you choose the honest life,
   Surely I will be your wife.
If you choose the life of crime,
   Prison boy do your time.

Late that night in his cell,
   Prison boy rang the bell.
Screws came running to the door,
   Prison boy was on the floor.
In his hand a note all red,
   In his hand a note that said:
Dig it wide and dig it deep,
   Plant red roses at my feet.
On my chest a turtle dove,
   Tell the world I died for love.

Thieving Little Simpkins
On the run from Hell and High Water

Urban and I walked up East Park View towards the Slip.
A group of dirty diggers were dossing near the phone-box
outside my nan's old house. They cluttered up the place and
made it look untidy. Nan never could stand clutter. As we

approached them, a white Mitsubishi pulled up, driven by a young Asian guy with another riding shotgun. Both wore the regulation baseball caps of the Great Satan.

'That's nice to see,' I said. 'It's rare we get any Asian visitors to these shores.' Apart from the shopkeepers, who came in to run their shops but lived elsewhere, East End Park was almost exclusively white. There were a few black and mixed-race people dotted about, but no Asians. This was probably because if any Asians moved in, they were immediately petrol-bombed by the local NF boys. The government tried to kid on that we lived in a harmonious multi-cultural society, but my eyes and ears told me different. In effect, a form of apartheid was in operation. Asians had their own communities, schools, social and family networks, places of work and worship. The only contact between the white and Asian communities was through trade. They had lots of stuff we wanted, like heroin, for example. As far as I could tell we had nothing they wanted, apart from money.

The smackheads were pushing each other out of the way, almost fighting, trying to get to the driver's window first. Bits of brown paper were hurriedly exchanged for bits of brown powder. As soon as both parties had what they wanted, they melted into thin air. They were gone, even before Urban and I reached the Slip.

The Slip Inn was the heart of East End Park, acting as youth club, community centre, sports club, social club, forum, pawnshop and black-market shopping mall. You could buy anything you wanted in there at one-third the standard price. Michael Harrington, the American writer and sociologist, once observed, 'In almost any slum there is a vast conspiracy against the forces of law and order.' The Slip Inn proved him right.

As a kid East Park View was my favourite street, because it was irregular, different on both sides. To the right was the standard assortment of gable ends going off into the distance, all different shades of red, orange and brown. To the left were gardens. Lovely, lovely, green and yellow gardens. They ran off in a straight line all the way down to the park. East Park View and, behind it, Londesborough Grove formed a kind of Maginot Line that divided the estate in two. Between those streets was a maze of ginnels and passages where we played kiss-catch and hide-and-seek. The View was paradise to me when I was little, a world of beauty and adventure. It seemed to go on for ever. If I came home late and Mum asked where I'd been, I'd always say, 'On the View,' and she understood.

Turning back, I looked along it for old times' sake. I saw that it had retained its magic. The squalor and decay only added to its splendour. The streetlights receded into the distance like glowing orange embers, the moon burned yellow in the sky and a billion tiny particles of broken glass reflected the moonlight and blazed like stars. The whole street crackled with energy, as stark and startling as a Van Gogh masterpiece.

At the bottom of the View, two bright white lights came into the picture. They danced around, like UFOs, got bigger and bigger, made a distant *b-vvuing* noise and finally resolved into a couple of headlights coming towards us at speed. For safety, Urban and I jumped on to the low wall bordering the Slip Inn car park. Tyson took refuge behind. At the top of the View, you had the option of turning left into the car park, or going straight ahead into the solid brick wall of the electricity substation. In short, East Park View was a dead-end. The car was approaching at forty or fifty miles an hour and showed no sign of slowing. As far as I could tell, it was about to smash into the substation wall, killing the occupant and plunging the whole estate into darkness.

As it came level with us, the wheels locked. The vehicle skidded, screamed and travelled sideways like a rally car. We were close enough to see the whites of the driver's eyes and his

Sox baseball cap. He wrestled with the steering-wheel for his very life. In the nick of time, the vehicle – the same one we'd encountered earlier in the day – skidded round a further ninety degrees, throwing up a blizzard of dust, grit and glass. Finally it shrieked to a dramatic halt, its rear bumper only inches away from the substation wall.

Urban clapped his hands in glee and ran excitedly towards the car. 'Wicked, man! Excellent hundred-and-eighty turn, Sparky.'

Sparky allowed his arm to dangle casually out of the window. 'Easy now, little bro. What's happening?' A showman, I gathered. 'I was just on my way to your mum's to find you. Just gunner park the car, then I'm off to the shed. Wanna lift?'

Urban rushed back to me. 'Now's your chance to meet the Shed Crew, Chop. You might not get another.'

'Wasn't that the Shed Crew I just met?'

'Some of them,' he said. 'The Outer Circle and the Arctic Circle. Now's your chance to meet the Inner Circle, the main monkeys. You're invited.'

An opportunity to meet the main monkeys was too good to miss. 'Is that car legal?' I enquired.

'Course it is,' he assured me.

Sparky revved the engine impatiently, in my view beyond its design specifications.

Urban pulled on my arm. 'Come on.' Out of the side of his mouth, he made that strange chuck-chuck sound that only dog-owners can produce. 'Tyson! Come on, lad!' He opened the back door and Tyson leaped in without a doubt in his mind. I was full of doubt – the driver was certainly no more than fifteen – but I followed the dog into the back seat. I sensed that this was my destiny. I would live or I would die, but it would be out of my hands. Fate would make the final decision.

Sparky spun the back wheels, creating a high-pitched, twirling screech but somehow managing to keep the car stationary. Take-off might come at any second, so Urban dived in the back door with me, then clambered over into the front. As the car accelerated away with the door still flapping, my head was pushed back into the headrest. Sparky achieved nought to sixty in an impressive five or six seconds, then kept to a constant velocity – no doubt considering that speed more than adequate in a residential area. I was able to pull the door shut when the G-forces eased. In seconds, we were approaching the bypass at the bottom of the View, but Sparky showed no inclination to apply the brakes. If anything, he was accelerating again. I looked over his shoulder at the speedometer: 60 . . . 70 . . . 80! With no time to protest and no prospect of escape, I hurriedly pulled the rear seatbelt across my chest and attempted to plug the male adaptor into its female receptacle. Nothing doing. The bastard wouldn't go in. 'Fuck,' I cried. 'Fuck, fuck, fuck, fuck.' We hit the bypass at ninety and flew – between an oncoming bus to our right and an oncoming truck to our left – straight over the road and into the park. With several heart-wrenching bumps along the way, we shot down the narrow service road between the bowling green and the playground, and continued to gain speed.

I gripped my seat. 'Slow down, you bastard,' I snarled, 'or I'll garotte your useless fucking throat with this useless fucking seatbelt.'

Sparky ignored me. He was too busy trying to keep us alive. He gripped the steering-wheel for dear life and reverberated like an astronaut on take-off.

I might have been screaming or something. Urban tried to comfort me. 'Can't slow down, Chop, else we'll never make it up the hill.'

'Hill?' I said. 'What fucking hill?'

I knew perfectly well what hill. I'd played on it as a kid, but I couldn't envisage anyone trying to drive up it. It was very bumpy, very steep and very covered with trees. We hit the hill at maybe a hundred miles an hour and, once again, I was thrown back into my seat. We cannoned up the one-in-two slope, narrowly missing several trees, any one of which would instantly have terminated our existence, demolished several bushes and saplings and finally came to a juddering halt at the top.

I opened the door, fell out, dazed, and threw up into the mud. I went into my own little world. They say it always comes in threes and that was the third time in one day that my life had been endangered. I heard Urban's voice: 'Chop, come away from the car.'

I didn't want to come away from the car. I didn't want to do anything. I was happy there, grovelling about in the mud with my face in vomit. I had finally found my true vocation.

'Chop, come away from the car.'

'Why? Why should I come away from the car? Why should I do anything I don't want to do?'

'Do you want to die, Chop?'

I had to think about it, but in the end I said, 'Not today, preferably.'

'Then, Chop, come away from the car.'

I looked up to see Sparky taking a petrol-can out of the boot. He opened it, poured some of the petrol on to a rag and the rest over the back seat of the car. He lit the rag with a disposable lighter, threw it flaring into the car and exited, stage left. I was already up and running, but the explosion blew me into the air and sent me rolling down the hillside like an avalanche.

When I stopped rolling, I performed a rapid inventory of my injuries. The back of my hair was singed and my ears were cooked. Other than that, the damage seemed superficial. Third-degree burns at worst.

Urban, Sparky and Tyson came running down past me. 'Come on, Chop,' Urban called. 'We have to chip, quick time, before the scuffers come. The parkie'll report the fire.' When I didn't move, he came back up the hill and offered me his hand. 'Come on, Chop. What's up?'

The sky was red behind me. The whole hill was ablaze. The flames reflected on Urban's pallid white face like some nightmare vision from *Apocalypse Now*. 'What's up?' I said. 'Petrol and oxygen are a very volatile combination, Urban. That's what's up. Are you all nuts, or something?'

'Got to torch the twocks, Chop. Fingerprints. The Babylon'll get us.'

'Oh,' I said. 'Fingerprints. That's all right, then.' I gave Urban my hand and allowed him to pull me to my feet. 'My ears are burning. Do you think someone's talking about me behind my back?'

'Don't be daft.'

'Anyway, thanks for saving my life,' I said.

'You're welcome,' he said. 'Ta for fishing me out the canal earlier on.'

'Don't mention it, but you'd have been okay on your own. You're a good swimmer.'

'Doesn't matter,' he said. 'It's the thought that counts.'

We joined Sparky and Tyson at the bottom of the hill. Hands on his hips, Sparky gazed at the summit, admiring his handiwork. 'Did I shit you up, mush?'

'Worse than that,' I said. 'You burned my ears and made me question the meaning of seatbelts.'

Sparky looked puzzled, shrugged, and said, 'Soz about the ears, mush.'

'Don't worry about it,' I said. 'Ears are ten a penny, this day and age. Do you know how many human ears are on the planet as we speak? About twelve billion of the cunts.'

Sparky slapped me on the back. 'You're a funny geezer,

mush. Mad, but funny. I'm just hoping you're not a nonce. Urban's one of us and we'd have to kill you if you was.'

The first question these kids seemed to ask about the adults they met was: 'Is he or she a nonce?' They were kids who lived on their wits and who responded quickly to their experiences. If that was the first question on their mind, I concluded that they must have come across a lot of nonces throughout their travails.

'I'm not a nonce,' I said. 'If you're calling me a kiddy-fiddler, I'll fight you here and now.' I didn't want to fight, but in the underclass if someone insulted or offended you, a show of aggression, or at least righteous indignation, was almost compulsory. Failure to stand up for yourself was taken as a sign of weakness. I had learned this working in the assessment centre. The staff and kids were permanently at war with each other and I took a good deal of flak from a little gang of thugs and bullies. My fellow countryman had pulled me aside as if he were the member of staff and I were the child: 'If ya let 'em, Chop, they'll run all over ya. Stand up to 'em, like. Ya dote have to hurt 'em, but ya gotta let 'em knar ya not a muppet, like.' When a girl was almost raped, I felt compelled to act. By simply grabbing the ring-leader by the throat and having a quiet snarl in his ear, I was able to convince him of the error of his ways. Not best social-work practice, but effective in an emergency. In short, with rowdy teenagers it's best to let them know straight off that you won't be taking no shit from them.

'Don't get shirty, mush, else you'll come off worst. I have to ask. Pissy, poncy nonces are crawling out of the woodwork everywhere you go.' Sparky had a point. The night before on prime-time TV I'd seen a Paris fashion show. The twelve-, thirteen-, fourteen-year-old 'models' were dressed in skimpy, sexy, revealing clothes. Children were being turned into sex objects on an international stage. Little wonder that the less aware among us were unable to control their baser impulses.

'I'm the oldest in the crew,' Sparky continued, 'so I have to look out for the younger ones. No nonces. That's a strict rule.'

Urban moved between us, which broke the tension as Sparky and I ended up looking at him instead of at each other. 'Sparky dun't like nonces, do ya, Sparky?'

'Don't know anyone who does,' Sparky answered.

'He's always beating 'em up, art ya, Sparky?'

'Someone's got to do it.'

'I'm not a nonce,' I assured him again. 'You don't have to worry.'

Tyson interrupted our conversation by barking and running round in circles.

'Sparky!' Urban yelled. 'It's on top! Let's nash!'

A police car, blue lights flashing, drove into the park at the bottom by the railway. We ran back along the service road and cut through the bowling green, which seemed like a bad move to me because it had only one entrance and was surrounded by a three-foot-thick privet hedge. We ran across diagonally, disturbing two youngsters, barely into their teens, who were having full sex in the middle of the green. The girl's long blonde hair fanned out across the grass, her top was pushed up over her breasts, her yellow summer skirt was round her waist, while her knickers and bra had been flung to the side. Ignoring us, the boy moved in and out enthusiastically with his trousers round his ankles. Sparky and I ran either side of the obstacle, but Urban leaped over the top, calling, 'Hiya, Molly,' as he passed. I noticed that Molly still wore her dazzling white ankle socks, which were even more startling now, attached to naked, wriggling legs against a dark-green background.

I was worried. I saw no way out of the bowling green and I thought we were trapped. If the police caught us, I would have too much explaining to do. Local knowledge, however, is indispensable in these matters. Tyson disappeared through a hole in the hedge, quickly followed by Urban, Sparky and me.

It was a tight fit, but I made it through with a few extra scratches. We ran across the bypass into Londesborough Grove, slowed to a walking pace and ambled along trying to look inconspicuous.

The Londesboroughs had a different character from the rest of the estate. Londesborough Grove was a narrow, tree-lined street, so narrow that two cars had difficulty scraping past each other. Residents' cars were parked half on the pavement to allow other road-users to get by without a struggle. Sleeping policemen at the top and bottom of the road warned drivers to keep their speed to a minimum. The houses were brick-built and in blocks of four. With small gardens at the front and larger ones at the rear, they were like stretched, semi-detached houses with two extra dwellings squashed into the middle. An arched ginnel ran through the centre of each block, giving residents of the middle houses direct access to their back gardens. The street had an air of decay. The houses were weatherworn and dusty, the trees and privets threadbare and dishevelled; the streetlights were the old-fashioned kind that gave off a bizarre purple glow like an Insecticutor. I used to avoid this street when I was young – too creepy and claustrophobic.

Half-way up the street, Urban pushed open a gate. A shared asphalt path ran between two front gardens. The one to our left was quite nice, laid out in a series of concentric squares with a birdbath at its heart. The one to the right had no discernible plan, and, unless I missed my guess, no one had disturbed it for years.

Urban was about to enter the ginnel between the houses, but Sparky grabbed his shoulder and pulled him back. The pecking-order was important to Sparky and there were established rules. He would walk down the ginnel first, as was his right. As he moved through it, his form was silhouetted against the greyer light at the end of the tunnel. This moody, evocative image at first conjured up *A Clockwork Orange*, where Alex and his little droogs beat up the old prestoopnik in the underpass. Then I thought of John Wayne silhouetted in the doorway at the end of *The Searchers*. Sparky turned back towards us, beckoned with a flick of his head and I was reminded of the Artful Dodger sneaking along some seedy back-alley in Whitechapel.

I told Urban what I was thinking. 'He reminds me of the Artful Dodger and you remind me of Oliver Twist.'

Urban was not so deprived that he'd never seen Lionel Bart's *Oliver!* on television at Christmas. 'Well,' he said, 'I guess that makes you Fagin, then, Chop.' Half-way down the ginnel, he jumped up, clicked his heels together and started singing: 'Consider yourself . . . our mate . . .'

I giggled as I watched him twirl and pirouette down the ginnel, and even joined in with a little jig of my own, but I couldn't help feeling guilty. The Fagin reference had been too near the mark.

Sparky came from a decent background. His dad earned good money and his family was affluent and respectable. He was doing well at school, popular among his peers, and looked to have a good future ahead of him. Things went pear-shaped for him as he entered his teens. Suddenly his dad wasn't around. Sparky would seldom talk about his past so I'm not clear if the problem was divorce or bereavement. Either way, it amounted to the same thing – Dad wasn't there any more. Mum shacked up with someone new and Sparky soon developed classic step-dad problems. His real dad was the only person he had ever truly respected. Sparky was an intelligent lad, a Holden Caulfield who saw most people as phoney. Nothing particularly fabulous about his dad, but he was straight and he was there. Without him, Sparky was cast adrift. With no one to guide him through the stormy seas of adolescence, he floundered. The new step-dad just didn't do it for him. There were problems – big problems – which culminated in him letting loose with his fists and giving the bloke a pasting. Sparky was a big lad. Gangly, but solid and muscular. The step-dad ended up in hospital while Sparky ended up in court and in care.

Sorted, he thought. Fair enough, then. Hunky-fucking-dory. He was on his own and he had to go to an attendance centre and scrub the floors and live in a children's home. Life just wasn't panning out as planned and he grew increasingly miffed. Care was shit. Nothing but inbred mutants who thought he was posh because he could string a sentence together without saying 'fuck' three times. A couple of half-decent birds, but otherwise the whole place was some kind of funny farm for disturbed, nonced-up, rat-faced, smegma-sandwich-eating doilems. Some weird people in care, boy. Very, very peculiar, some of them. Some perverted little rent-boy tried it on, so Sparky took him into the tool shed and impaled him on a pitchfork. Court again. Detention centre this time for a short, sharp shock – the same as he'd given the rent-boy. Perhaps the magistrate was trying to make the punishment fit the crime.

Sparky went to DC just after his fourteenth birthday, which made him about the youngest there. One or two people thought they could take him for a Joey, but even though some were bigger, he wouldn't bow down. There were many fights. Some he won, some he lost – and was taken to hospital – but he soon found his place in the pecking-order and gained the respect of his fellow inmates. He lost a couple of weeks' remission, but the screws never heard about most of the fights. No one told them anything. Inside there were rules, and rule number one was: 'No Grassers'.

When Sparky got out of DC, they stuck him in Bulwell House, the main clearing-house for disturbed, delinquent or destitute children in the care of the local authority. Sparky hated the place the moment he set foot inside it. To him, the staff were pigs who made his life a misery. Bulwell House was mainly for the older kids, thirteen and upwards. The worst kids in the city were dumped there and they weren't always happy about it. The staff were underpaid, under-trained, underfunded and under pressure, which made for a volatile situation. They and the kids were at each other's throats, morning, noon and night.

Sparky had toughened up nicely inside and he was at the top end of the pecking-order in Bulwell House. In different circumstances, he might have been made head boy. He might have led by example. Unfortunately, there were no head boys or girls in the home, only Chief Disappointments. Instead, Sparky got in with the older kids, the twockers, and learned how to nick cars. For the first time in a very long while he was happy. He enjoyed the freedom, the speed and the rebellion. He loved the buzz of twocking because it brought him closer to Death.

Even the callous Social Services recognised that Bulwell House was not a happy environment for younger children. In general, they tried to keep the under-thirteens as far away as possible. There was, however, one boy who was under thirteen. His name was Urban Grimshaw and he was twelve. He'd been through every children's home in the city, constantly fighting with the staff, constantly refusing to go to school, constantly leading the other kids into trouble, constantly sniffing solvents, constantly smashing his room and constantly running away. After several years in care, he had a hard-earned reputation as a prominent and influential refusenik. To the other kids, he was a legendary, if remote, figure, the Che Guevara of Social Services. Consequently, he was kept isolated and under observation to stop him running away, with a member of staff allocated to watch him 24/7. Sometimes there would be four or five different faces a day, all strangers, all watching him shit, piss and bathe.

The mysterious figure upstairs had a profound effect on Sparky, who saw him as a symbol of Hope, Redemption and Freedom. He only ever came among the other kids at meal-times, when he sat at his own table with his own member of staff, cursing him and calling him all the bastards under the sun. If that didn't provoke a response, he spat at him or pelted him with food. Eventually the guy would crack and drag Urban, kicking and screaming, back to his room. Sparky knew the game. It was self-defeating, but a good way to make your point. In a way you were doing what everyone else wanted to do but didn't have the bottle for. In a way you were doing it for them and everyone appreciated it. Sparky figured that some-one who was willing to suffer for others like that was someone well worth their salt.

The home was divided into two units, one for the bad children and one for the very bad children. They were called The Haven and The Hollies respectively. The girl in the room next door to Sparky's called them Hell and High Water. Her name was Thieving Little Simpkins and she was fourteen. She'd been all the way through the system with Urban Grim-shaw and was inordinately fond of him. She wanted to help him and she quite fancied Sparky. That night, as she snuggled up to Sparky in bed, the plot was hatched.

Sparky wasn't into it at first. 'Can't,' he said. 'You don't know how much trouble I'm in already. They'll send me back to DC.'

But she kept at him until he couldn't take any more. 'Okay, okay, fucking hell,' he said, relenting. 'I'll do it. Whatever you say, but you better write to me when I get banged up.'

So, next night, they did it. Thieving Little Simpkins went up to Urban's room and asked to see him. The night staff said no, but she'd expected that. It got him talking to her and that's what mattered. She'd seen how he looked at her, the specky-four-eyed, perverted, smelly nonce. Naturally, the dirty muppet fell for her come-on, straight off. She took him down to the sleeping-in room where Sparky was hiding and, on cue, Sparky cracked him over the head with a cricket bat.

The plan had worked lovely. Thieving Little Simpkins had been in care since she was six and she'd learned a few tricks. Main thing was that you needed a plan. If you didn't have one, people walked all over you. You had to be as clever as them. Sometimes a plan worked, sometimes it didn't. If it didn't you had to blag your way out of it, but mostly it did. She went through Gary's pockets, got the keys and freed Urban from his cell. Same as always, she shouted, 'Urban! My little baby!' It was like their trademark and he rushed towards her, tears in his eyes. She hugged him and kissed him, because he really was her little baby. She loved him to bits. Then they climbed out of the window and did a nash up to East End Park.

Best place, because Urban's mum was hanging out up there and Thieving Little Simpkins had a Joey called Burner Brown. Burner's mum had booted him out of the house and made him live in the shed. They could doss there for a while. Burner was only a Joey so they could take over the gaff. If Burner got funny, Sparky could terrorise him and that ought to shut him up. There were loads of ways to control a Joey. Burner wasn't a problem. His mum might be, but he wasn't. Anyway, she couldn't think of anything else, so that was the plan. Burner had bunk beds in the shed, so at least they'd be warm and comfortable.

SIX

SCARS AND STRIPES

She was born and raised in Halton Moor.
She was sexually abused when she was four.
Educationally, she was very poor,
So she won't be getting jobs galore,
And that's for certain, that's for fucking sure.

Like Mum she liked to read the stars.
Like Dad she liked to drink in bars.
Like Sis she liked to shag in cars.
On moral grounds, she was locked behind bars,
Whereupon she got it up the arse.

So the task my friends is simply thus:
To stop them from taking the piss out of us
And we do it best by being riotous!
Whoops. Mustn't let on to the Lies 'Я' Us –
Bring Babylon down with insidiousness.

Sparky
Talkin' bout a revolution

We emerged from the ginnel into a triangular area barely two metres each side. A solid wooden fence topped with snarling barbed wire gave the space a tight, claustrophobic feel and prevented any view beyond. Two latched gates, one either side of the triangle, gave access into the gardens.

Sparky pushed on one of the latches and we followed him

in. The house itself was in darkness, but the light pollution from the city and the moon gave the garden an orange-silver glow, which was decidedly eerie until you got used to it. Everything was wrong, like the negative of a photograph. My eyes were drawn to a small fire burning at the centre of the garden, which scorched the retina and made things seem even weirder than they already were.

To our right, as we entered, two steps led up to the back of the house, which if anything was in a worse state of repair than the front. The paint was bubbling and peeling away from the door- and window-frames. The windows were grey with years of grime. The net curtains had ragged black holes, promising perspectives into alternative dimensions and paradoxical realities. A metre-wide concrete path ran along the base of the house and was littered with all manner of crap, including plastic toys, two wheelie-bins overflowing with pizza-boxes, a plastic bucket of something nasty and a rotting wooden kennel.

The garden was perhaps twenty-five metres long by ten metres wide. The high wooden fence continued all the way round, topped off with swirling razor wire that sparkled in the moonlight. A crazy-paving path staggered madly down the middle, effectively splitting the space in two. To the right, the grass was waist-high and untended; a green and purple swing stuck out of the savannah like a lonely giraffe. To the left, some effort had been made to keep it under control: patches of grass more than a foot high had been trodden into submission and the molehills patted down. A ring of cobblestones encircled the fire in the centre and a surrounding patch of scorched earth indicated that larger fires were not uncommon.

Two teenage girls were sitting on beer crates, one smoking from a homemade bong, the other toasting bread on the end of a stick. Both were completely shit-faced and seemed almost oblivious to our presence. Beyond the fire, a rickety garden shed stood beneath the boughs of an ancient horse-chestnut. There were signs of habitation everywhere. Clothes hung on a washing-line strung between the shed and the tree. A couple of bulging black bags, which I assumed to be full of rubbish, hid among the shadows. A loaf of bread and a margarine tub warmed themselves by the fire. A pile of wood with a saw for a friend waited patiently against the fence, while bits of rubbish lurked in every corner of the garden.

If the kids were living in the shed, they were not entirely without home comforts. An electric cable emerged from the kitchen window, flew over our heads, attached itself to the fence, bobbled along, and eventually disappeared into the shed through a hole in the side. Light escaped from the half-open door and a low, melancholy, wailing rap music, which I learned later to be Cypress Hill, emanated from a gigantic Technics speaker standing sentry beside it.

Urban offered me a crate and I sat down by the fire with the two girls. The one with the bong examined me blearily. The other seemed to be watching an imaginary fly buzzing about the end of her nose.

It was ten o'clock on a clear summer's evening with hardly a cloud in the sky. The music was low. Above me, I could hear the trees rustling gently in the breeze. A line of them ran down between the two streets to the park. The moon seemed to nestle among the leaves, making them shimmer and dance in a thousand different hues.

It was nice sitting outdoors by the fire. There was something rustic and primitive about it, like being back in the Stone Age. Rousseau would have loved it. Primitive man. The noble savage. A return to nature. Man is born good, but he is corrupted by institutions, the love of luxury, the desire to please social superiors and economic dependence on others – all contribute to his downfall. The benefits of science and technology had made us lazy and servile on the one hand, greedy and avaricious on the other. We needed a revolution. Not the old-fashioned type, with firing squads, more a revolution of thought, of consciousness. The Romantic Ideal seemed to take on a solid existence as I rubbed my hands together and warmed them in the fire. I was close to Nature and God. For the first time in a long while, I felt truly alive.

Much of my later commitment to Urban and the crew sprang from that moment. Somehow it felt right. It felt like I belonged. I even had a vague notion that one day I might write about them. Maybe I had my first religious experience. I somehow got the idea that forces greater than I were at work. Normally I would dismiss such a crazy thought out of hand, but this wasn't so much a thought as a warm feeling in my belly.

Sparky ambled over and dropped a pile of wood on the fire. Urban was sitting on a log, sharpening the end of a stick with his penknife. The two girls remained in their own little worlds. No one was speaking. It was like the family home where everyone gets in exhausted at teatime and can't be bothered talking. The silence was comfortable. Everything was fine. The world was a good and decent place.

The girl to my right came round and began to prepare another stiffener. She acknowledged my existence by holding up her little finger for a second, as if to say, 'I know you're there, just got something to do and I'll talk to you in a minute.' A stout, mixed-race girl in her middle teens, she had frizzy Afro hair tied up into a bun. Her face flickered red from the heat of the fire and she looked to me like one of Gauguin's young Tahitian women. She held a three-litre Quite Frightening cider container. She wasn't drinking but smoking from it. The blue plastic bottle had revealed itself as the Frankenstein's monster it was: it had been crudely operated on and turned into a bong. Silver foil covered the mouth and a transparent plastic tube, six inches long, stuck out at an angle from the body. The girl gripped it with both hands, like an experienced flautist, and sucked heartily on the tube, causing the embers on the foil to glow red and the bottle to fill with smoke. When it was full, she daintily released her index finger from an air-hole at the back and sucked the contents into her lungs. She savoured it for half a minute, then exhaled into the cool night air. Eyelids half over her pupils, she finally spoke: 'Easy, charver. I'm Pinky.'

'Chop,' I said, moving my head from side to side, trying to stay within her field of vision. 'I'm Urban's friend.'

'I know who you are,' she said. 'I'm not fucking stupid.'

The other girl carried on toasting. Asleep, or so stoned as to be comatose, she was slumped over the fire holding a twig with a slice of bread on the end into the flames. Dreaming, perhaps, that she was on a distant boat upon a distant ocean, she rocked in her stupor. The bread danced in and out of the flames, toying with them, daring them to blacken it. God alone knows what they put in the loaves these days, but that slice suddenly flared up like a roman candle.

I knew instinctively that this was Thieving Little Simpkins. I'd heard so much about her. She was one of Urban's favourite people: he ranked her up there with Tyson in the great scheme of things. With her eyes half closed and her mouth half open, she looked like a bewitched, bewildered, psychedelic doll. Her hair was pitch-black, cut above the shoulders in the thirties burlesque style. Liza Minnelli had worn the same cut in *Cabaret*. A grown-up cut for a fourteen-year-old, I thought, but who was I to judge? She wasn't quite slim and she wasn't quite fat. She wasn't exactly childlike or precisely womanly. She was somewhere in between, a child-woman. Most young girls were wearing masculine or unisex fashions. She wore girly clothes, and her bra straps, skimpy top and sleeveless crew-neck jumper all jostled for position around her shoulders. Below her skirt frilly pink socks disappeared into short, elfin boots, which seemed inadequate given her nomadic lifestyle.

Like one of those crying dolls whose eyelids work of their own accord, her eyes creaked open and she saw me studying her. 'Want a photo?' she sneered.

She had caught me by surprise and I didn't know what to say. She had very long eyelashes.

'If you do, say so,' she said. 'They get dearer the longer you wait.'

I still didn't know what to say and I couldn't pull my eyes from hers, but I had to speak to break the spell. Thinking I was being funny, I said, 'Your toast's on fire, Thieving Little Simpkins. I'm from the council. I've come to take you back to the nonces' home.'

Thieving Little Simpkins suddenly looked sad. A tear dripped from her eye and rolled down the china-doll face. Dejectedly, she stood up, turned to Urban and whimpered on to his shoulder. 'Oh, my little baby,' she sobbed, 'my poor little darling.' Urban looked at me over her shoulder reprovingly, then took her in his arms and gave her a hug.

'What have I done?' I asked.

Urban snorted down his nose. 'Come and have a look.'

'What?' I said.

'This.' He took hold of Thieving Little Simpkins's arms and moved her away at an angle. 'Look.' With his middle fingers, he gently pulled her jumper down at the neck. With his other hand, he pulled her top and bra back to reveal a tattoo on her left breast. It was homemade, the letters scratchy, untidy and ill-formed. Nevertheless, clearly legible, in blue-black Indian ink, it read: 'Council Property'.

I was sickened and enraged. I gritted my teeth, clenched my fists and turned to Sparky. 'Don't look at me,' he said, in alarm. 'I didn't do it.'

I love the rush of adrenaline you get when your head goes, a mixture of anger and fear, rage and humiliation, the fight-or-flight response in action. Just for a second, it's like the best drug you ever had. You could smash any opposition, or you could run like the wind. But when I saw Sparky standing before me with his guard raised, I suddenly felt stupid. 'Sorry,' I said. 'It's not your fault. It's not my fault either. What am I thinking?'

Sparky forgave me instantly, but before I could stop him, he whipped off my glasses and put them on his nose. He ruffled his hair, took up a Jimmy Cagney stance and tried for all the world to sound like Michael Caine: 'You're a big man, but you're art ov condition. Wiv me, it's a full-time job. Nar sit darn, before I knock you darn.'

'Boo-hoo,' said Thieving Little Simpkins, from behind a frilly pink handkerchief, which she had produced like a stage prop.

Sparky licked his finger and smudged the tattoo all over Thieving Little Simpkins's breast. It wasn't a real one. They were playing with me, winding me up. What was more, they were all in it together. I must have looked confused or disconcerted. 'We're only fucking with your head, mush,' Sparky said. 'Don't take it serious.'

'Only teasing, Chop,' Urban said. 'We've all got scars and bruises. Take a look at this.'

He undid his jeans and dropped his trousers to his ankles, revealing a massive scar on his left shin. An upturned U-shape, it ran from his ankle up to his knee and most of the way back down to his ankle again. Deep purple against a pure white background, it was the worst scar I'd ever seen. The skin must have been dangling off him like a bed-sheet. You could have stepped on a landmine or been bitten by a shark and got away with less. 'My God,' I exclaimed. 'What happened there?'

'War wound,' he explained, doing himself up. 'We've all got them.'

Sparky presented his two fists, thumb to thumb, for my inspection. The fingers of his right hand said 'LOVE' and those of the left 'HATE'. I knew several people with exactly the same tattoo, so I failed to be impressed. 'Only kidding,' he said. 'That's not it.' He wore a bottle green Adidas sweat-top, which he pulled over his head to expose his back. A thin red line ran several inches across his shoulder-blade. Every inch or so another thin red line ran across it where it had been stitched; it looked like a railway track on an Ordnance Survey map, or the type of scar you draw on people's faces in newspapers. 'Got striped,' he said, squinting at me from under his arm like Quasimodo. 'In DC. Argued with the wrong mush.'

A stripe is a phenomenon of the British penal system. I knew this from my own experience and from watching cult underclass films such as *Scum*, which nearly always featured Ray Winstone saying, 'I'm the facking daddy!' A clean, shallow cut, usually inflicted with a Stanley knife, or similar razor-sharp blade, it serves to reinforce the pecking-order, rather than to disable permanently. You had to represent a serious threat to someone's authority before they took the trouble to give you such a stripe. In my eyes it gave Sparky a very high rank. In aristocratic society, he might have been a baron.

'I dub thee Sir Twockalot of the Stripe,' I said, pulling the sweat-top down over his back. 'What horrors will you show me next?'

Sparky pointed to Pinky. 'Show him yours, Pinky.'

'No,' Pinky said, loading yet another bong.

'Show him,' Sparky insisted.

'No.'

'Go on.'

'I said fucking no, din't I?'

'Oh,' he said, finally getting the message. 'She doesn't want to show you it.'

'Fair enough,' I said, to her rather than to Sparky. 'Can you describe it?'

'No! Fuck off!'

'Oh,' I said. Whatever it was, I suddenly didn't want to know.

Urban said, 'Show him the tattoo, then.'

'No, he's a mush.'

'He's not a mush,' Urban insisted. 'He's sorted. He's one of us.'

'He's a mush,' she said. 'Else what the fuck's he doing here?'

Urban grabbed my collar like a school bully and dragged my face down towards Pinky's. 'Tell her what you're doing here.'

Having been put on the spot, I had to say something. The air of expectation was almost palpable. Everyone was looking at me, waiting for me to speak. I'd given the day to Urban Grimshaw and this was where I'd ended up – or been led. Now that I was here, I couldn't quite work out how to play it, or what my motives were. I was a man who went with the flow and the flow had brought me here. I'd been reading the *Tao Te Ching* and was trying to lead my life according to the teachings of the ancient Taoist philosopher, Lao Tzu. The following verse sums up my philosophy at the time:

> *Can you coax your mind from its wondering and keep*
> *to the original oneness?*
> *Can you let your body become as supple as a*
> *newborn child's?*
> *Can you cleanse your inner vision until you see*
> *nothing but the light?*
> *Can you love people and lead them without imposing*
> *your will?*

*Can you deal with the most vital matters by letting
   events take their course?*
*Can you step back from your own mind and thus
   understand all things?*

No, neither could I, but at least I was trying. 'When the best student hears about the way he practises it assiduously. When the average student hears about the way it seems to him one moment there and gone the next. When the worst student hears about the way he laughs out loud.' I was, at best, an average student. Nevertheless, I really got into it and not-doing, not-saying, not-thinking, not-deciding and not-wanting were big things with me. This might have affected my decision-making capabilities. One thing was certain, I couldn't easily ignore the Shed Crew, no matter which dream world I was living in.

'None of this is right,' I said. 'I might be able to help.'

'None of what is right?' Pinky queried. 'What are you talking about?'

'The way you lot are treated, the way you have to live, the way nobody cares about you, the way society has washed its hands of you, the way the children's homes are a national disgrace, the way you can't claim any dole or relief until you're eighteen, the way you've missed out on your education, the way you're preyed upon, the way you're criminalized and excluded, your lack of basic human rights, your poverty, the scars you bear—'

'Okay,' she interrupted. 'I get the picture. Sit down, I'll show you the tattoo.'

She took her trainer off and pulled back the sock to reveal a blue-black tattoo, a Borstal spot, half a centimetre in diameter, positioned just above the ankle.

'Is that it?' I asked, disappointed. 'I expected something a bit more snazzy.'

'That's it,' she said. 'It might not seem like much, but it's important to us. Everyone in the crew has the same tattoo in the same place and if you're planning on joining you'll have to have one too.' Then she went to the shed and came back with the following drawing on a sheet of A4:

'It's beautiful,' I said. 'What is it?'

'The shed, the tree and the sun,' she said. 'It's our trade-mark.' The sun was the same colour as the sun on the Japanese flag. 'That's the design I'd like to do, but we haven't got any red ink and the needles are a bit blunt.'

'Never mind,' I said. 'I'll take whatever's going.'

Urbie told Thieving Little Simpkins that he'd met this bloke. *A bloke with eyes*, he said, whatever that meant. Not a Joey, a proper bloke, and he wanted him in the crew. *We can't have grown-ups in the crew*, she said. *They're all nonces and grassers, all on the make. This one's not*, Urbie said. *I've tested him and Trudi checked him out when Mum was in the hostel. He isn't a nonce, he isn't on the make and he isn't a grass. He's proper sorted, not like most people, almost like he gives a shit. He's already done loads of stuff for me and Mum and he's gunner teach me how to read.* She didn't like the idea, but Urban seemed to know about people instinctively, so she'd go along with it and see how things panned out. Urban never knew his real dad, so he probably had the bloke down as a father figure or something like that. The guy had a van, a pad and a few quid, by the sound of it, so he might turn out all right. If he was in he'd have to have the tattoo, was all. Everyone had to have the tattoo. She didn't fancy another winter in the shed, so she'd give the bloke a chance. Urban's hunches mostly paid off. That was yesterday and they all agreed to keep shtum and test the bloke out before they made a final decision. Urban and Sparky said they'd bring him round. Her and Pinky would check him out with their feminine intuition. Play a few games with him. That was the plan.

Her and Pinky had a way of talking without using words, little nods and grunts and faces. Pinky liked him. You could tell. She was always drawing and writing poems and the bloke came out with a dirty big mouthful of words. That was all it took to impress Pinky. But she wasn't so easily impressed. *Actions speak louder than words*, her dad used to say. She saw the way the bloke looked at her, the same way everyone else looked at her. The only person who didn't look at her that way was her dad and he just gave her grief every time he saw her. And Urban. Urban was her little baby and loved her for what she was. Urban could have anything he wanted. If he wants a new daddy, he can have one, she decided.

'Well?' Urban enquired.

Everyone had settled down in a circle round the fire. Thieving Little Simpkins looked round the company, collecting nods from Urban, Sparky and Pinky. Tyson kept his head between his paws and failed to give an opinion. 'Okay, but three conditions,' she said. 'He has to have the tattoo, he has to tell us who he is and he has to tell us a story.'

Urban raised an eyebrow at me. 'All right with you?'

I was among the Inner Circle of the Shed Crew and Urban had proposed me for membership. They worked on the principle of one member, one vote; applications for membership, changes to the Shed Crew rules or to the unwritten constitution to be carried unanimously. They didn't want casual members, people just coming in and playing with them or spying on them, then clearing off. They wanted 100 per cent loyal, committed people, like any family, organisation, business or terrorist cell.

A tattoo served as a permanent reminder of your affiliation, but it presented me with a problem. I hated tattoos. I didn't like the idea of being branded, marked out as belonging to a certain group. I saw myself as something of a rogue elephant, wandering the savannah alone, going my own way. I joined the odd herd, here and there, when the loneliness became too great, but I never made it any secret that my affiliations were purely temporary. Rogue elephants like to come and go as they please. A brand meant that you were domesticated, no longer free. I was aware that I was making a decision that would change the course of my life and tie me to the herd.

I was a superfluous man, superfluous to society's needs, no matter how hard I tried. I felt like a spare prick at a wedding. Which firm was going to give me a job when they knew full well that I'd start a union, nick anything that wasn't chained down and quite probably Luddite their computers? Which woman was going to settle down with me when I drank like a fish, smoked like a chimney, took drugs by the boatload, and owed out a fortune. Some people thought me a moron; others considered me too clever by half. I couldn't find a place anywhere. But after long years in the wilderness, I found that I wanted nothing better than simply to belong to something, anything. I liked the Shed Crew's style. They, too, were superfluous, so I thought I might as well have the tattoo, despite the age difference. What harm could I do? How could things be any worse than they already were?

The second task she set me was even more impossible. I had

to tell them who I was, but how could I do that when I didn't know myself?

Last, but not least, I had to tell them a story. But which? There were so many of them and I couldn't always tell them apart. In truth, everything I said and did was a story. I had no real substance.

What kind of talk was this from fourteen-year-old street trash in any case? Weren't they supposed to be mindless zombie ants? Thieving Little Simpkins had the wisdom of the goddess Athena, saw into my very soul, knew my deepest fears.

'Don't worry, Pinky's a top-class tattooist,' she assured me. 'She won't hurt you a bit.'

SEVEN

SPINNING CRAZY

Isolated, confused, feeling distant?
Why aren't humans hurt-resistant?
Stepping back I watch the spin
Of this tumble-dryer world I'm in.

With socks for feet and gloves for hands,
Nothing goes as it is planned.
Out of programme, spinning crazy,
Makes my vision blurred and hazy.

Spinning, twisting, turning rapidly,
I hope this story will end happily.
This tumbling mess fills me with horror,
I hope the cycle ends tomorrow.

The spin has stopped but everything's wet,
So it's back into the dryer I bet.
Tomorrow is another day.
Maybe then I'll break away.

Kara MacNamara
Flapping in the wind

Pinky squinted and looked me over at length. I offered her my profile. 'Give me your honest opinion,' I said. 'What do you think?'

She damned me with faint praise. 'You're just like us. Fucked in the head.'

She was fifteen and struck me as a nice kid, relatively normal compared to the rest of them. The others dressed in brand-name clothes, but still presented as windswept, weatherworn and crumpled. She had style, panache and a certain fifties-America air. She wore white Fila trainers, skin-tight DKNY slacks and a black Nike cardigan with amber piping, all very respectable labels. She reminded me a little of the young Marilyn Monroe but with a different complexion. She had coffee-coloured skin, freckles across her nose and mahogany eyes with unusually large pupils. Medium build, she carried some extra weight, but nothing that wouldn't shake off under a regular fitness regime.

She flicked her head in the direction of the shed. 'Come on. I'll have to find my tackle.'

Approaching the shed, I noticed graffiti on the gable above the door. There was an A in a circle, the Anarchy symbol, an E in a circle, the Ecstasy symbol, and a smily face with a crooked mouth in a circle, the symbol of the chemical generation. 'The Shed Crew' was written bold above the door. Above that in a smaller script was scrawled, 'The Untouchables!'. As I entered the shed, I was struck by how warm and comfortable it was. It smelt of damp earth, Calor gas, sweaty socks and glue, but it was surprisingly homely. Approximately three metres long by two metres wide, it had bunk beds positioned against the right-hand wall, which took up half the floor space. The bedding was clean and the quilt plump and inviting. The wall opposite had a small window draped with gingham curtains, like a Wendy house. A chest of drawers and a gas heater took up most of the wall space. All manner of junk and paraphernalia was littered about – makeup, tapes, felt-tip pens, a ghetto-blaster, an electric kettle and a vicious-looking machete. A lit table lamp bathed the shed in a warm orange glow. The floor was nicely carpeted, wall-to-wall. Three wholesale boxes of lighter gas were stacked up neatly in the corner by the door, each containing a dozen cans.

I couldn't resist doing my Loyd Grossman impersonation: 'The bunk beds, the tapes, the felt-tip pens, the machete, the industrial quantities of butane . . . Who . . . would live in a house . . . like this?'

'Not funny,' Pinky said, rooting about in one of the drawers. She pulled out a piece of black cloth with sewing needles threaded through it and a bottle of Stewart Houghton finest Indian ink. She jumped up on the top bunk and patted the mattress invitingly. 'Come on. Get your shoes off.'

I was still in two minds. I'd lived alone for many years and I fancied the attention that was being offered, but I didn't want a tattoo, least of all on my ankle where everyone would be able to see it when I went swimming. In the end, after careful consideration, I decided to be impetuous. 'What the hell?' I said, kicking off my shoes and climbing on to the bed. 'You only live once.' I confess that reservations returned when I noticed the state of the needle. 'Shouldn't you sterilize it first? Just in case? I'll put the kettle on if you like.'

Pinky shook her head vigorously. 'No. When we get nicked, the Babylon takes our DNA. That's all we've got in the world, our DNA, and still they take it. You can't say no, because they take it by force. They kick the shit out of you if they have to and they take it. They're bastards for doing this and we hate them for it. You can have our DNA free, because we kinda like you. I only use this needle to do this tattoo. You'll get exactly what we've got. "Share and share alike." That's rule number four.' She pointed to a list of rules scribbled on a scruffy piece of A4 pinned to the wall.

'And that includes AIDS, hepatitis B and meningitis, does it?' I enquired.

'Yes,' she said. 'It includes everything.'

Pleasantly surprised that they'd even heard of DNA, I

weighed up the risks. I knew that the kids were sexually active, but I figured they'd had dozens of partners, rather than hundreds. I therefore calculated that the risks were small, if not insignificant.

'Have Trudi or Molly ever been tattooed with that needle?' I asked. They struck me as the only ones who posed any major threat to my safety.

'Yes,' Pinky said, 'but in their cases I made an exception and popped it into boiling water afterwards.'

'Fine,' I said. 'Go ahead and add me to your culture.'

She pulled off my sock and roughly thumbed the area where she was about to work, sending a shiver up my spine. 'That's a funny thing to say,' she mused. 'Culture has two meanings, doesn't it, as in "where people live" and "germs"? That's quite clever, is that. Not many people come out with stuff like that, you know.'

'As in "Untouchables" above the door,' I said. 'Did you write that?'

Nodding, she dipped the needle into the ink and ever so lightly outlined a circle on my foot. I tensed immediately and gripped the quilt. I was nervous. She was working on the second most sensitive part of my body and I wasn't sure if what we were doing was legal.

She gave my foot a reassuring shake. 'Chill out, silly. I'm not going to hurt you.' I wasn't sure if she was talking to me or to my foot.

'Do you draw a lot?' I asked, as the dot took shape.

'All the time.'

'Me too,' I confessed.

'The rest of the crew'll get pissed and glued up and start ripping each other's clothes off with their teeth. I'll be sitting there doodling and drawing and trying to capture their essence.'

'Been there, seen it, done it, worn the T-shirt,' I said.

She licked the needle, dipped it into the ink and prepared to jab it into my foot. 'What is it, then? Like a disease or something?' she asked. She had black ink all over her tongue and looked as if she'd recently contracted some terrible disease herself.

'Could be,' I agreed, 'but probably it's something to do with temperament. Best way I've heard it put is that there are two types of people in the world, artists and scientists. Most people are scientists. We're artists.'

'Is that what it is?' she asked, spitting on my foot.

'Something like that, I reckon.' We knew what we were talking about, even if no one else did. If you came from the underclass and you had any interest in learning, literature or the arts, you soon learned to hide it and to feign stupidity and ignorance. Those were the qualities that really counted in the underclass. Learning, literature and the arts counted against you. Where this anti-learning culture came from none of us knew, but some of us were acutely aware of it. We went through life in disguise, but recognised each other on sight.

I couldn't tell her exactly what it was, because I wasn't sure. I have always had difficulty pinning down the precise nature of the difference. As a child, I thought it was because I was fat and wore glasses. In films, the fat kid with glasses was the clever one who was always called Piggy or Brains. It got to the point where if anyone called me anything, I punched them in the face first and asked questions later. So then I thought it was that I was violent and always getting in trouble. When my marks at junior school stood out despite this, I thought I was simply a cut above the average. When Judo died, I imagined myself a lightning rod for death and destruction, a Jonah or a jinx. In my teens, my dad took me picketing. I became politicised and started to see things in terms of class. That wasn't it, though, because I felt different even from my own class. When Bowie started being Ziggy Stardust, I thought maybe I was gay. Tried it. Didn't like it. That wasn't it. Thinking it was artists and scientists, I applied to do a fine-art degree at Bradford University. The tutor said he'd give me a go, because he needed to fill his places to stay in a job, but that I was crap and could never hope to earn a penny as an artist. How right he was. That wasn't it. I did social work instead and imagined myself an enlightened superbeing stalking the earth doing good, but the *Tao Te Ching* teaches that you can't help people by helping them, they must help themselves.

Years of research brought me to Jung, who believed that everyone was either male or female, introvert or extrovert, and any one of four different 'types': intellectual, intuitive, emotional or touchy-feely. I was a male introvert intellectual, as only one in sixteen people were, which perhaps explains why I felt different. People like me were few and far between. As far as I was concerned Jung was the man. He also talked about the Shadow, the other side of your nature, the dark side . . .

Pinky smiled maliciously and brought the needle down into my heel. She was definitely one of us. Pain as art. I admired her originality. The tattooing process involved dipping the needle into the ink, then jabbing it into the skin over and over again as quickly as possible, so that the ink got underneath the skin. In effect, she was creating a bloody, open wound with a blunt needle. The pain was alarming and prolonged. As she progressed with her work, I kept letting out little gasps and whimpers.

'You okay?' she asked.

'I'm fine,' I said. 'I just don't like tattoos.'

'Could have fooled me,' she said.

We chatted while she worked and I got to know more about her. Until recently, she had lived at home with her mum, dad and brother. She wasn't a care kid: she came from a normal, respectable, working-class family. They were so normal that they drove her mad. Mum and Dad worked all the time so she hardly ever saw them. She and her brother lived on frozen foodstuffs warmed up in the microwave. They weren't poor. They had everything they needed: widescreen telly, computer in every room, DVD player, the lot. Pinky hated it.

The other problem was that her mum and dad were white and she was black. It didn't take a genius to work out that something wasn't quite right. Questions were asked in the house, but few answers had been forthcoming. Questions led to arguments and arguments to recriminations. Eventually, Mum admitted that Pinky's real dad was a Rastafarian by the name of Carlton Jenkins. Pinky soon ran away from home and went in search of her roots.

She broke every stereotype and preconception about homeless people. She was refined, articulate and intelligent. She was fun to be with; you could relax in her company; she accepted you as you were. She had a knowledge of religious theory, describing herself as a Rasta-Buddhist. 'Mum's a Buddhist and my real dad's a Rasta,' she explained. Relatively speaking, she was politically aware. She hated churches and governments and war and anything that destroyed the environment. I filled in a few gaps in her knowledge by telling her about the worldwide struggle against economic globalisation. 'The Yanks want to turn the whole world into Detroit,' I told her. 'People all over the world are organising to stop them.' She was glad to hear that she wasn't alone. She liked art, poetry and music and adored the singer Tracy Chapman. She had a good general knowledge, good self-awareness and a good sense of self. How she had achieved such balance in a mere fifteen years on the planet, I can't say. I marked her down as the introvert intuitive type.

After a quarter of an hour she finished her work, wiped away the excess ink and blood with toilet paper, spat on the tattoo, rubbed it in, smiled, and said, 'Welcome to the Shed Crew.' I had done what had to be done, however insanitary, and had passed the first test. I put my sock back on, stuffed toilet paper down it to soak up the seepage and refitted my shoe. It was good to belong.

Pinky changed the tape and we went outside to join the others round the fire. I showed everyone the new addition to my body, as the strains of Tracy Chapman singing about a revolution rolled gently across the lawn.

The crew had put the bong aside and were making supper. Thieving Little Simpkins had her toast on the go again, Urban was warming a 9p tin of Kwik Save baked beans on the fire, while Sparky took care of the beverages. He disappeared into the shed and came back with five steaming cups of tea. Feeling drained by the tattooing process, a dripping bean toastie was just what I needed to replenish my strength. Swilled down with sweet, milky tea with a bong for afters, nothing could have been finer. Those kids certainly knew how to live.

After her supper, Thieving Little Simpkins wiped the bean juice from her mouth with the back of her hand. 'You must tell us who you are,' she said, pretending to be formal. 'Now is the time.'

I'd already prepared my speech. 'I'm Chop to my friends. I come from Eastie, Leeds, Yorkshire, England, Britain, Europe, and, one day, hopefully, the world. Politically, I can't fault the Bolsheviks. Philosophically, I'm a citizen of Ancient Greece, a follower of Socrates, a corrupter of the youth like myself. Religion: lapsed atheist. Anti-feminist, anti-capitalist, anti-Nazi, at your service. Loyal to the land.'

'What's your favourite colour?' Urban asked, chasing a gang of renegade beans back into his mouth.

'Red.'

'Favourite car?'

'Mini,' I said. There were stares of disbelief around the fire.

Urban spat the beans out of his mouth and fell into a fit of coughing. He'd given me my big chance and I'd embarrassed him. I could have chosen a Colt Mitsubishi Evolution III Turbo, a Cossy, or even a Cavvy GSi. 'I used to have a firm called Mini Magic. We bought old Minis and either did them up or stripped them down for parts. I can strip a Mini with my eyes closed and I know their inner workings. Mini Magic made loads of money and I had a de-seamed Mini pick-up with a chopped-down roof and three-spoke alloys finished in British racing green. I had the engine bored out and it went like shit off a stick. I loved that car more than anything in the world.'

'What happened to it?' Pinky asked.

'Smashed it up, drunk.'

'If your favourite colour's red, why did you paint it green?' quizzed Thieving Little Simpkins.

'It wouldn't have looked right in red. It had to be green.'

'Cars have their own personality,' Sparky explained. 'Sometimes I hate to burn them out. It's almost like they're alive.'

Thieving Little Simpkins knew when she was getting out of her depth. 'Got any kids?'

'One,' I said. 'She'll be your age now. I haven't seen her since she was three.'

'Typical dad,' she said, to a murmur of agreement.

'It's not my fault. Her mum's from Hong Kong and she took her back there. I didn't get a say in it. I'm going to see her the minute I've got the plane fare.'

Sparky was astonished. 'You mean to say you've got a half-chat Chinky kid running about?'

'Us half-chats prefer the term *mixed-race*,' Pinky admonished.

'Oh, sorry, Pinky,' Sparky said, realising his mistake.

'Chop, did you love the car more than you loved your daughter?' Urban enquired, out of the blue.

The conversation went on in similar vein for another half-hour. I was asked about all my favourite things and I gave honest, direct replies. Urban's friends never ceased to amaze me. They didn't know anything about psychology or interview techniques, yet they had devised a way to find out who and what they were dealing with. They were young people in a vulnerable position. They had to be careful. The main danger to them was from predatory adults. How better to expose them than to sit them down and ask them about their favourite things? Some key words to look out for were: 'hammer', 'chisel', 'rubber' and 'rope'.

I believe I'd passed their test by the time the nocturne began. Out in the street the contralto screech of troubled tyres pierced the cold night air, quickly followed by the 'woo-woo' of a police siren descending the scale. The drum beat of an engine over-revving led to a deafening crescendo as the car containing the engine crashed into another parked in the street. The movement drew to a close with the cymbal-clash of doors being slammed, with another melancholy 'woo-woo' for a finale.

Five seconds later, the gate flew open and Pixie, the baseball-capped little girl from Greta's house, ran gasping into the garden. In a perfect sine-wave, she curved into the long grass at speed, narrowly missing the swing, came back in our direction, hopped between Thieving Little Simpkins and Sparky, skipped over the fire, jumped on to the giant speaker like an antelope, flicked up on to the roof of the shed like a flea and disappeared over the fence like a gazelle. 'It's on top,' she could be heard wailing, as she faded into the distance.

Three seconds after that, Urban, Sparky, Pinky and Thieving Little Simpkins were gone. It was as if they had never been there. Each jumped up without a word, threw their cups into the bushes, their toasties into the fire and scattered to the four points of the compass. Urban followed Pixie over the shed,

Sparky used the kennel as a springboard to bounce over the fence, Pinky climbed the tree in record time and leaped from one of the branches and Thieving Little Simpkins dived into a small bush behind the tree and disappeared under the fence. When the police walked into the garden, I was alone with only my faithful old dog for a companion.

There were two of the big bolshy bastards, a young blond one with a moustache and an old bald one with an attitude. They wore body-armour, but no headgear. Assorted paraphernalia hung down from their belts: torch, walkie-talkie, handcuffs, expanding truncheon, CS gas. I almost felt sorry for them, idiot centurions overseeing the decline and fall of the new-age Roman Empire.

The young one said, 'Did a lass just run through here, mate? A little bastard?'

'She did,' I said. 'She jumped into next-door's garden, the little bastard. What's going on? Has there been an accident?'

The old one looked round the garden suspiciously while the young one got on the walkie-talkie. 'Crrrck . . . target vehicle crashed, driver and passenger bailed, driver disappeared into thin air, suspected misper jumped into next door's garden, Victor Four . . . crrrck.'

Meaningless gobbledegook came back over the walkie-talkie and I could see that the scuffer didn't understand it any better than I did. 'Er . . . Roger, ten-four . . . crrrck.'

The old one came over and started sniffing around the fire. He spotted the bong on the ground and nudged it with his foot like an explosive. He looked at me, as if to say, 'I know what you've been up to.'

'My only vice,' I told him.

'Do you live here, sir?' he enquired.

The way he said *sir*! You wouldn't have thought it was possible to get so much venom into one word. I wasn't fond of scuffers. They were supposed to be our servants but they talked to us like shit. What the police didn't seem to understand was that criminals were also the victims of crime. Quite often, people turned to crime only after credit-card companies, banks and other vicious criminals had cleaned them out. No good telling the scuffers. They didn't care. Best just to steal it back when and where you could. If you were a member of the underclass, the police weren't there to protect you: they were there to arrest you.

'Yes, I do,' I said petulantly. 'I live here. Why? What's it to you?'

'Merely making my enquiries, matey.'

'Nice use of alliteration,' I said, 'except *enquiries* doesn't begin with an M.'

He looked me straight in the eye and fingered his trusty canister of gas. 'Are you some kind of a clever cunt, *sir?*' he asked.

I was deliberately being cheeky to keep his attention away from the shed. If he saw that kids were sleeping in there, the goose was cooked. On the other hand, I didn't want to push him too far. He had the riot gas, the armoured cars, the armed-response units and the helicopter gunships backing him up. 'Certainly not,' I said. 'I know my place. Look, the wife's kicked me out and I'm stuck out here in the garden with the dog.' Tyson tried to look pathetic in an effort to back up my story. 'I could break the door down and beat her up if that's what you prefer.'

'That won't be necessary, sir. I'll just call this in. Could you tell me your name?'

Just when I was almost out for the count I was saved by the bell. We heard another commotion out in the street, the wail of an over-revved engine, the screech of tyres and the smash of one car slamming into another. A pained woo-woo confirmed that it was the police car that had been rammed. 'Brian!' the young scuffer exclaimed, and the two of them blundered down the ginnel getting in each other's way like real-life Keystone cops.

Tyson and I followed them out into the street. A blue Cavalier, driven by Skeeter, the scarred boy, with Sam, the baseball-capped little boy, as a passenger, had driven into the back of the police car. Further up the street, another twock was crashed into a resident's car. The owner was only now coming out of his garden and scratching his head. He was just an ordinary Joe, in his thirties, starting to go fat round the middle like me. Skeeter slammed his car into reverse and took off backwards down Londesborough Grove. The scuffers dutifully jumped into their car and reversed after him. The front end of the Cavalier and the rear end of the police car were badly crumpled and glass was left scattered across the road. Skeeter did a snazzy little reverse-handbrake on to the bypass and soon both cars were lost from sight. A deep, angry woo-woo pierced the night air.

The bloke up the street called down to me, 'What's going on? Look at my fucking car.'

'Kids, by the looks of it!' I called back. 'Bloody kids again!'

'Bloody hell,' he said. 'Little bastards.'

'Maybe you should call the police,' I suggested, but he shook his head forlornly. 'Night, mate, anyway. Sorry about your car.'

'Night, mate,' he said.

I went back into the garden, bolted the gate, sat by the fire and loaded myself a bong. Holding the bottle with my left paw, I put a light to the weed with my right. I filled the bong with smoke and sucked it down my throat like a hungry wolf.

Tyson waddled over, nuzzled up and rested his chin on my lap. Gawping at me with big brown eyes, he let out a long, anguished 'mwoooorrrr'.

I patted his head a couple of times. 'I know, Tyson,' I said. 'I know. Never mind, lad. There's a good dog.'

EIGHT

A BOOK AT BEDTIME

Coleridge was a smackhead – at least, that's what they say.
I don't know if they tell the truth and I don't care anyway.
Dylan liked a drink, they say – a glass of beer, or two.
I don't see anything wrong with that. I take a drink myself,
    don't you?
Blake lived in a dream world . . . dreaming all the time . . .
Rabbie was a Jock, you know, for the sake of auld lang syne.
Kafka was a man from Prague who had a metamorphosis.
Jung wrote on psychology, but had a slight psychosis.
Let's not forget young Rimbaud, in his anguish and his
    sadness;
Dried himself in the air of crime, played some fine tricks on
    madness.
Dickens, a Victorian novelist, whose dad owed a few bob out –
Great Expectations and *Oliver Twist* his best without a doubt.
Emily is there with the big boys, but took ill and sadly died –
Read about Cathy and Heathcliff in a book called *Wuthering*
    Heights.
None of them was perfect, Shakespeare taught us this –
If you sit down and read his comedies, you'll thinketh he
    taketh the pith.
But the story I like best of all is a noble and cautionary tale,
Retold over and over, King Arthur and his Grail.

Chop
On a mission

After just a few minutes the kids drifted back. Urban and Pixie were the first to return, appearing on the shed roof again as if by magic. 'All clear?' Urban enquired. Not knowing for certain either way, I shrugged and finished off my bong. Tyson, feeling sure the coast was clear, ran round in circles and barked excitedly. Sparky came next. 'Who's locked the fucking gate? I can't get in.' Pixie opened it for him. 'Ta, chicken,' he said. A few moments later, Thieving Little Simpkins popped her head out of the bushes at the back of the garden. 'What's happening?' Urban gave her the all-clear and she climbed out of the hole, closely followed by Pinky and Frank.

Frank had been driving the car that had crashed in the street. 'Fucking hell,' he said. 'That was close.' The scuffers were chasing him, not realising that Skeeter was chasing them. When Frank had got into trouble, Skeeter had gone to his assistance, using a basic diversion technique.

That brought the company to seven, which I thought was more than enough, but still they kept coming. There was another knock on the gate and three more walked in: Trudi, Kara and Molly. No army was complete without its camp followers and the girls had brought provisions: a bottle of vodka, a bottle of Coke, two family-size bottles of Quite Frightening cider, paper cups and a bagful of munchies. 'Trudi had a result,' Molly informed the assembled company. 'Get the gas out.'

'Not yet,' Thieving Little Simpkins said. 'Chop's gunner tell us a story, soon as Skeet and Sam gets back.'

'Who the fuck is this silly fat cunt anyway?' Molly asked.

Urban said, 'You've already met him twice today, you tart.'

'Shut your face, Clockwise,' Molly threatened, 'else I'll push it in the fire.' Molly called Urban Clockwise, because he couldn't tell the time. Pinky coughed, implying that if any face was going into the fire it would be

Molly's. Molly got the message. 'Sorry, Urb,' she said. 'Only joking, precious.'

It was clear that Urban, Sparky, Pinky and Thieving Little Simpkins formed the core of the Shed Crew. They stayed at the shed most of the time, while the others lived elsewhere but came and went according to whim. It was also clear that Sparky was the hardest boy, while Pinky was queen bitch.

Skeeter and Sam arrived back twenty minutes later, out of breath and looking flustered. With them was a boy I hadn't seen before. Sparky grabbed him unceremoniously by the scruff of the neck and dragged him into the shed. 'I want a word with you, you little shit.'

I asked Urban what was going on. 'I think he grassed someone. Sparky's not very happy with him.'

Skeeter was a man of few words. He requisitioned a cupful of vodka and the bong and settled himself in front of the fire. 'Wow!' he said. 'What a buzz!'

Sam was left to explain how they'd outwitted the police. 'Fucking hell, right. They chased us all over t' place, right up Gipton and right back down up through the bottom end of Seacroft there.' His voice was soft and lilting, which made you listen all the harder because you didn't want to miss anything. 'Eh? Wan't they Skeet, man? They were right up us arseholes. Skeet was doing ninety past the Asda, foot t' floor, but we cun't shake 'em off. Fucking T5 joined in on Selby Road, so Skeet shot into Halton Moor and rallied over the bumps.' Sam jumped to his feet, using his hands to demonstrate the stresses and strains that can be placed on a vehicle by unruly speed bumps. 'Every time we hit one we took off, din't we Skeet?' He slapped his hands together with glee. 'We lost t' fucking T5 on Halton Dial cos some kids was in the street. Skeet fired down the path to avoid 'em, but the T5 went and crashed into a van. Din't it, Skeet? Crash straight into this fucking van? Anyway we still had the Panda on us and we were shitting us sens in case the copper-chopper turned up, so we fucked off up Tempsy, din't we Skeet?' He meant Temple Newsam Park. 'Road wa' fucked, man, but we kept going. Scuffers can't a been three inches behind us. Fucking trying to knock us in t' ditch, wan't they Skeet? Good job the golf course gate was open. A little ninety-degree handbrake and we were bombing across the greens. Skeet shouts "Fore!" out of the window, daft cunt, and we shot down the hill towards the power station. For some reason, I don't know why, they wun't follow us on t' golf course so we was in the clear. We came back along the sidings, torched the twock on the park, and here we are,' he concluded, with a final flourish of his arms and a bow. A small ripple of applause ran round the company. Sam could tell a story.

'They play themselves,' Skeeter said, swilling vodka in his glass and downing it in one go. 'They know we'll trash half the holes before they can stop us. They don't give a fuck about us, but they worry over their precious greens.'

The new boy emerged from the shed with a bloody nose and his hand over his eye. Ignoring everyone, he went and sat dejectedly on the doorstep. I thought about saying something, but by now most of the kids were half pissed or stoned and I didn't want to make things worse for him.

Sparky popped his smiling face out of the shed; he was looking pleased with himself. 'Anyone fancy an old favourite?'

The speaker crackled into life, letting out an anguished, haunting wail, like the sound of a high wind howling along a deserted, desolate street. I recognised it immediately as 'Ghost Town' by the Specials. The beat built up until the vocals came in.

Sparky came out of the shed waving the machete, doing a kind of Red Indian dance. He approached the fire and skipped and danced in a circle around us. His swordplay was rather erratic. Most people ducked their heads to avoid losing them.

Urban jumped up to join him, quickly followed by Skeeter, Molly and Sam. Soon everyone was dancing in a lithe, liquid ring about the fire. Only Pinky and I remained seated.

The kids all screamed the last line together like a deranged and degenerate choir. They twirled around the fire like whirling dervishes, patting their mouths, woo-wooing like Apaches, howling and moaning and wailing to the refrain.

Pinky and I looked into each other's eyes. I saw fear, pain, bitterness and grief in hers and I guess she saw the same in mine. She toughed it out, but my stomach tightened and tears rolled down my face against my will. I looked across to the boy sitting on the doorstep with his head in his hands. He was crying too. Our culture had disintegrated so much that we were now little more than savages. If I'd had a pig's head in my possession, I'd have stuck it on a pole and called it God.

There was nothing to be done until the children had finished their dance. That's if you could call them children. Pixie was ten and already promiscuous. At fourteen, Skeeter would stab you without a thought. When the song ended the kids gathered round the fire, breathing hard and flushed with excitement. They were laughing and giggling, happy to be young.

I wiped my tears away. For a moment, I envied them. They were wild, but they were truly alive. Looking in from the outside, things were bleak, but human beings are hardy and resourceful. They make the best of any given situation. Dancing and singing helps you to forget your troubles.

'Right then, Chop,' trilled Thieving Little Simpkins. 'Time to tell us our bedtime story.' She called everyone to order: 'All right! Shut the fuck up! You all know Chop. Chop, show 'em your foot.' I displayed my tattoo and there were a few raised eyebrows and murmurs.

'No one asked me if he could join,' Molly said petulantly. 'I thought we all got a vote.'

'You were too busy shagging on the park,' Pinky said. 'Now, shut your fucking ring.'

I had imagined the Shed Crew to be a democracy. I saw now that the Inner Circle formed a kind of Politburo, which dominated the decision-making process. Democracy was fine in principle. It just didn't work in practice. I counted thirteen in the garden all told, including the new boy but not Tyson. Thirteen was an auspicious number, resonant with symbolism and precedents, like Jesus and his twelve disciples, or King Arthur and his knights.

In fact, I got it wrong. Tyson did count. He was standing in for Greta. It was the new boy Burner Brown who didn't count, even though we were in his mum's garden. He was a Joey and Joeys were beneath contempt. They got no say in anything. Nevertheless I called him over and made him sit with the group.

Urban and Sparky loaded up the fire. Skeeter loaded up a bong. Trudi poured a splash of vodka into everyone's cup. I sat on my nice kitchen chair, while everyone else sat where they could, mostly on the grass, logs, stones or crates. I had decided to give them an allegory, the story of King Arthur, Excalibur and the Holy Grail. Maybe Urban wasn't merely an illiterate ignoramus: maybe he was a king in waiting. Maybe Pinky had the royal blood of Mesopotamia in her veins. Maybe Sparky, Skeeter and Frank were modern-day knights, riding twock cars rather than horses, carrying screwdrivers and flick-knives instead of swords and lances. Maybe in the process of telling the story, I could teach them something.

King Arthur, although of high birth, was a foster child and for the common people. I figured the story would educate the kids and give them hope. To add a touch of colour and excitement, I asked Sparky for the machete, climbed up on to the roof of the shed and whacked it into the woodwork.

'Excalibur!' I cried.

I climbed down and rejoined the company. I looked at the expectant faces and said, 'Are you sitting comfortably? Then I'll begin . . .'

It was the Dark Ages and the land was in chaos. Armed men roamed the roads of Britain, loyal to no one but themselves. Some groups of men found common cause, banded together and dominated whole swathes of the countryside. Soon they were in a position to levy taxes on local farmers and tradesmen. In return, they offered protection against other marauding bands of men. In effect, they ran an early protection racket. The leaders of these armed gangs came to be known as barons, like tobacco barons in prison. They became immensely rich and built themselves great and imposing castles, which set them apart from normal people. Soon, they began to see themselves as special, a cut above the rest. They took on airs and graces and called themselves 'sir'. There was no television in those far-off times, or sport, so the barons organised great jousting tournaments where they could test their skill and prowess as warriors. The very best warriors wore shining suits of armour and called themselves knights.

Then, like now, people wanted to be rich and famous, but there was no television, no Internet, no pop music, no football, no lottery, so this was no easy task. Becoming a knight was your best hope, but there were other ways. The two really famous people at the time were Uther Pendragon and Merlin the magician.

Uther had a dream. He wanted to forge all the warring regions of Britain into one big united kingdom. He, of course, would be the man to rule the newly formed domain. Merlin was a bard. He told stories, made music, told fortunes and horoscopes, performed miraculous firework displays, told you when something funny was about to go off in the heavens, cured your warts, acted as judge and jury in your disputes, turned base metals into gold and provided mind-altering potions. Some people believed him to be a real magician, some saw him as merely a wise man who could be trusted, still others saw him as little more than a con-man and a drug-dealer.

Uther almost achieved his dream of uniting the kingdom, but he was betrayed by his peccadillos . . .

'What do you mean "peccadillos"?' Urban interrupted.

'Foibles,' I said. 'Human weaknesses, base impulses, urges, like lust, vanity and gluttony. In those days, they called them the seven deadly sins. They aren't sins, really, more like addictions or obsessions. Kids tend not to suffer from them so much – at least, that's what I thought until I met you lot – but adults often fall prey.'

Urban said, 'Like smackheads and nonces, you mean?'

'Erm . . . yes,' I said, 'like smackheads and nonces. Anyway . . .'

Uther battered all the other barons into submission, until only Yorkshire stood against him. Yorkshire was an ancient land and we were a brave people. Even though we were vastly outnumbered, Uther couldn't finish us off. In desperation, he called on Merlin to find a solution. Merlin gave him Excalibur, the sword of power, but cautioned that it might only be wielded by a brave knight and true. With Excalibur in his hand, Uther was invincible and Yorkshire had to yield. In those days, you didn't take it personally if you lost a fight. You simply shook hands and owned up to the fact that the better man had beaten you. To celebrate his defeat, Sir Geoffrey, Tsar of all the Yorkshires, threw a big party for Uther and everyone got pissed. Unfortunately, Sir Geoffrey's wife, Igraine, who was a real Dark Ages cracker, did a lap-dance and Uther got turned on. He forgot all about England and duty and only wielding the sword if you're a brave knight and true. He wanted to shag her and that was the end of it. Even Merlin couldn't bring him to his senses. 'I must have her!' he cried. When Geoffrey realised that Uther was just a dirty old lech, he threw him out of his castle. The two armies squared up once again and prepared to make war.

Uther wasn't really into it, though. He couldn't get Igraine out of his mind. He wanted to make love, not war. He begged Merlin to help him get into her knickers.

'You are weak,' Merlin said. 'You will never be the true king. Still, I will do as you ask, if you swear that any child born of the union belongs to me.'

'Whatever,' Uther said. 'Just work your magic and we'll worry about everything else in the morning.'

Merlin devised a scheme whereby Uther's army would retreat, thus luring Geoffrey's army out of the castle in pursuit. Uther would then sneak into the castle and shag Igraine disguised as Geoffrey. Everything went to plan. Uther slipped it to Igraine still wearing his helmet and she didn't know the difference. What was more, Uther's army lured Geoffrey's into a trap and kicked seven bells of shit out of them. Geoffrey was killed, so Uther took the castle, the girl and the victory.

Uther's kingdom now stretched from Cornwall and London in the south, all the way to the Scottish borders, but we weren't happy in these parts. We considered Uther sneaky and dishonourable. Maybe people sat in front of a fire on this very spot all those ages ago and plotted their resistance campaign. A tribe called the Leodites lived here in those days, which is how Leeds got its name. We were one of the many Brigante tribes of the north. 'Brigand' is now taken to mean 'thief, thug or vagabond', so you can tell that we haven't changed much in fifteen hundred years. Uther never properly quelled us. Indeed, we spread our rebellion to the south. By the end of his life, Uther's kingdom was in turmoil again. When he passed away, the land returned to a state of anarchy.

'This is interesting,' Sparky said. 'I always knew I was a vagabond, but I didn't know it was part of my cultural heritage.' There were a few raised eyebrows around the fire, because not everyone knew what 'cultural heritage' meant. Sparky was easily the best educated of the kids, had an excellent vocabulary and wasn't afraid to use it. I half-expected Sam to say, 'Here, who you calling a cunting heretic?'

'There's more,' I said. 'I could go on for ever. You're sitting in one of the most interesting places on the planet, right now, as we speak. Every now and again, the spotlight focuses on one particular place at one particular time: Egypt three thousand years ago; China and India two and a half thousand years ago; Palestine two thousand years ago; Mecca fifteen hundred years ago; continental Europe a thousand years ago; America five hundred years ago. Why not England now? Why not here? For all I know, this could be the very spot.'

Sparky shook his head. 'I'm not with you.'

'Things happened in those places at those times that rocked the world. Jesus, Buddha and Muhammad were born, new worlds were discovered, amazing things like the Great Wall of China were built, concepts were invented. Big things are happening in England today. I don't know what exactly. Maybe a new person will be born, a new world will be discovered, or a new concept will be invented. Something's going on. That's all I know.' I lost my nerve. 'People think I'm nuts when I talk like this, but that's what I think.'

'Get on with the story, Chop,' Urban reminded me.

I haven't told you what Merlin was up to behind the scenes. A child was indeed born to Uther and Igraine, and Merlin exacted his pound of flesh. He took the child away from the couple like a self-righteous and overbearing social worker. Igraine screamed and wailed, but Uther had given his word, so there was nothing to be done. The knights had a code of honour, a little like the Shed Crew rules, which included honesty, justice, brotherhood, compassion and chivalry. Lying to each other was against their code. In those far-off days, a man's word was his bond. Merlin foresaw that things in the kingdom would get worse before they got better, so he took out a place-of-safety order on the child, whose name was Arthur. Merlin called in a few old favours and got a mate of his, Sir Hector, to foster the child. Hector lived out in the country, where it was safe. Merlin left strict instructions that Hector should not tell the child its true identity.

Years passed. Hector brought up the child as his own. He also had an older son, Sir Kay, a brave knight and true. Arthur, being younger, acted as his squire. A squire was like a knight's Joey, who looked after the horses and cleaned all the blood off the armour after a battle. Still, Arthur didn't grumble. He knew his place in life and was content.

Anon, news travelled round the kingdom that Uther Pendragon was dead. He had died without an heir and civil war was brewing as the barons argued over the succession. Merlin stepped in and called for a great joust to be held in London to find a new king. Excalibur, the sword of power, had been thrust into the magic stone at Westminster Abbey. 'Whosoever shall pull the sword from the magic stone,' Merlin prophesied, 'shall be the rightful monarch of all the land.' Soon, all the knights in the kingdom were making their way to London. Sparkling armoured columns were on the move along all the highways and byways of England. Sir Hector accompanied his son, Sir Kay, to challenge for the prize. Arthur accompanied them as squire.

Come the day of the great joust, the colour, the crowds, the noise, the glamour, the splendour and the majesty of the occasion overwhelmed Arthur. Joust followed joust, each a graceful symphony in the noble art of war. Sometimes the jousts were over quickly, with one rider knocked from his horse or skewered on the end of a lance. Others went on for an eternity, with both riders unseated, clashing into each other with swords like Titans. To great cheers, the victors were then allowed to try and pull the sword of power from the stone. Despite strenuous efforts, no one had yet succeeded.

'You're next up,' the steward told Sir Kay.

Sir Kay went into a panic. 'My sword, Arthur! My sword! Where have I put my sword?'

Arthur didn't know. He rushed back to the jousting tent, but he couldn't find it. He looked all over, but it was nowhere to be found. Kay's sword had been stolen and it wasn't even insured! Arthur was distraught. He didn't know what to do. He couldn't let his brother down at such a vital moment. The only thing he could think of was to grab the sword out of the stone and put it back later. Hopefully before anyone even noticed it was gone. Arthur approached the sacred stone with trepidation in his heart. He was just an ordinary person and he felt unworthy to touch the sword of power, but he was in a fix. What else could he do? As he gripped the hilt of the sword, a surge of adrenaline pumped through his body and he pulled with the force of ten men. Sure enough, the sword came out, the sun glinting on the metal. Onlookers fell to their knees in awe and wonder.

Relieved, Arthur took the sword and handed it to his brother, who stopped dead in his tracks at the sight of it. 'Arthur,' he said, 'this is the great sword of power. How did you come by it?'

A crowd gathered round, murmuring and whispering. Arthur thought he was in trouble. 'I never touched it,' he said. 'I bought it off a gypsy over there.'

Merlin emerged from the crowd. 'We have found the true

king! Arthur of the Britons! Rightful heir to the throne!' It looked like a straight set-up to Arthur, but the crowd didn't care. They carried him on their backs through the streets of London and partied for days.

And that, people, is how Britain got its first true king. He was noble and brave and he united the land. Even we brutal savages in the north fell under his spell. His rule was peaceful and prosperous. Camelot was his court, a place of beauty and wonder, and he ruled there with the good Queen Guinevere. Believing in equality for all, he built a great round table for his council of knights so that none should have precedence over another.

It wasn't all plain sailing, but there again, it never is. Guinevere had it off with Sir Lancelot, which caused a great deal of wailing and gnashing of teeth. Everyone fell out for a while and their only redemption was to go on a quest to find the Holy Grail. Many of the knights of the Round Table were killed in the process.

'What the fuck's the Holy Grail?' Molly interjected. 'I've never heard of it.'

'It's a cup,' I informed her.

'A cup! What did they want to go chasing after a cup for?'

'It was a very special cup.'

'Why?'

'Because it was the cup Christ drank from at the last supper.'

'Who?'

'Never mind,' I said. 'It's a big golden magic cup worth loads of money. Okay?'

'Right,' she said. 'Get on with it, then.'

The main problem was that like Molly none of them really knew what they were looking for. Eventually Sir Percy, the most modest and unassuming of knights, found it and saved everyone. When asked the secret of his success, he said, 'I probably found it because I wasn't really looking for it, to tell you the truth.' When you discover what your own personal Holy Grail is, then you're getting somewhere in life, and you, too, will find your redemption. That's the real message that comes down to us through the ages from Sir Arthur and his knights.

Today we remember Arthur's time as a golden age in our history, when justice ruled and chivalry was all the go. Legend has it that, one day, when Britain is in its time of direst need, Arthur will come again to rescue us from evil and strife . . .

'Now would be a good time,' said Kara MacNamara.

I stood up and pointed to our own version of Excalibur sticking out of the shed roof. 'Now is the time!' I boomed. 'Whosoever shall pull the sword from the shed shall be the rightful monarch of all the land! Go to it, my hearties!'

Bedlam ensued. As one man the kids jumped to their feet and raced towards the shed, each wanting to claim Excalibur. They were punching and kicking each other like lunatics, screaming and scratching. Oddly enough, the Joey, Burner Brown, looked favourite to acquire the prize. He was already standing on the speaker, trying to clamber up on to the roof. His long years of serfdom almost at an end, he was determined to give it his best shot. I didn't think Urban stood a chance, but he was light and nimble and destiny called. He leaped on to Pinky's back in defiance of gravity, sprang weightlessly on to Sparky's head and launched himself on to the roof as light as air. Balancing precariously, he drew the noble sword from its anvil, swung it round his head three times in triumph and brought it scything down on to the shed roof. From my vantage-point, it seemed certain that he had sliced off Burner's hands.

As Burner Brown fell screaming from the shed, I knew that my allegory had gone horribly wrong.

NINE
BEDKNOBS AND BROWN STUFF

If all be true that I do think,
There are five reasons we should drink;
Good wine, a friend, or being dry,
Or lest we should be by and by;
Or any other reason why.

Henry Aldrich, 1647–1710

If all be true that I construe
There are five reasons to sniff glue:
Pink wood, a zlak, an octopus,
A dog that turns into a bus,
Or an underground car park chasing us.

Urban

Nothing's true I see around
So that's why I toot lots of brown:
Fucking, fighting, writing verse,
Doing 180-spins in reverse,
And going from bad to worse.

Skeeter

From Burner's vantage-point, it must have seemed that he'd at least lost a finger. The blade actually lodged between the third and little fingers of his left hand and there were millimetres to play with in either direction. That didn't register with Burner, because his reptile brain had already decided to push away from the shed and hope for the best. Unfortunately, he landed on a rock and bust open his head.

Sparky rushed over in a panic and tried to pull Urban's shirt off his back. Instinctively, Urban struggled to resist. 'Give us your shirt, you daft little bastard,' Sparky demanded. 'We have to stop the blood.' Urban pulled his shirt over his head and handed it to Sparky, who returned to the victim and wrapped it round his head. I was glad to see that someone had taken charge of the situation.

I couldn't move. I must have been in shock. I had suddenly seen things as they really were. I was in a back garden, drunk and stoned, with a team of mad kids, who were also drunk and stoned. As the only adult, any court in the land would naturally assume that I was the ring-leader. Already I had been a witness or a party to illegal swimming, trespass, underage substance abuse, teenage promiscuity, dumping smackheads, aggravated twock, arson, assaulting the police, bullying and *Lord-of-the-Flies*-style savagery. The situation had been certain to end in disaster all along. What did I think I was playing at?

Pixie, long blonde hair tumbling to the small of her back, came over and took my hand. No doubt she felt insecure. In the mayhem, she had lost the baseball cap that shielded her from the world. 'I don't like this,' she said.

Once things had calmed down, Thieving Little Simpkins was dispatched next door but one to use their phone. Burner was a bit concussed, staggering about and talking incoherently, so we got him off to hospital as quickly as possible.

Sparky grabbed him before he left and planted a message in his mind. 'Don't grass, cunt, else you really will get your head smashed in next time.' Trudi and Molly were the only ones not actively on the police wanted list, so they were nominated to accompany him to the hospital. I didn't go, because I didn't want to get on to the police wanted list.

Burner's head had bled profusely and several of us had blood on our hands. We were a ghastly crew and everyone was looking at me to decide the next move. They were just kids, trying to be tough, having to be tough to survive, but underneath not very tough at all. As the only adult, I knew I would have to take a hand. After all, Greta had taken control when the kids lost it. Why shouldn't I?

'Right,' I said. 'This is what we do.' My voice didn't carry like Greta's, but in my own way I like to think that I conveyed a certain authority. 'Erm . . .'

An embarrassing hush descended on the garden, but Urban helped me out, as always. 'Best get cleaned up, Chop. We'll go to yours.'

'No, we won't,' I protested. 'Are you mad?' Half the people in my block were pensioners who fainted at the sight of a teenager. Imagine ten teenagers crammed into the lift, dripping blood and looking like they'd been involved in a small-scale massacre. 'We'll have to go to your mum's,' I said. 'Nothing else for it.'

'I'm not going nowhere,' Sparky said. 'Burner'll keep his mouth shut, so I don't know what all the fuss is about.'

Just then the lights came on in the house, first downstairs, then upstairs. 'Burner's mum's back,' Sparky said.

I voiced my feeling that this was too big a disaster to keep quiet. 'Someone will have to tell her what's gone off.'

Everyone nodded sagaciously and nominated Thieving Little Simpkins with their eyes. She agreed that she and Pinky would break the bad news. The two of them could probably get round Burner's mum, comfort her, house-sit for her if she wanted to go to the hospital, and use her bathroom to get cleaned up. The lads would have to clear off for the night and sort themselves out as best they could. Sparky didn't like the idea – the shed was his home – but eventually concurred.

Some of the kids nipped into the shed to grab provisions as, one by one, a bare-skinned Urban in the lead wielding the sword of power, we jumped into the bush at the back of the garden. We emerged into a dark, narrow ginnel overhung with trees and tangled barbed wire. Like a troupe of dwarfs sneaking through the caves of Mordor, we zigzagged along the maze of back passages until we surfaced at the top of Scargill Grove, directly opposite Greta's house. No sooner had Urban poked his nose into the street than he poked it straight back into the ginnel, causing a minor pile-up. 'Scuffers,' he whispered in alarm.

Flashing blue lights filled the street. Two police cars and an ambulance were parked by the midden yard where Cod had been dumped. A small crowd had gathered and half a dozen people were straining their necks to peer into the yard. The scuffers were taking them aside, one by one, asking them questions and writing things in their notebooks. Among them, I recognised the two scuffers who had interviewed me earlier in the evening. In due course, two medics carried a lumpy stretcher out of the yard, put it in the ambulance and drove it away. With lights flashing, but no siren, the ambulance drove down East Park View, indicated left and turned sedately on to the bypass.

As I was the oldest in the party, Sparky asked me to go over and find out what was happening. Naturally I refused point-blank. It was clear to me that the black-toothed dirty digger was in a bad way and I didn't want the scuffers to associate the event with me in their minds. Scuffers are simple people. To them, two and two makes four and they don't believe in coincidence.

The Shed Crew were between a rock and a hard place. We couldn't go back to the shed and we couldn't go out into the street, so we stayed where we were. I was peeping round the corner of the fence, observing. Kara inserted her head into my armpit and shoved me out of the way. 'Hey up, Chop. Let's have a look.' Pixie came next – 'Mind out' – quickly followed by several others. I was pushed back into the middle of the group where it was warm and secure. I didn't mind. I liked being warm and secure, but everyone else was trying to push to the head of the ginnel to see what was going on. In consequence, Kara and Pixie were ejaculated into the street.

Pixie was spotted straight off. 'There she is, Brian!' cried the young, moustachioed scuffer. 'Over there, the little bastard!'

'Bowling green!' Urban yelled, and everyone scurried back down the labyrinth of ginnels like rats in a sewer. Luckily, Kara and Pixie had the good sense to fly across the Slip Inn car park and draw the Babylonians away from the rest of us. Blindly, I followed Urban and Tyson through the complex maze of passages. We came out by East End Park, scampered over the road and met up with the others in the bowling green. I held on to a horribly defaced park bench, coughing and choking, and threw up into the rosebushes. It just wasn't my day.

Sparky whacked me on the back. 'Go on, lad. Cough it up.' Tenderly Urban rubbed the back of my neck and said, 'You've got to stop smoking, Chop. You know that, don't you?'

Even Skeeter showed a hint of humanity. He pulled the bottle of vodka from the inside pocket of his Berghaus waterproof and offered it to me in lieu of medicine. 'Here y'are, chor. Tek a slug on that. That'll fettle you on.'

I'd had enough for the day. I wanted to go home, but it didn't seem right to abandon the rest of them and just take Urban. I doubted he would come with me, in any case. Rule number five clearly stated, 'No Go-offs.' Of the original company, only Urban, Sparky, Frank, Skeeter and Sam remained. A manageable number, but Sam was a problem. It was clear which provisions he had salvaged from the shed: he was already refilling himself with butane. With his golden hair, he did a good impression of a yellow disposable lighter. Urban could stay at my flat, because I had his mum's permission. Sparky, Frank and Skeeter were all right too, because they were boys of an age at which I couldn't be accused of anything. But Sam couldn't stay because he was only ten and seemed to have a red adaptor permanently inserted into his mouth. He was already on the way to Zombie Voodoo Land and I wasn't willing to put myself in a position that I couldn't justify in a court of law. Ten is a child, fourteen is a teenager: two very different things, in my mind at least.

In a moment of clarity, I decided to act. Sam had to go home. He was sitting on the bench next to mine. I marched over, snatched the can from his hand and threw it over the hedge. He cried out in pain and anguish as if I had stolen his very lifeblood. 'No! No! It's mine,' he wailed.

'You're going home,' I told him, grabbing him by the arm and pulling him to his feet. 'Where's he live?' I asked the others.

They all looked blankly at me.

'Where's he fucking live?' I demanded, raising my voice a decibel or two. 'He's ten! He's going home. Lose the gas and the rest of you can doss at mine. We'll worry about everything else in the morning.'

The kids were initially confused. No one told them what to do and if anyone tried they got it. There were murmurs of discontent and Skeeter was fingering something in his coat pocket. It didn't take too much imagination to work out what it was.

I didn't give a shit any more. It had been a long, hard day. 'Come on, then, Skeeter. Come and stab me if you're a fucking hard man, but remember I've been in this jungle three times longer than you have. I'll rip your fucking head off if it comes to it. Butane is a super-cooled liquid gas. It'll freeze your larynx or your lungs if you're unlucky and your breathing days will be over. I'm not even going to tell you about the long-term damage to your kidneys and your liver. He's ten. If you care about him at all, he's going home. If you don't care, then you can all stay here and sniff yourselves to death and I'm out of here!'

Silence reigned in the bowling green. Skeeter was astonished. I could almost see the cogs turning in his brain. We stared directly at each other for something like half a minute. It took all my courage to keep looking into those vacant black shark eyes. No one else said a word. This was between Skeeter and me. Finally he nodded, more to himself than to me, and dropped his eyes. 'Scargill Mount,' he said, taking his hand out of his pocket. 'We're prob'ly best going along the tracks.'

'Good,' I said, relieved. 'Thank you, Skeeter. Welcome to the human race.'

This was probably the make-or-break moment in my relationship with the Shed Crew. Had it gone a different way, I dread to think what might have happened. I couldn't have defended myself against more than one of them. If Skeeter had gone for me, Sparky's code of honour might have dictated that he side with him. Frank would have joined him without hesitation and I have little doubt that Skeeter would have used his trusty flick-knife. I might have been left for dead in the bowling green under deeply suspicious circumstances, just another bizarre headline. Fortunately, I must have played it right and I got away with it. You can't tell kids like Skeeter what to do: they'll do precisely the opposite. You can, however, open a dialogue with them, give them the information they need and allow them to make the right decision for themselves.

We got Sam home by walking along the railway line as Skeeter suggested. At the bottom of Scargill Mount, he climbed up the embankment, waved to us from the top and scrambled over the railway wall. He seemed relieved to be going home. Maybe he'd wanted to all along, but didn't want to breach the 'No Go-offs' rule. When I got the chance, I planned to call together a legislative sub-crew and put forward new provisions: the No Go-offs Act (Ashtrayland), Exceptions and Exemptions, 1996. Something was rotten in the state of Ashtrayland if a kid couldn't go home whenever he chose.

The rest of us continued down the line as far as Richmond Hill, then came off and headed cross-country. I lived in Lincoln Green, which was a fifteen-minute walk away. Keeping to the shadows wherever possible, we walked down Upper Accommodation Road, crossed York Road via the underpass, cut through the Ebor Gardens estate and circumnavigated the swampy rec at its heart. The rec was like the Twock Graveyard of legend, with a dozen rusting, burnt-out cars scattered haphazardly across it. Our party claimed only two, so it was clear that the Shed Crew weren't the only gang of miscreants on the patch. We crossed Torre Road, sneaked through the tight, poorly lit streets of Stoney Rock and were into Lincoln Green. My block was at the top of Lindsey Road, overlooking the hospital and the graveyard.

My flats weren't all bad. Sometimes I was almost happy there. Slab-like and overbearing, they were thought ugly by most people. I considered them an architectural wonder. Using a standard Le Corbusier 'domino' pre-stressed concrete frame, they soared sixty or seventy metres into the sky. Clad in grey pebbledash concrete, they weren't pretty, but they were clean, dry, reasonably priced and (with the exception of the under-floor heating) cheap to run. I wasn't house-proud and I needed somewhere to sleep: they did the job. Our block had a mixture of one- and two-bedroom dwellings, a washing-line on the roof, a nosy caretaker and heavy security doors at the communal entrances. Most of the residents were well past their prime, elderly couples, or middle-aged loners like myself.

What residents there were at the younger end of the scale were mostly alcoholics, drug addicts and other social inadequates, all on long-term benefits. I'd be willing to bet that there weren't a dozen people in the block who worked.

They didn't work but they could talk, and if anyone saw me walking in with four teenage monkeys and a Staffordshire bull terrier, they'd talk like parrots. Luckily, it was getting on for half past one in the morning. Most eyes would be asleep, but the walls had ears.

'Listen,' I said, 'we can't all walk in together. We'll have to go in two by two.' I went in first and told the kids to ring up on the intercom. Urban, Sparky and Tyson rang first, Skeeter and Frank following two minutes later. We were safe and warm, with the minimum of fuss.

Like the Shed Crew, I had a couple of rules by which I ran my life. First and foremost among them was 'Don't shit on your own doorstep.' I had a drug-dealer living next door to me who would boot your door off and shoot you quicker than you could boil an egg. My other next-door neighbour was an old man who collared you in the lift and gave you an earful. To my mind, discretion was the better part of valour. Either one of them could have made my life unbearable. I operated a policy of 'Hear no evil, see no evil, speak no evil.' I treated them both like they were my dearest friends, but had never been into either of their flats. Living in the inner city, my relationship with my neighbours was important to my survival so I took the matter seriously. I needed to translate this concern into a rule that the kids could understand. I laid down the law to them before they even got out of the hallway.

'You might have ten rules in the Shed Crew,' I said, 'but that's the Old Testament. I can't be bothered with all those rules. Here, we go by the New Testament. Only two rules. Rule one is "Do what you like, just don't hurt nobody else." Got that, Sparky? Skeeter?' They nodded hungrily. 'Rule two is "Don't annoy my neighbours." I don't bother them and they don't bother me. We're like little dictators of our own private countries. They do things I don't like, I do things they don't like, but we give each other space because we're sick of war. Now, we have a deal. They don't try to impose their culture on me and I don't pour petrol through their letterbox in revenge. In short, if any of you gives my neighbours any cause for concern, I'll ban you from this flat immediately and for life. Do I make myself clear?'

'Crystal,' said Urban, handing me the machete as if it were an umbrella. 'What's for supper?'

The kids took it in turns to use the bathroom and I put their clothes in the washer. I broke out every pair of boxers, Bermudas, trackie bottoms and shorts that I had in an effort to clothe them. When they had cleaned themselves up each was issued with a T-shirt. Urban went first as he'd been walking round for half an hour without a top and was shivering. He came into the kitchen wearing my Bermuda shorts, my Ray-Ban sunglasses, my flat cap and my CCCP T-shirt with the hammer and sickle on it. It was like having a party of refugees in the flat, except that the Shed Crew were refugees in their own country and had nowhere else to turn.

Everyone was starving so we decided to cook something, despite the hour. I had to show them how to make a curry. They had no idea. To tell the truth, they didn't even know how to use knives. More fingers were almost lost as they chopped the vegetables. I don't think they even knew what vegetables were. Pot Noodle, McDonald's hamburgers and children's home gruel were the heights of their culinary experience. I showed them how to defrost a pound of mince in the microwave, how to slice vegetables so they looked pretty, how to cook the powder rather than just throw it in at the last minute and give yourself indigestion, and how to make rice.

We were just about to dish up supper when the intercom

rang again. 'Open the fucking door, then, you silly fat nonce.' Who else but Greta? She came marching in, accompanied by Trudi and Molly, and we all got smaller portions because of it. Once they were in I locked and bolted the door and turned off the intercom. That was it for the day. I'd had enough. I was clocking off and the rest of the world was on its own.

I only had a two-seater settee in my living room, so most people sat on the floor to eat their supper, which was fine as I had scatter cushions and a nice carpet. It turned out that Greta had suffered one of her asthma attacks and been taken to hospital. My diagnosis was attention-deficiency syndrome, but I kept my thoughts to myself. Trudi and Molly had put Burner into safe hands, reminded him that he'd better not grass, and then bumped into Greta, who was coughing up blood in the gutter outside A and E with a fag in her hand.

Greta didn't seem too far gone, all things considered. If she was smashed earlier in the evening, she had coughed herself sober again. She organised the washing-up and the sleeping arrangements. For my own safety, I wouldn't have let the girls stay if she hadn't been there. She held moral rights over the girls, so I allowed her to make the decision. She thought they'd be 'all right'.

I have a two-bedroom flat. At the time, the spare bedroom had a double bed and an old settee in it, so Greta told all the kids to sleep in there. In mild weather, I usually left the under-floor heating on low in the hallway, which kept the whole flat nice and warm overnight. The flat was basically one long hallway with all the other rooms coming off it. The wallpaper in the hall was hanging off in places and the paintwork had yellowed. Opposite the front door, I had an old Labour Party poster on the wall, which showed a silhouette of a half-starved mother and child and bore the legend: 'LANDLESS'. I liked to keep my hallway destitute and decrepit, so that I knew where I stood. The other rooms weren't half bad. I was particularly proud of my bookshelves, which covered a whole wall of the living room.

Once the children were all tucked up in bed, Greta told me that she had something for me. In my room she pulled out a bag of brown wrapped in clingfilm, which was an unexpected boon. I got the foil out and we wound down the day with a nice, grown-up toot, away from the prying eyes of children.

Greta was like a precision engineer when it came to tooting smack. I watched the intricate origami as she prepared the foil and the tooting tube. As always, she was completely engrossed in the operation and at one with herself. Eventually, she sprinkled the powder on to the foil and played the lighter underneath it until it melted into a brown, glutinous bead of stinking sludge. Her preparations complete, she got on with the business at hand. The lighter in her right hand, the foil in her left and the tooter in her mouth, she warmed the bead from below so that it ran down the foil, following its progress with the tube and hungrily sucking in the resultant fumes. This is known as 'running a line' or 'chasing the dragon'. Greta ran half a dozen lines for herself, which was a little more than etiquette dictated, then handed me the tooter. 'Not bad gear,' she croaked.

Tooting brown is a delicate operation. If you aren't careful with the flame, twenty quid's worth of brown frazzles into nothing in front of your eyes and all your blagging and thieving has been for naught. I had never mastered the art: I reasoned that if I couldn't run it, I was unlikely to become addicted to it. I asked Greta to do the honours. Happy to oblige, she ran the beetle down the foil and I inhaled the evil-tasting smoke. After three lines, I was already feeling its soothing, melancholy power.

It had been a bad day. I had suffered the humiliation of walking around soaking and stinking of shit; I had looked death in the eye at the bottom of a river and at the top of a hill;

I had relived the agony and the ecstasy of my childhood and adolescence; and I had sustained multiple injuries, a tattoo and a dog bite. Worst of all, I finally understood that my world was in ruins. I'd known it in my head all along, but now I felt it as an emotion in the pit of my stomach.

A few more lines of the sweet brown lady and I no longer cared. All my pain, fear and bitterness evaporated and I was at one with the universe. Just before the gouch came, I fancied I heard Lao Tzu whisper across the ages: 'Much speech leads inevitably to silence. Better to hold fast to the void.'

PART TWO
ON TOP WITH THE PENTHOUSE POSSE

If once a man indulges himself in murder, very soon he comes to think little of robbing; and from robbing he comes next to drinking and Sabbath-breaking, and from that to incivility and procrastination.

Thomas De Quincey
Confessions of an English Opium-Eater

'One day, lad, all this'll be thine.'

TEN
A BIG HEAVY LOAD

So, now, little man, you've grown tired of grass,
Amphetamine, downers, acid and hash.
Someone pretending to be your best friend
Introduced you to Lady Heroin.
Well, honey, before you start fooling with me,
Just let me inform you of how it will be:
I will seduce you and make you my slave;
I've sent stronger men than you to their grave.

You think you could never be a disgrace
And end up an addict to poppy seed waste?
You'll swindle your mother, just for a buck,
And turn into something vile and corrupt.
You'll rob and you'll steal for my narcotic charms
And only find peace when I'm there in your arms,
And when you realise the monster you've grown,
You'll solemnly pledge to leave me alone.

You may think you've got the mystical knack,
But, honey, try getting me off your back.
The vomits, the cramps, your guts tied in knots,
Nerves screaming out for those much-needed shots,
The hot sweats, the cold chills, the withdrawal pains,
Can only be cured by my little brown grains.
You gave me your conscience, your morals, your heart.
You're mine now forever, TILL DEATH DO US PART.

Thieving Little Simpkins
Just married

143

The next morning I had a big job, shifting the contents of a two-bedroom house to Aberdeen. I woke at dawn to find the naked Greta in bed with me. The wise removal man seldom toots smack the night before a big job. It kind of saps your strength. I felt like death warmed up.

I pulled back the curtains to reveal a glorious sunrise, which lifted my spirits immediately. A blood-red ribbon of light ran across the horizon like a river, bottom-lighting the clouds in a furious kaleidoscope of oranges, pinks, crimsons and mauves. The colours were so rich and powerful they made my head spin. The moon hung low in the sky to the south-east, with a brilliant star above and to the left of it, far too bright to be a normal star, probably Venus or Mars. The vista was achingly beautiful. It was either proof of the existence of God or there'd been a nuclear explosion in the night. I wasn't sure which.

Weeks back I'd promised to take Urban to Aberdeen with me. He'd never been to Scotland. He'd never been anywhere to speak of. I decided to wake him because I didn't want him to miss the sunrise. Life was harsh and good sunrises were few and far between. He was lying on the settee in the spare room with his head on Molly's naked chest. Tyson was balanced precariously on the back of the settee, keeping watch. Trudi slumbered serenely in the double bed, blissfully hemmed in between Skeeter and Frank, her two true loves. Sparky had made a kip for himself on the floor, disdainful of the whole sordid business.

I gave Urban a shake and he got up straight away. 'I lost my cherry last night,' he told me in the kitchen, as I fried bacon.

'That's nice,' I said, turning the rashers with a fork.

'Four times,' he insisted. 'Trudi twice and Molly twice.'

'I didn't hear anything,' I said. I wouldn't have done. I was in Zombie Voodoo Land with Greta, but Urban didn't know that. 'Anyway, I thought you didn't like Molly.'

'Well, I didn't but . . .'

'But what?'

'But . . . well . . . you know.'

'You discovered another side to her personality, did you?'

'Something like that.'

I passed him the bread and margarine. 'Do the honours.'

He stood by the table and layered the margarine an inch thick on to the bread. 'We made enough noise. I was frightened you'd come in and tell us off. Fucking nymphos, the pair of them. Proper little orgy. Even Frank got his nuts, the big puff.'

'Sauce?' I asked, when the bacon was done.

He shook his head. 'I'm only twelve. Four times, two different lasses, that's pretty good going, don't you think?'

He seemed to want my approval. Losing your virginity is a big thing when you're a kid and I wasn't making enough fuss about it. It meant very little to me at my age. I might have shagged his mother the night before or I might not. I couldn't remember. 'Pretty good,' I agreed, ruffling his hair, trying to be enthusiastic. 'That's my boy! I'm proud of you.' I made a mental note to tell him about sexually transmitted diseases when I got the chance, but I didn't want to raise it over breakfast. 'My first time I had one girl once and I was sixteen.'

'Times change,' he said, taking a chunk out of his bacon sandwich and swilling it down with sweet, milky coffee.

The smell of bacon drifted down the hallway. Attracted to the source, Tyson waddled into the kitchen and plopped himself at his master's feet. Urban dropped a slice of bread on the floor, which the dog wolfed in a swift gulp. Carrying our sandwiches and coffee, Urban and I went into the living room to watch the remainder of the sunrise. It was getting light and already the splendour was fading, the colours less spectacular, the mood subtly changed.

'I want to tell you something, Urban. It won't mean much to you now, but remember it for the future. Nothing is permanent. Everything changes all the time. Remember that, will you? It's very important.'

He didn't have any idea what I was talking about. 'Wha' um that?' he chewed, nodding towards the future. In the distance Ferrybridge A and B power stations belched thick black smoke into the atmosphere. Venomous vapours poured from the cooling towers and blended in with the clouds, which loomed off into the distance across the horizon. The rising sun lit the scene maroon from behind so it seemed almost as though the power stations were manufacturing the sky.

'It's the cloud factories hard at work,' I explained. 'That's where they make acid rain for Scandinavia.'

I wasn't looking forward to the job. The house was easy enough, just the usual collection of junk and electrical equipment. I even told the punters it would be cheaper to buy new junk in Aberdeen rather than cart all their old junk up there, but they wouldn't hear of it. People get attached to their junk. Only the removal man sees things as they truly are. Shifting junk was easy. The problem was distance. Aberdeen was a long way off, in a foreign country, four hundred miles away by my reckoning, the other side of Hadrian's Wall. I'd spoken to my uncle Archie and brushed up on my Rabbie Burns in preparation. Uncle Archie gave me this advice: 'Dinna gar off the main route, Choppie. Warritis, see, we no like fucken Sassenachs.' Rabbie Burns had given me the following advice, which I delivered to Urban as bacon fat dribbled down his chin:

> What tho' on hamely fare we dine,
>   Wear hodden-gray, and a' that;
> Gie fools their skills and knaves their wine,
>   A man's a man for a' that.
>   For a' that, and a' that,
>   Their tinsel show, and a' that;
>   The honest man, tho' e'er so poor,
>   Is King o' men for a' that.

I recited it for Urban's benefit. He was the most honest person I'd ever met. He was a thief, a vagabond and a sniffer, yet his heart was true. He had a sharp tongue, which could cut you to the bone, but he always spoke his truth without bitterness, deceit or pretension. I certainly didn't consider myself an honest man. Most people thought me 'dodgy', 'iffy', some said, a few even alleged that I was 'double-bent'. None of them were even close. I was as crooked as a politician.

My yellow box van, a 3.5 tonne, D-reg, Leyland-Daf Sherpa, had no tax, insurance or MOT. Her name was Elsie and she'd done more miles than the starship *Enterprise*. She was an old lady, but allowing her to die with dignity was out of the question. She earned me too much kelly. I kept her going with blood, guts and will-power. On the windscreen, I displayed a stolen tax disc I'd bought for a fiver in the Slip. The legend on the side of the van, 'Chop's Man 'n' Van Service, Distance No Object, Full Insurance Cover', was something of a misrepresentation, but your junk was probably safer with me than it would have been with a proper firm. Because I had no insurance, I took special care not to break anything. It was my proud boast that I'd never broken anything worth mentioning during my entire career as a shifter.

'Looking forward to it?'

Urban gazed into the Lowryesque distance, turned Turneresque by the sunrise. 'Yeah, man.'

'Feeling strong?' Together, we were easily able to handle most people's lightweight junk. The odd washer caused problems, but then I roped in the punters to give us a hand.

'Yeah, man.'

'Shall we take the air-gun and the tent and make a trip out of it?'

'Yeah, man. Can Tyson come?'

'Yeah, man.' I was looking forward to getting out of the shit for a while too.

Various negotiations were essential before departure. I agreed with Urban that Tyson would be leashed if there were humans in sight and locked in the van if there were animals in sight. Urban would be paid a flat fee of twenty pounds for the job, which I expected him to spend on something useful, not solvents, gas or glue. Not a great wage, but budding union officials should note that I also provided free gloves and overalls, free work-based learning, free education, free counselling, free food and free temporary accommodation for his dog, friends and family.

We got everyone up, except Frank, who was impossible to rouse, and Greta made more bacon sandwiches. Molly helped, chatting to Greta in the kitchen and ferrying the rations into the living room when they were ready. When the bacon ran out, which was pretty soon, the unlucky ones had to make do with eggs.

Over the second breakfast sitting, Skeeter implied that Urban and I were go-offs for clearing out and leaving everyone in the lurch when there was trouble. 'How come he gets to go? That's not fair. We're in trouble if Cod dun't make it. What we supposed to do? Fuckin' go-offs, man. An' it's all his fault for electrocuting the bastard in the first place.'

'You're lucky,' Sparky said. 'At least you get a bacon sarnie. All I get is egg.'

Molly came into the living room and plonked two more sandwiches on the coffee-table. 'Here y'are, starvers.'

Trudi was sitting on the window-sill, sipping tea. She didn't eat much as a rule. 'Pair of you can shut your gobs anyway. He's put us up for the night and fed us and all you lot do is moan. You oughta be saying "Ta very much, Chop", not having a go at him.'

'Not having a go,' Skeeter said. 'Just telling him straight.'

I explained that I had to make a living. Without money, the world was a harsh, cruel place and I couldn't cope. Skint, I was a suicide waiting to happen. Flush, I was generous, gregarious and caring. Which did they prefer?

'You ought to draw lots then or summat, see who goes,' Skeeter insisted. 'Who's he, like? God Almighty?'

He was jealous. He wanted to go. To him, and to the rest of us for that matter, a trip to Aberdeen wasn't work but a holiday. I kept the peace by saying that I'd already promised Urban the trip but would rote it in future and give everyone a shot. Out of the corner of my eye, I saw Urban twist up his face and stick out his tongue at Skeeter. Clearly there was a minor battle of wills going on between them. The other kids, the girls especially, let Urban have his own way much of the time, probably because he was the youngest. Skeeter was more interested in fighting his corner. Immediately he got to his feet in a rage. 'Stick your tongue out at me again, you little bastard, and I'll rip it out your face.'

'Go for it,' Urban goaded him, then stuck his two little fingers into the corners of his mouth and fired off a piercing whistle. 'Tyson! Here, boy!'

Tyson romped in from the kitchen, but so did Greta. She pushed Skeeter back into his seat and stamped on his toe. 'Don't start, Skeet. Give it a fucking rest.'

Skeeter folded up his leg and hugged his foot. 'Ow! You stupid fucking bitch.'

If Urban thought he'd got the better of it, he was mistaken. Greta pulled him to his feet, slapped him across the face, pushed him back into his seat and stamped on his toe too, just to keep things even. 'Chop, you think he's all sweet and innocent, but he's not. He's quite capable of winding Skeet up just to get him banned from the flat. They don't like each other, in case you haven't noticed. Next one who starts gets a crack round the head with the frying-pan and I'm not kidding.'

And you,' she said, coming towards me, 'Skeet's right. You are a fucking nonce. Eastie is on top to fuck. We're all starving and we've nowhere to go and you go swanning off to Aberdeen.' I ran round the other side of the settee so that she couldn't slap my face and stamp on my toe. She came after me, but I kept the settee between us and she wasn't fast enough. 'Bastard,' she said, giving up the chase and heading back to the kitchen. 'Wait till I get my hands on you.'

'Come on,' Sparky said, when he'd stopped laughing. 'All lads together. No point falling out. See what we're up against.'

I was left with little choice but to leave Greta the keys to the flat. Urban cautioned against it, but we were already late for the job and I couldn't be bothered arguing. I gave her a tenner to settle my smack tab and left the kids a score to get food. 'Food, not substances,' I stressed, handing Sparky the money. 'We'll be back in a couple of days.'

It was hard work loading up. Luckily Urban was young and enthusiastic, so I let him do most of the work. I made the punters and their kid get stuck in too. The head of the household was some kind of albino freak. I told him I had a touch of pneumonic fever and I wasn't at my best. We picked up at ten and we were on the road by twelve. Tyson behaved impeccably throughout.

I wanted to break the back of the journey so I hit the A1 and kept my foot down all the way to Edinburgh. A decent van would have done the journey in three hours; we took five and hit Edinburgh in the rush-hour. We were tired and hungry. Tyson was getting snappy.

'Can't we just stop and get something to eat?' Urban asked.

'No. How can we? Don't talk stupid, Urban. We'll never cover any ground.'

'But we've covered hundreds of miles.'

'Yes, and we've got hundreds more to go. Don't you under-stand? Aberdeen is half-way up my arse. They've got oil-rigs there, for fuck's sake.'

The mood lightened somewhat as we approached the Forth Bridge. Urban loved it. 'Wow! Look at that.' The wind caught the van and toyed with it as we drove over the wide, wild and beautiful estuary. Urban was enthralled. He'd never seen such a place in all his life. Indeed, he had seldom been out of Leeds so suspension bridges, estuaries, oceans, forests and moun-tains were all new to him.

'This is the Firth of Forth,' I said. 'This road bridge is one of the longest single-span suspension bridges in the world. Only Yorkshire has anything better – the Humber Bridge. That over there is the Forth Railway Bridge, built about a hundred years ago and an equally impressive piece of engineering at the time. It's called a cantilever bridge and it works like a chain of men holding hands. That's how all things should work. Thus endeth the architecture lesson.'

'Wow!' he said. 'The Firth of Forth!'

He was so enamoured of the place that I decided to stop. In North Queensferry, on the other side of the estuary, we found a little pub-restaurant virtually underneath the bridge, which welcomed dogs, children and Sassenachs. There, before an open fire, we tucked into shepherd's pie and chips and made our plans for the remainder of the journey. The waitress was friendly but I couldn't understand a word she said. After the meal, I spread the big, fold-up map across the table and gave Urban his geography lesson. 'England and Scotland,' I said. 'The Auld Enemies.' I gave him a crash course in Anglo-Scottish history, mainly featuring Edward Longshanks, the Hammer of the Scots, then turned the map over and focused on the Grampian region of Scotland. 'We're here,' I said, sticking my finger on the map, 'and we have to be there by tomorrow morning.'

'What's all that?' he asked, pointing to the mauve bits.

'Hills, mountains, lakes, forests and beautiful country-side.'

'Can't we go there?'

'It's a bit hilly,' I said. 'I don't know if the van will make it.'

Urban ruffled Tyson's ears as he surreptitiously ate the leftovers under the table. 'Course she'll make it, Chop. Have some faith.'

There were two possible routes, so far as I could tell. The M90 went to Perth, but there the road forked. The A94 continued up the coast to Aberdeen and was the flattest and most sensible approach. The alternative, the A93, ran directly north to Braemar on the edge of the Cairngorms, then took a hairpin right and followed the course of the river Dee to our destination. I explained the two options. Urban voted wholeheartedly in favour of the latter.

'Yes, but look,' I said, running my finger along the A93. 'The road follows the course of the Black Water river in the Forest of Alyth. It sounds like something from *The Hobbit*. What if the Dark Lord comes after us? Look how close together those contours are. The closer they are together, the steeper the hills. Contours can't get any closer than these ones, trust me. Look here. Balnaglar Castle, near Clackavoid. What's that all about? Here. The Spittal of Glenshee. I'm not stopping there, sounds disgusting. Look at this! "Devil's Elbow" with little chevrons on the road. That means it's impassable in winter. I'm worried, Urban. This isn't a good idea.'

'I can't believe you're scared of a load of in-bred Jocks,' he said. 'You just told me they're the last vegetables of our empire. What would Longshanks have said? I've got Excalibur, you've got the air-gun and Tyson's got his teeth. Happen they should be more scared of us.'

A valid point, but Uncle Archie's words were preying on my

mind. 'Dinna gar off the main route, Choppie. Dinna gar off the main route.'

'I'm not scared,' I said. 'I'm just cautious. And it's *vestiges*, not vegetables.'

It was dark and drizzling as we pulled off the main road at Blacklunans on the river Black Water. I drove up into the hills a while and we camped in a 'carnivorous' forest, as Urban called it, on the foothills of Mount Blair. By coincidence, someone called Blair had recently entered the public consciousness as the new Labour leader. He had promised to liberate us from the long years of Tory oppression at the general election that was looming the following year.

Once we were safe and warm, I read to Urban by the light of a candle. 'In a hole in the ground there lived a hobbit . . .' He was so enthralled that he fell asleep even before Gandalf started chalking runes on Bilbo's door. I went outside, sat on an ancient tree stump rooted in the earth, opened my secret can of Tennent's, lit myself an enchanted spliff and gazed up at the stars through the trees.

I had planned to get up at five a.m. and drive the scenic route to Aberdeen. The punters would forgive us if we were an hour or two late. Unfortunately I slept in. It was eight o'clock before I stuck my head out of the tent into the mist. We packed up quickly and went down into the village. The punters had given me a contact number in Aberdeen, so I rang them and told them we'd broken down. The albino wasn't happy, but what could he do? I told them I'd ring back at lunchtime and give them a clearer idea of our revised arrival time. We got back on the road and headed north.

The van wasn't happy. I've seen quicker road-sweepers. The cam was on its way out, without a doubt, emitting a constant 'tut-tut-tut-tut' as it rattled along. The springs creaked like barn doors blowing in the wind. Worst of all, the brakes felt spongy, not something you needed on such a road. I decided to stop as soon as we hit a garage, check her over and maybe top her up with brake fluid and oil.

We found a garage at the Spittal of Glenshee, which was quite a nice village, nothing disgusting about it at all. While I was busy with the van, Urban and Tyson ambled over to a church opposite to kill some time. They were gone five minutes, then came running back across the road. Urban seemed agitated. 'Come on! Let's go! Let's go! Come on!'

'What's up?'

'Nowt. Come on. Let's go.'

I thought maybe they'd seen a ghost or Tyson had attacked the vicar. A couple of miles up the road, Urban started pulling banknotes out of his pocket, large amounts, of all conceivable currencies. After interrogation, he confessed to having robbed the donation box at the church. I was disappointed with him, and I told him so, but I wasn't going to lose time by taking him back to face the organ music. The last thing we needed was the Jock Babylon on our case.

We were climbing. The countryside was more open, moorland scrub to the left and right of us, vast mauve mountains leering in the distance. I was giving Urban his economics lesson and I was quietly hopeful of getting to Aberdeen by teatime.

He had the loot spread out across his lap. 'These?'

'French francs. You get about ten to the pound. You can pay four quid for a beer in Paris, less if you stand in the gutter outside.' I mainly conducted his education by means of these question-and-answer sessions. He'd ask a question. I'd ramble on, telling him all I knew on the subject.

'These?'

'Italian lira. I once had a fight with a bloke in Turin because he tried to charge me three thousand liras for a round of drinks. I thought the spic bastard was trying to rip me off, but it turned out to be about one pound fifty. Liras are bollocks.'

'These?'

'American dollars. There've been many great empires in the history of the world – China, Egypt, Mesopotamia, Rome, Mongol and British, to name but a few. At the moment, we're subjects of the American empire. America dominates the world economy with its mighty dollar. Subject nations are powerless against the Americans and they spread their values and culture around the globe, willy-nilly. Some of us are sworn to resist them.'

'These?'

'Deutschmarks. The Krauts suffered massive inflation before the war. You had to carry your wages home in a wheelbarrow. Money became worthless. That's why they started the Second World War and slaughtered six million Jews.'

Urban hadn't heard of the Holocaust so I told him all about it. As his self-appointed teacher, I considered it my duty. Suddenly he wasn't interested in economics any more. He shovelled the money into the glove-box, then sat in silent contemplation for a while and let the landscape roll by. Wild geese were flying across the heather.

It was time to give him the last verse of the poem I'd learnt:

> Then let us pray that come it may,
>   As come it will for a' that;
> That sense and worth, o'er a' the earth,
>   May bear the gree, and a' that.
>   For a' that and a' that,
>   It's coming yet, for a' that,
>   That man to man the warld o'er
>   Shall brothers be for a' that.

Meanwhile, we had to get to Aberdeen. We were soon clawing our way up the Devil's Elbow in first gear. I didn't think Elsie would make it. I gripped the wheel, rocking backwards and forwards, trying to give her some extra momentum, but she struggled on at her own leisurely pace. She was slow but tenacious, and bore her load to the crest of the hill. The road continued like that for another four or five miles. The map forgot to mention the Devil's Knee, the Devil's Armpit, the Devil's Crotch and the Devil's Arsehole. Aberdeen seemed a million miles away. Time was altered. We were a sorry ship, adrift upon a twisting, turning ocean with mountains for waves. Just when we thought to abandon ship, the storm abated. We were on our last supplies of rum as we sailed into the Glen Clunie Ski Lodge and Services.

A petrol station, a ski shop, a restaurant and several other buildings were dotted around the complex. We were high in the Grampians and a huge mountain reared up behind the lodge. A chair lift ran from the lodge to the top of the mountain. Little feet dangled down from yellow chairs looming high in the sky. Urban rarely asked for anything, but he was determined to have a go on it. 'Please, please, please,' he begged. 'I'll pay. Think they'll take Deutschmarks?' I was powerless to resist. We left Tyson in the van, took the lift as far as it went, then climbed the rest of the way to the summit on foot.

At the peak, we gazed across the foreground scree to the hazy mountains, green and purple, receding into the distance seemingly for ever. Urban didn't speak: his eyes and face said it all. He held out his arms and spun round in an attempt to express the immense, infinite wonder of it all. We were on top of the world!

I pointed into the distance and said something I'd always wanted to say: 'One day, lad, all this'll be thine.'

We liked it so much at the top of the world that we went hiking for a couple of hours. When we returned to earth, Urban took Tyson for a run while I checked the van again. I had no hope of getting to Aberdeen that day, so I rang the punters and told them we'd be there in the morning. We had to wait for a camshaft to be delivered from Dundee, I told them. We couldn't move an inch until it arrived, sorry for the inconvenience.

In Braemar, we visited the castle then took Tyson hunting in Ballochbuie Forest. In a dappled clearing, we chanced upon a deer nuzzling in the undergrowth. It stood its ground and stared back at us defiantly. It's a magical thing to catch a deer's eye. Even Tyson froze, not wishing to destroy the moment. I breathed too loud and broke the spell. Startled, the deer bounded off into the bushes with Urban and Tyson in hot pursuit. They might as well have been chasing a chimera. We followed the course of a stream, uphill, for miles, and it was teatime and chilly when we returned to the van. We were now within thirty miles of Aberdeen. In theory, it would be simple to drive there in the morning. We were worn out from all the walking about, so I unfolded the map and looked for a place to camp. Only then did I notice how close we were to Balmoral.

'Mmm,' I said, a whimsy forming in my mind. 'Fancy spending the night with royalty, Urban? We have here a perfect opportunity to poach the Queen's venison.'

We spent the night in the grounds of Balmoral. We pitched up by a fast-running, rocky river and had the time of our lives trying to catch fish with homemade harpoons. We were like two wild things. 'This is how the other half lives,' I told Urban, as we tucked into Wacky Salmon, a concoction of my own invention, which we cooked on an open fire beneath the stars. We hadn't actually caught the fish: Urban stole it from a supermarket in Braemar while I was on the toilet. He stashed it in the van and by the time I noticed it, it was too late to do anything except eat it. It tasted sensational. The only thing more impressive than the Scottish fish was the Scottish sky. These days, light pollution blocks out the stars near major cities. Urban had never before just lain back and observed a clear night sky in all its glory and munificence. He had certainly never seen the Northern Lights before, possibly the most awesome sight on the planet. 'This makes up for everything.' He sighed enigmatically. The fire below and the *aurora borealis* above entertained us into night like a moving, flickering picture show until the lullaby of the rippling river soothed us to sleep.

At dawn, we took the air-gun and tried to scare up a rabbit for breakfast, but Tyson scared all the rabbits away, as well as the birds. Urban tried shooting fish, but that didn't work either, due to refraction, which neither Urban nor the pellets understood. Tyson splashed through the shallow water like a whippet on crack, as happy to be chasing invisible, fast-moving, whistling pellets as anything else. When we heard shots echoing in the distance, we feared a gamekeeper was firing at us. We beat a hasty retreat and were on the road to Aberdeen by eight.

As we rolled into the Granite City, I felt an immense sense of relief. The nightmare was over. Aberdeen did exist. I had begun to doubt it. I was tremendously excited and light-hearted. 'Here we are at last, Urbie. I can't believe it. Aber-fucking-deen!'

I wasn't really watching the road. My mind was still at the top of a mountain somewhere. 'Watch it!' Urban cried.

Too late, I saw the low, arched railway bridge in front of us. There was no time to do anything. With a monumental thwack and a heart-wrenching jolt, we hit the bridge at forty miles an hour, knocking the box-unit clean off the chassis, blocking the road and converting the albino's junk into matchwood.

Stupidly, we weren't wearing our seatbelts. Urban cracked his head open on the windscreen, while I bust a couple of ribs on the steering-wheel. Elsie, unruffled, shook herself down, revved herself up and carried on going as if nothing had happened. If anything, she seemed refreshed by the lighter load.

I chucked Urban the first-aid box, said, 'Fucking hell, that was close,' and we headed back towards the jungle via the coast road.

ELEVEN
THE QUIET ZONE

Do you know what it's like to be alone
By yourself
No one home
Going insane
Racking your brain
No boyfriend
No child
Don't care for the wild
But you know in a while you'll become like a child
Sucking your thumb
No one will come
To save you from the sadness
Madness
Loneliness
They won't help you up or fill up your cup
So you do it yourself
Don't trust no one else
Keeping it real but your soul won't heal
So you do it to them
Till they know how you feel

Teezer
Desperately seeking someone

We got back to Leeds around midnight to find a thick metal sheet across the door of my flat. Loaded up with bags, weapons and camping equipment, we stood before it and looked on in disbelief. We were tired and wanted to go to bed.

I knocked on the metal. 'Anyone home?' I whimpered. Events were spiralling way beyond control.

Urban dropped his rucksack on to the floor and sat on it despondently. 'Told you not to give Mum the keys. She spoils everything.'

Normally I'd have slept in the back of the van and worried about everything else in the morning, but the van was now a chassis-cab and had no back to sleep in. Nor was there any way into my flat through the sixteenth-storey windows. We had little choice but to get back into the van and head for East End Park in search of Greta.

Charlton Mount was in complete darkness, the door and windows locked, the curtains drawn. I peered through a gap in the curtains and tapped on the window. I was getting my first taste of homelessness. 'No one's in,' I said to Urban, through the open van window. He hadn't bothered disembarking.

'We're wasting our time,' he said. 'She's gone. Once she's gone it can take weeks to track her down. She could be anywhere. Best kip in the shed.'

We were running out of options. Had I been alone, there were several places I could have stayed. For example, I only had to turn up at my dad's, the prodigal son, to be given refuge and respite. Urban, however, was an added complication that was difficult to explain. Dad wasn't ready to adopt a grandson, least of all a common-or-garden urchin from the streets, so the shed seemed our best bet. I parked the van at the Slip, where it had least chance of being stolen, ransacked or vandalised, and we made our way through the ginnel to the back of Londesborough Grove. When we got there, the lights were off in the house and the shed was deserted. Urban and Tyson took the bottom bunk, I took the top and we went out like lights.

*   *   *

Something brushed down my cheek and lingered on my lips, something small and bulbous with a hard, flat top. I didn't know what it was, because I was in that bizarre dimension between sleep and wakefulness. One thing I was clear about was that it didn't taste nice. I pulled the quilt up round my face, rolled over and turned the other way, only to find ten more of the smelly little creatures trying to wriggle into my mouth. I woke up and discovered, to my horror, that I was topping-and-tailing with Trudi and Molly. I jumped out of bed like a jack-in-the-box and cracked my head on the roof, adding a fractured skull to my growing list of injuries.

I didn't want to be accused of anything. 'There's no smoke without fire,' they say. The slightest thing would have given people an excuse to call me a nonce. Why else would I have been involved with the Shed Crew?

Dazed, I staggered outside in my boxers and T-shirt and pushed my toes through the morning dew. The birds were twittering and singing in the trees. My watch said six o'clock. Summer was almost at an end and the first hint of autumn was in the air. There was no sunrise to speak of, just a boring grey half-light coming up on the horizon.

I sat on the doorstep, made myself a roll-up and mulled things over in my mind. I saw beauty in young people, no doubt about it. I couldn't deny that I found some of the older girls attractive. Did that make me a nonce? The idea of actually doing anything with them had never entered my head. They were kids and you didn't touch kids. That was rule number two. It might even have made rule number one, but as Sparky had so rightly pointed out on another occasion, 'No grassers has to be rule number one, else we'll all be in jail and we won't be able to kick fuck out of the nonces.'

Molly emerged from the shed tugging a comb through her hair. She wore a scraggy old dressing-gown and slippers.

'Morning, Fatboy,' she said. 'Hope you wasn't fiddling about with us in bed last night, you dirty old nonce, you.' She sat beside me on the step. 'Got a roll-up I can have?'

I made one and handed it to her.

'Cheers there, Fatboy.'

I thought I sensed a hint of disrespect in her voice. 'Molly,' I said, 'don't call me Fatboy, love. Names are important. You should always call people by their proper names. It's a simple matter of respect towards what Schopenhauer would call your fellow sufferers. How would you like it if I called you Slagheap or Slut-face or something?'

'Call me what you like,' she said. 'I couldn't give a fuck. And who the fuck's Schopenhauer? I've never heard of him. Where do you get this shit from? If you're so clever, how come you have to go round sleeping wi' little girls?'

I looked at her like I'd never seen a human being before. 'Hang on,' I said. 'What are you trying to say?' I pointed out that I had gone to sleep in all innocence and that it was she who had climbed in with me. I couldn't be held responsible for that. 'And why do you always have to have a dig at people, always some barbed comment? What's the need, Molly? You don't have to put someone else's light out for your own to shine.'

'Only having you on,' she said. 'Don't get carried away with yourself. Tyson wouldn't let us get in with Urbie, so we had to bunk up with you. Got a light?'

We sat together on the step, smoking our roll-ups in silence. She had a peculiar way of holding a cigarette, up in the air, fingers fanned out and wrist bent at ninety degrees. She inhaled the smoke deeply, relishing it, as if nicotine were nectar. She was extremely slight, almost malnourished, the original waif and stray. Her long blonde hair tumbled over her ears and eyes like a waterfall. She had stars in her eyes and dirt in her ears. She was no stranger to curling tongs.

I was about to ask what had happened to my flat, but she jumped in first. 'I know your dad,' she said. 'He's always in the bookie's.'

'That's him,' I confirmed. 'We never got holidays when we were kids because he always lost all his money on the horses.'

'What's an 'oliday?' she enquired glumly.

'I know your dad too,' I said. 'I drink with him in the Slip.' Not only was it a small world but East End Park was a microcosm of it. The Slip Inn was like Crewe station. If you stood in the taproom long enough, you'd meet everyone you knew; and many people did just that. I'd seen Molly with her dad at the kids' discos on Sundays. The Slip has a taproom, a snug and a lounge. Kids aren't allowed in the taproom or the snug, but they can go into the lounge, which in effect means they can roam free throughout the building. On occasion, you even find them playing dominoes with the old men in the taproom. The Sunday disco is where Eastie kids are traditionally introduced to the drink culture. It was a regular event even when I was a child. The Slip always reminded me of those lowlife haunts in Dickens novels with kids lurking in the corners. The only thing missing was clay pipes and gin, although Lambert and Butlers and alcopops substituted adequately.

Molly and I were on a similar wavelength. We had been brought up in adjacent streets. Twenty years separated us, but nothing had changed. People were still people. Molly had been through everything I'd been through. We immediately accepted each other in a way that is only possible with someone who comes from your patch. We understood each other. We knew what we'd got up to and how we'd got away with it. We had similar problems of the head. She acted out her disturbance by means of sexual promiscuity and harsh words dressed up as comedy. I liked to get drunk and violent every once in a while. Same problem. Different solutions.

'You quite like Urban, don't you?' I said. 'I can tell by the way you're openly abusive to him.'

'He's all right,' she said. 'I'll make a man of him yet.' Suddenly she elbowed my arm, as if she'd just thought of the most important thing in the world. 'Have a guess what the best thing in life is.'

'Erm . . . candy floss at the seaside on a rainy Tuesday?'

'No, it's getting photographed. You know when you're little, everyone photographs you all the time, dote the'? Right? And when you get older no one photographs you any more because the' dote love you any more, that's why. So t' best thing is being photographed.' She was talking pure, genuine Eastie, the real McCoy. The way we used to talk it in the old days. I was filled with joy. I thought the language was dead, but Molly was as common as muck. Our culture had not been overwhelmed. There was still hope. Okay, she was having trouble at home but, then, which teenager wasn't?

I constructed another couple of roll-ups on my knee and passed one to Molly. I couldn't help but lapse into the vernacular myself. 'What'd ya dad say if he knew ya wa' down 'ere?'

She came straight back with the best possible answer. 'What'd *your* dad say if he knew *you* wa' down 'ere?'

'Fair point,' I conceded. 'I wote grass if you dote.'

'Just one thing,' she lamented, accent back to normal, voice full of disgust and loathing. 'He's not my dad. He's just a little Irish bloke and I hate his fucking guts.'

There was always this pit of horror and despair. Everywhere you went you came across it. Just when you thought you had an intelligent conversation going, there it was, like an ugly wart distorting the beauty of nature and humanity. Everyone was different, each individual case was unique, but everyone was tormented with anger, fear, confusion, resentment or hatred. They were all messed up, one way or another. Something was rotten and corrupt at the heart of our society. In the ageing body, the circulation ceases first at the extremities. We were at the edges of society where the bloodflow had already packed up.

There wasn't much I could say to her about her dad. 'Fancy a walk up the Slip to get the van?' I asked. 'We'll get something for breakfast.' I had nothing to hide, so I had decided on a policy of doing whatever I thought was right. If we were seen together and her dad asked questions, I knew I could look him in the eye. Whether he would be able to do the same was another matter. After all, it wasn't my daughter who was sleeping rough. But I didn't blame him. I didn't blame any of their parents. Most had done their best in impossible situations. Many were victims of illness, madness, depression or addiction. Some had lost hope. Few were nasty or malicious. I often got in trouble as a social worker because I refused to follow the party line that the individual was always at fault. I was more inclined to blame corrupt and incompetent executives, public servants, law enforcers and politicians who made life for the average underclass parent a living hell until they cracked.

'Sorted,' Molly said. 'I'm starving. We can nick milk off doorsteps while we're at it.'

She told me on the way what had happened while Urban and I were in Scotland. The scuffers were making a big fuss over Cod, she said, who had barely survived his near execution at Urban's hands. They knew about the shed, about my flat, about everything. 'Burner must have grassed,' she said.

The bobbies must have put two and two together. 'Brian, could it be possible, in case of point, that the spate of twocks in East End Park is linked to the teenage runaway problem? If so, how can we tackle it and improve our pensions at the same time?'

'Good job your flat's five hundred foot in the air,' Molly went on. 'We saw 'em coming a mile off.' Everyone got out in time, but the police kicked the door off just to be on the safe side. Greta had a Joey in Chapeltown and everyone was hiding out there. The girls had been sent as scouts to find us. 'The scuffers want the ring-leaders,' she said, no doubt meaning me and Greta, 'and it's on top to fuck.'

After breakfast, Molly and Trudi took us to Greta's new hideout where we put a story together. I believe that if you're going to lie, the best way to do it is to approximate the truth. We agreed to tell the exact truth, but to leave out one detail. Instead of Cod being dragged out of the house with his head banging along the floor, he had staggered out under his own steam. If he had stumbled into the midden yard and nearly died, that was his own affair and none of us could be held accountable. He was only a smackhead, after all. 'Maybe leave out the bit about electrocuting him as well,' I added, as an afterthought.

Once everyone had been reminded of rule number one, Greta and I marched into the Bridewell and gave ourselves up. Molly, it transpired, had most of her facts wrong. They didn't give a toss about the smackhead, but *Squealer* Brown, as he was soon rechristened, had complained about an unprovoked attack on his person and they wanted to speak to Master Urban Grimshaw in connection with their enquiries.

The council were slow putting a new door on my flat, but not as slow as I'd thought they would be. My expectations of public services were nil, so any time within a month was fine by me. They did it in less than a week, which was mustard. I spent most of the intervening time at my lockup garage playing with the van. I gave her a full service, including a new cam, and fitted new shock absorbers and brake-pads. I rang round the scrapyards and found a box unit at Jack Straw's in Middleton.

All I had to do was reverse into the yard and four of the lads plopped it on the back for me. It was a simple matter for me to bolt it to the chassis, making certain this time to do a good job of it. It cost me the last of my savings, but I was back on the road, back in my flat and back in business with the minimum of fuss.

As soon as I had a new door, the Babylon came banging on it again with renewed vigour. Urban was Public Enemy Number One. We all rallied round and hid him, of course. I even went so far as to build a priest-hole for him, something not seen in England since Elizabethan times. I had a big walk-in cupboard in my flat, a good three metres square. By pushing my filing cabinet forward a little, I was able to make a space behind it big enough for a young person to hide in. Disguised with shelves, boxes, bike tyres and assorted junk, the police were far too stupid to find it. They came daily over the next few weeks and became increasingly frustrated at their inability to lay their hands on one little boy. They turned petulant, even moody, some resorting to abuse, calling me a nonce and a Fagin-type character. One WPC looked me in the eye and spat, 'I hate people like you. You're a disgrace to humanity.'

Had the world turned upside-down? Didn't she know I was High Church? You got to the point where you didn't even try to justify yourself any more. She was a happy slave who thought we were just troublemakers and nuisances. I beckoned her with my finger, as if I fully intended to grass all my friends, and she pushed her ear towards me in an involuntary reflex. 'Avoid the loud and the ignorant,' I whispered into her shell-like, 'for they are vexations to the spirit.'

No good arguing with the police. They thought they were right on every issue, which precluded any meaningful dialogue. I simply got on with my life under constant harassment. I began to see the situation as akin to the Roman occupation of Britain. The big-nosed, breastplated bastards were in control and there was little to be done about it. All you could do was take the piss, hit back as and when you got the opportunity and wait for their empire to fall.

I began to see Urban as the heir to the throne of all the Yorkshires, the Messiah come to liberate us from oppression, the World Teacher prophesied by the Theosophical Society, or the reincarnation of King Arthur of the Britons, and the Babylon would have him over my dead body. I saw something noble and courageous in him. I admired his honesty, so untainted by the socialisation process the rest of us had suffered at school, college, home and work. I saw in him a symbol of innocence, like the newborn Christ-child, updated for the modern age. I even envied him his ignorance, for ignorance is bliss. In some indefinable way, he was untainted by the world. This, of course, meant that I had an uncontrollable urge to protect him.

Urban loved every minute of it. From being an illiterate nobody, I had convinced him – or had he convinced me? – that he was something very special indeed, something so special that the forces of darkness were on his case in no uncertain terms.

Over the next few months things changed a great deal. Greta abandoned the house in East End Park, refusing even to go back to collect her stuff. 'Too many bad memories,' she claimed. She had started from scratch so many times that it was second nature to her. She preferred to have nothing. She found possessions a burden. As was her practised habit, she simply found a new Joey and moved in with him.

Yeah-yeah Ken didn't think of himself as a Joey. He knew the concept, but didn't see how it could ever be applied to him. He was one of the boys. He was twenty-three, young by Greta's standards, with a lightweight build and pasty skin. He had sunken cheeks, furry blond eyebrows and beady, piggy eyes. He liked a drink and a smoke and a laugh and anything else if it was going: he'd try anything once, the life and soul of the party.

'Aw right, mate? How's it goin', like? Aw right?'

'Fine. Yourself?'

'Aw right, mate. Yeah, yeah, not bad, not bad.'

I felt like saying, 'How come we're both from within half a mile of each other and I talk like this while you talk like a fucking parrot? Now, get out of my face before I smash your beak in, you bastard.' He was that despicable.

'Yeah, yeah, I met Gret in Big Lil's an' that. Know what A'm saying? She's aw right an' that.' He had a way of speaking without saying anything. I detested him on sight. Nature gives no reasons for its gut reactions: he just set my alarms off. There was something vacuous and lewd about him.

Greta didn't care. Yeah-yeah Ken was a good Joey and she had everything she needed. He was a semi-competent thief who brought plenty of money into the house, knew his place and did as he was told, so the kids could come and go as they pleased. He even took the kids to work with him on occasion and tried to teach them a good, honest trade. His house was in Chapeltown, a largely West Indian suburb of Leeds, and Greta was soon able to get down to some serious drug-taking, Chapeltown offering a veritable cornucopia for drug-users of all denominations.

Perhaps understandably, Burner's mum was seriously pissed off about his head injury and disconnected the shed from the national grid, leaving the Shed Crew homeless. They renamed themselves the Penthouse Posse and tried to move into mine. However, two-bedroom flats aren't built for a dozen people, their friends, their family, their sexual partners and assorted hangers-on, especially when the police call round every morning looking for one or all of them.

So I had to introduce new house rules. Anyone who wanted

to visit had to ring up first. No more than four in the house at any time. No more than two staying overnight. I couldn't cover their every need, but I could provide an emergency service. If they were really desperate or stuck, I'd help them out. Otherwise, I expected them to give my place a wide berth. I'd already had my first warning letters from the council, threatening to throw me out if I didn't calm things down. I'd agreed to help the kids, but I wasn't willing to lose my home because of it and I let them know this in no uncertain terms. Having said that, I must give them their due. That I managed to keep the flat, and run a safe-house for disturbed, delinquent, alienated, violent, rootless and homeless young offenders for several years testifies that, in general, they respected my wishes.

We called Greta's house in Chapeltown 'the mad house' and my flat 'the quiet zone'. If you wanted to get smashed or go mental, you went to Greta's. My flat was mostly for reading, writing, drawing and quiet contemplation. I taught Urban the alphabet and tried to get the other kids interested in the arts. The philosopher Epicurus mentions three things essential to human happiness: a group to belong to, freedom, and the requirement to lead a 'considered life'. We had everything but freedom, so we were two-thirds happy. Our group was each other. Art and poetry were our way of leading the considered life. We drew pictures and cartoons, made paintings and generally scribbled and scrawled our way through the afternoons. Pinky showed most talent as an artist, Kara and Sparky as poets, but all the kids had a go at anything and everything without shame. Even Frank and Skeeter showed the artistic side of their temperaments. Frank was a dab hand at chess. Skeeter studied the noble art of chivalry, most often with Trudi – especially against the washing-machine, I heard, the moment I went out.

We played lots of chess. Chess, at its best, is a form of

meditation. At its worst, it's a cheap hobby, and a way of learning to plan ahead and concentrate. Most of the kids liked the game and I thought it would do them some good. At least, it would do them no harm. In the months between summer and Christmas '96, the chessboard was on the go 24/7.

TWELVE
PAWNS IN THE GAME

In Stone Age times
Men in animal frocks
Drew squares in the soil
And played with rocks

In Bronze Age times
Having mastered tools
They cut men from bone
But played like fools

In Dark Age times
On the Isle of Lewis
They carved ivory men
Though their play was crude

In modern times
We have Staunton sets
And opening theory
Which we always forget

Chop
Playing nice

The sun came up later and later every day, until it was full-blown autumn. The nicest thing about living a hundred metres in the air was that you could watch the onset of the seasons and follow their changes, day to day. October and November were my favourite months. I loved the way all the colours were bleached from the landscape. The only survivors were the faded hues of the fallen leaves: red, yellow and brown. Leaves gathered in piles at the communal entrances, occasionally blown up into bothersome tornadoes by passing gusts. On windy days, the panes in the rotting wooden window-frames in my flat whistled and rattled alarmingly, threatening to fall out and double-glaze someone's head. I wrote to the council outlining my fears, as did many of my neighbours, but all we got was promises.

The penthouse, as I was now beginning to think of it, over-looked an old municipal graveyard with a blue plaque on the gate. No one had been buried there for a hundred years or more, and the whole place was overgrown and unkempt, but it was the nearest thing we had to a park. A good sixty acres, in summer it was covered with a dusty blanket of ancient, leafy trees. Urban liked the graveyard. By now, he was staying at mine once or twice a week on average, if we had work or if he needed a break from the mad house. Whenever he stayed over, we'd take Tyson there for a run the next morning.

'See you! Hey! Wee boy! Weer'd ye get the doggie? That's mar dog. Ye stole it frum me, ye wee thief!'

Ginger Geoff sat on the benches in the graveyard every morning drinking Special Brew from golden tins. He was in his fifties, an ageing teddy boy with a giant quiff who, somewhere along the line, had accidentally become a tramp. Urban once told him he was wasting his life, sitting on benches, drinking Special Brew all the time. Why didn't he check into a safe-house for treatment with an eventual view to finding a job? What did he hope to achieve by just sitting there drinking alcohol all the time? 'Wee boy,' the tramp had replied, 'ye nar jack shit. Away wi' ye now an' Ah've an idea that's mar dog.' Since then, he had maintained his claim to Tyson, come fair weather or foul.

All the posh graves were at the front of the graveyard, mostly built by rich Victorians. Some must have cost a small fortune. There were big, square tombs with grandiloquent carvings and ornamentation, huge Gothic monuments, miniature mausoleums and all manner of statuary, from cherubs and angels to rampant, roaring lions. I often read out the inscriptions to Urban as we ambled along and there was always something new to discover. 'Look at this one, Urban.' A tall, thin column reared five metres into the air. An inscription ran round it in a spiral pattern and it looked like a giant upturned barber's pole. I had to walk round it three times to read it. 'It's about a bloke called Thomas Jeffreys, who died in 1884 aged forty-eight. He was grand master of the Ancient Order of Juveniles. It says, "He was noble in thought, generous in spirit and a willing worker for his fellow man."'

'Nice,' Urban agreed, throwing a stick through the trees for Tyson. 'Go gerrit, boy!' Tyson ploughed through a hedge as if it wasn't there and brought the stick back, slavering. He dropped it at his master's feet, then stood, gasping and panting expectantly. Urban picked up the stick and threw it again.

Towards the back of the graveyard were the 'guinea graves'. Here, the cemetery was heavily wooded and overgrown. Vast stones two metres high, covered in lichen and ivy, contained up to twenty interments. These were the mass graves where the Victorian poor had been buried at a guinea a time, their only hope of a decent funeral. 'No inscriptions here, Urban, just endless lists of names: "Agnes Wilson, died 1882, aged nineteen; William Povey, died 1882, aged twenty-seven; Bertha Hernshaw, died 1882, aged two." I expect Thomas Jeffreys and Agnes Wilson led quite different lives. Maybe Agnes was a prostitute addicted to laudanum and Thomas was her client when he wasn't being a philanthropist. What do you reckon, Urban? Urban?'

Urban was moderately interested in English social history,

but there was a time and a place for everything and this wasn't it. Bored or worse, he had disappeared into the trees to play with his dog. All my chat sometimes distracted him from the basic pleasure of simply being alive. I was addicted to nicotine so I didn't experience things like Urban. The receptors in my brain were filled with goo. There was nothing else for it. I took out my tobacco tin and sat on a tomb to await his return.

I did go on a bit, I admit. I tried not to, but it was a learning curve. I gave a lot to the kids, Urban especially, but it wasn't one-way traffic. I got something special in return. I was slowly learning how to chill out and enjoy myself, to live in the moment, to be at one with myself and the universe. It's a hard trick, but if you can master it it makes life worth living. Only children are really good at it. With Urban's help, I was remembering how to be a child again. Some of the older kids in the crew, however, were already forgetting.

At Greta's things were going from bad to worse. The lads were getting nuttier by the day. Skeeter and Frank were living with Greta, while Sparky was staying with friends in Morley, a slightly better neighbourhood than most of us were used to. They were twocking day and night and taking who knew what combination of drink and drugs. Sparky had brought a new character into the equation: Spurry, a lad of similar age and temperament to himself. Sparky, Spurry, Skeeter and Frank, the Four Horsemen of the Apocalypse. The lads were heading for big trouble and we all knew it. The rest of us were steering a wide berth, hoping to avoid the worst of it when the shit hit the fan.

One afternoon, in a fit of dejection with life, I'd visited Greta. She and I went to the local pub and returned about midnight to find her kitchen floor swimming in blood. Skeeter was stood at the sink with chunks missing from his arm. Sparky, Spurry and Frank were sitting at the kitchen table rubbing their brows and shaking their heads in dismay. Greta was too shocked even to kick off about the mess. 'What the . . .' Apparently, the police had devised a new tactic. Tired of twock drivers bailing out of their cars and running away, they now carried highly trained Doberman pursuit dogs as pillion passengers. When the twockers ran for it, these hounds of hell were loosed upon them. 'One got Skeeter,' Sparky told me, 'but I whacked it over the head with a scaffy bar and put it out of its misery.' We spent the night in A and E where Skeeter added twelve chevrons to his coat-of-arms.

Also, Yeah-yeah Ken had disappeared into thin air and no one would tell me what had happened to him. Urban later confided that the lads had beaten him up and scared him away, but made me promise not to say anything, fearing he'd be beaten up as well for grassing. I realised, perhaps belatedly, that I hadn't been seeing the lads as they really were. I had some kind of idealised image in my head, which they never quite lived up to. What was more, I never really witnessed their dark side. They always treated me with kid gloves. They saw something in me that they didn't want to destroy: an adult who genuinely liked and respected them, who didn't blame them for the situation in which they found themselves and who was willing to give them time and energy. It was a rare and precious commodity in England towards the end of the twentieth century. They couldn't risk alienating me and losing my friendship. But I was beginning to understand that Sparky, Frank and Skeeter were a dangerous, volatile combination. Each one was heading for the big house.

When the three of them came round to my flat one day to escape the madness at Greta's, I asked them what had happened to Yeah-yeah Ken. Urban sometimes made things up to get people into trouble and I wanted to hear their side of the story. 'It's on a need-to-know basis, Chop,' Skeeter said. 'Don't ask.' I didn't push it as Urban was still there, having been around for two or three days. He was sitting at the dining-table in the corner engrossed in building a model aeroplane. Tyson was under the table, sniffing glue.

It was a school for scoundrels, I was dean of the academy and chess figured large on the curriculum. All the lads liked it and Frank, in particular, showed a real aptitude for the game. I encouraged them to play with financial inducements. There was ten pounds on offer to anyone who could beat me and I often handed out a fiver brilliancy prize if anyone came out with a good combination or a well-conceived attack.

My many years on the planet gave me some advantages over their youth: I had seen most of it and I had done most of it. They could still shock and surprise me, but I possessed a certain equilibrium, which they were seldom able to upset. My usual method was to get stoned and conduct their lessons by means of diatribe. They could take notes or not as they preferred. Mine was a free school.

'Do you know why there's sixty-four squares on a chessboard? I'll tell you why. It's because of the *yin* and the *yang*. *Yin* and *yang* are the two opposite forces of nature, like good and evil, male and female, light and dark, up and down, that sort of thing. In China, three thousand years ago, where they first spotted these forces, they called them the white tiger and the azure dragon. They also had these fortune-telling cards, called *I Ching*. There were sixty-four in a pack and they laid them out in an eight-by-eight grid. That's where they got the chessboard from. It was how they interpreted the Tao. The Tao is like the way everything works in the universe.'

Frank said, 'Shut up, Chop, we're trying to concentrate.'

Frank had the better position, against Sparky. Skeeter and I were looking on from the side. 'You lot obviously don't understand the meaning of numbers, that's all I can assume. There's a Jewish sect called the cabbalists who are really big on numbers. If you knew anything at all, you'd know about them.

If you add six and four together, you get ten, which represents the earth. Add one and nought together, you get one. So sixty-four is linked to ten and one. And one means . . . one . . . the one true God and all that – i.e., heaven. So you've got heaven and earth mixed up in one little game, which can't be bad. They teach you fuck all in school, these days, that's all I can say.'

'We don't go to school, Chop,' Sparky reminded me.

'No, that's true. I forgot about that. Anyway, there's a nice story about the bloke who invented chess. This bloke invents chess, right? And he sells it to this prince in India.'

Sparky was on the ball as always. 'I thought you said it came from China.'

'Same thing. Don't interrupt. So, the prince says to him, "This is the best game ever invented, my man. How can I ever repay you for this delightful addition to my life? Surely I will win many a battle with this tool. Name your price." So the bloke says he wants one grain of rice for the first square, two for the second, four for the third, eight for the fourth, and so on and so forth, doubling up every time to the sixty-fourth square. So the prince says all right. Well, what a Joey! He couldn't pay the bill! There wasn't enough rice in the whole of India! It goes one, two, four, eight, 16, 32, 64, 128, 256, 512, 1024, 2048, and so on till you can't even work out what the next one is. Pretty soon it's millions and billions. The prince emptied every silo there was, then handed over the whole country and had done with it.'

Frank lifted his eyes from the board and looked at Sparky. 'What's he on about?'

'I think he's trying to teach us math on the sly.'

'*Maths*, Sparky. *Maths*. Not *math*. *Math* is American. You know how much it injures me when you talk in their filthy barbaric tongue.'

Sparky liked baseball, basketball, American football and

rap. 'America's all right, Chop. I don't know why you keep going on about it.'

'It's not all right. You don't know. You weren't there.'

'Weren't where, Chop?'

'There . . .' I said, waving vaguely out of the window into the distance, somewhat confused by a surfeit of dope. 'China and India . . . places like that.'

Frank made the winning move by crashing his knight down on the board and sending half the pieces flying across the room. 'Have it, motherfucker!'

'You're supposed to say checkmate, Frank,' Skeeter said.

I'd had enough of them all by teatime and sent them back to Greta's. Urban rang up again within the hour. 'Please, Chop, can I stay there tonight? We'll go scrappying in the morning if there isn't any work.' When there wasn't much work, I was in the habit of driving around at random looking for scrap metal. A half-decent load would bring in twenty or thirty pounds. 'Please, Chop. Please, please, please, please.'

'No, Urban. You can't stay here all the time. It's not doing you any favours.'

'Oh, it is, Chop, it is. Trust me on this one. I can't stand it here. They're all fucking fruitcakes. Everyone's fucked out of their faces all the time. Trudi's got six lads in the bedroom and she's going through 'em all one at a time.'

'No, Urban, I'm sorry. Maybe tomorrow.'

'Fuck you, then.' He slammed the phone down.

Urban hated the mad house and would have stayed with me every night had I let him, but I limited him as much as I could. I didn't want to shield him too much from reality. The mad house was his lot and he had to make the best of it.

Unfortunately, I forgot about his iron will. Greta rang me half an hour later and ordered me to get my arse down there, quick time. 'You won't fucking believe this. I'm gunner kill the little bastard if you don't do something about him.'

When I got there, she grabbed me by the scruff of the neck and pointed me towards the phone box opposite, its melted carcass still smoking and smouldering.

Frank and Skeeter had been winding Urban up, tormenting him, driving him to distraction until he snapped. He had rung me looking for refuge and I'd turned him away. In protest, he doused the phone box with petrol and put a match to it. 'Do you know how much stress I'm getting off those big black bastards next door because of this?' Greta yelled. 'They're fucking Yardies, man. Fucking drug-dealers and pimps. They don't need this shit. They like to keep a low profile. We had four fire engines and three police cars in the fucking street earlier on.'

'Well, he's your son,' I protested. 'What's it got to do with me?'

'My son? That's a laugh. He thinks more about you than he does about me!'

'Well, maybe that's because—'

'Yeah, go on. Finish your sentences. Because what?'

It wasn't worth getting into it. The only way out was to be stupid. 'Because you're an ugly fucking tart,' I yelled, head-butting her in the belly and knocking her down into the flowerbed. I followed up by diving on top of her and pinning her down. 'Give us a kiss, you little spunker.'

'Gerroff me, you silly, noncing pervert,' she screamed, punching me in the face as hard as she was able. It wasn't always a simple matter to read her correctly. I'd thought she'd find it funny.

I got up, rubbing my cheek, to find a six-foot-four, eighteen-stone Rastafarian watching me from the next garden. 'Yow, chess mon, beat ya bitch indoors. Want play some gay-ems?'

Greta pushed me through the threadbare bushes that separated the two gardens. 'Go on! Fuck off and play chess, you fat stinking knobhead.'

I landed in a pile next door and Big Sink offered me his spade-like hand. 'Come den, white boy.'

'Usual terms?' I enquired.

'Aye.'

The deal was that I could smoke as much draw, snort as much coke and lick as many rocks as I could handle while I was there, and that West Indian gear is five times better than the crap they sell us, I don't mind telling you. I'd been playing there for weeks and getting smashed for free. Four black guys lived there and sat around all day smoking draw and playing chess. Girls came and went on the batter and punters came and went for their drugs. Greta had seen them playing and happened to mention that I was good. They were bored playing each other. They wanted an outside yardstick against which to measure themselves and I was that yardstick. Bizarrely, they insisted on having the black pieces every game. I explained that this was a distinct disadvantage. White has the first move and that's quite important in chess. Sometimes it's the difference between victory and defeat. They understood, they said. Chess was like life in that respect, they said. Beating white, despite the odds, was part of the game as far as they were concerned.

They kept me there for hours trying to beat me, all the while building bigger and more magnificent reefers, trying to get me out of it so they could win. When that didn't work, they got the rock pipe out, which was a very bad move. Boy, did I play some phenomenal chess! They never had a prayer. Big Sink showed some promise, but the rest were little more than beginners. I could have beaten any of them blindfolded. I neglected to mention to them that I was one of the top amateurs in the city and an automatic selection for the county.

Then I made one of the biggest mistakes of my life. I'd won about twenty games on the trot and Big Sink was getting agitated, slamming his fist into his palm over and over again. I wasn't sure whether he was trying to intimidate me, or whether he was merely frustrated. Either way, he succeeded in intimidating me. The other three guys had nicknames like Slasher, Stabber and Killer, and their body language was no more inviting than Sinky's. I decided it was time to take Greta's advice. She'd suggested before that I let one of them win a game to keep them in the net. 'They must get fed up losing all the time. Give them a game,' she suggested. 'Let them have some hope. Why kill the goose that lays the golden egg?' Like a fool, I decided she was right. Big Sink put up a half-decent showing in the next game so I accidentally blundered a piece and let him polish me off. They all went crazy, dancing and shouting excitedly and slapping each other on the hands. I've never seen people so delighted. I was just setting up the pieces for another game when Big Sink ragged me out of the house by my hair, threw me over the hedge into Greta's and told me that if he ever saw me again he'd kill me without hesitation.

To this day, I don't really understand what was going through their heads. I can only assume that they rationalised the problems of the world in terms of skin colour. I didn't see it like that. To me, we were all in the same boat. You were either inside the system or outside it; and if you were outside it, you were in trouble.

It was almost midnight when I stumbled into Greta's. 'He's only checked into the fucking Safe House now, that's all.' When Urban couldn't stay at mine, he stayed at the Church of England Safe House more often than not. This was a haven for runaway kids, one of only two such experimental projects in the country – one in Leeds and one in London – and Urban was well known to them. He'd been going there on and off for a number of years. Their rules allowed a twelve-week stay, but then you weren't allowed in again for another twelve weeks. He'd also been banned for a while for nicking their car, but was back in their good books. He loved the place and they seemed to like him. It was his regular bed-and-breakfast establishment when he had nowhere else to go. 'They only let you in when you're in trouble, so have a guess what? He'll be telling 'em I beat him up and torture him and nonce him up and lock him in the cupboard. We'll have the fucking social workers round here in droves. What do you say to that, then?'

What could I say? Greta was developing a dependency culture and was in the habit of blaming me for everything that happened. 'Greta,' I said, 'for fuck's sake, he's not my responsibility. He's not even your responsibility. He's on a care order. They've taken the job upon themselves so he's their responsibility. After that, we're all only doing what we can. You've got a house together for him – and I know you don't like paying bills, love, so that's quite a big thing – but if he won't stay in it, what can you do? Vast masses are on the move internationally, Greta. It's out of our hands. There's nothing we can do about anything.'

'That's bollocks,' she said, 'absolute fucking bollocks. If you cared about him at all you'd let him stay at yours whenever he wanted.'

'And if I do that, you'll accuse me of trying to steal him away from you. I can't win whatever I do.'

'No, cos you're a fucking man, that's why. All the fucking same . . .'

There was no arguing with Greta when she was in a certain mood. 'Got any gear?' I asked, changing the subject. 'I could murder a line.'

THIRTEEN
SUGAR AND SPICE AND ALL THINGS NICE

I saw him, I did.
I know that I did.
He said, 'It's a dream.'
But that was no dream,
Cos I know what I saw,
If you know what I mean.
Cos I know what I know,
And I know what I mean,
And I see what I see,
If you see what I mean.

Sam
ICU

Urban didn't stay long at the Safe House and was out in time for his birthday, which fell on Bonfire Night. Thoughtfully, Greta had organised a little get-together for him at the mad house. I got freaked out just walking down there. In the old days, Leeds people built a huge bonfire in every street. While organised displays had cut into this tradition, there were still minor fires ablaze round almost every corner. Some were well attended, with rockets and Catherine wheels going off all over the place, others had only two or three visitors, or at best a nuclear family, letting off feeble bangers and fountains, while some blazes were mysteriously deserted, like the *Mary Celeste*.

I passed a burning settee, a burning car and even a burning piano, and it was against this nightmare, post-apocalyptic backdrop that I composed my thoughts. I was thinking that the best thing to do with fires was to let them burn themselves out.

That's why I wasn't too worried about the lads, even though they were having wacky races out in the street when I arrived. I knew it was going to be one of those nights when Urban whizzed past me driving a stolen Cavalier with Sam in the back seat and Tyson sticking his snout over the dashboard up front. Yes, the lads were out of control, but I'd been a lad myself and I couldn't remember being any different. We didn't steal cars because we didn't have the technical know-how, and we didn't take so many class-A drugs, but we were just as violent and rowdy. I figured they'd all settle down in the end, probably after they'd been to prison for a while. Boys were much the same as boys had ever been.

The girls worried me more. The girls were different from girls in my day. It had been hard work to get a girl into bed when I was a lad, often requiring weeks of planning and determination or a fortuitous Christmas party. The girls had known what they had and kept it in a box until that special someone came along. When you finally got a girlfriend, there were strings attached and commitment required. Nowadays, the girls gave it away and asked nothing in return. Much had changed between times: the pill, sex education, readily available condoms and abortions, but mainly attitudes. There was no longer any stigma attached to getting pregnant out of wedlock. The girls were now free to enjoy sex as much as they pleased, which made it the best ever time in the history of the world to be a boy, as far as I could tell. The only clouds on the horizon were the rash of teenage pregnancies and sexually transmitted diseases, which were reaching epidemic proportions: underclass girls

seldom used the pill, condoms or took any other prophy-
lactic measure.

I hadn't been at the party an hour before I'd had enough. I
was bored. Greta and Spacey Tracy were blathered on who
knew what combination. They had two similarly blathered
blokes in tow who I didn't know; one seemed more interested
in Thieving Little Simpkins than he was in Greta or Tracy.

Pinky pulled me aside and said, 'You'd better tell that nonce
to leave off or Sparky'll do him.'

I put a spliff in the bloke's hand and told him straight:
'That's my daughter,' I said. 'She's fourteen. She's got three big
brothers outside, and I mean big, and two little brothers, who
if anything are more disturbed and dangerous than their big
brothers. Watch yourself, mush. You're on dodgy ground.'

'Roger,' he said. 'Get your drift.'

'My name's not Roger,' I told him bluntly. 'It's Chop.'

Apart from me and the two nonces, everyone else at the
party was female. Trudi was so pissed off with the situation
that she wasn't even out of it. She was sitting in an old red
armchair with her legs crossed, angrily filing her nails. Pixie
was sitting among the adults, which worried me until she
winked at me, as if to say, 'Don't worry, I know what I'm
doing. Just gunner nick a nice lump of weed off these muppets,
then I'll be out there with the normal people.' Pinky, Thieving
Little Simpkins, Kara and Molly settled down in the kitchen
away from the nonces to drink alcopops and share a spliff.

I joined them and cracked open a rusty orange gin-and-
something-or-other. 'Fuck me,' I sighed as I slumped down,
'what's the world coming to?'

The girls were just chatting about old times. 'Remember
how we used to go in the Slip as soon as it opened?' Pinky said.
'And—'

'And we used to get washed and put us makeup on in the
ladies',' Thieving Little Simpkins interrupted. 'And you told

her in t'kitchen that we'd been raped an' she gave us bacon sarnies.'

'Kara wouldn't come in,' Molly laughed, 'in case her mum or any of her mates saw her.'

'What about you?' Kara asked caustically. 'Shagging every boy in there under twenty just to prove you could do it.'

'Shut up, Kara. There's no need to be like that.'

'Truth hurts,' Kara said.

'So did some of the boys,' Molly confessed.

The conversation went on like this to the accompaniment of various noises from outside. I had become so well versed in the ways of the twocker that I could tell one manoeuvre from another simply by the sound: the wailing handbrake-turn, the screeching doughnut and the roaring 180. But the noise I heard next was the high-pitched wail of the burn-out, where a vehicle is made to remain stationary – say, by putting the front bumper up against a wall – and then the engine is revved up 'to the max' until it explodes. It wasn't long before sirens were heard and Urban, Sam and Tyson ran in, gasping for breath.

'Urban, have you been twocking?' I demanded straight off.

'No,' he said, with just the right amount of righteous indignation. 'Have I fuck.'

'What's all the noise out there, then?'

'Fireworks,' he said. 'It's Bonfire Night.'

The boy had a quick mind. I could never make excuses that fast because, first of all, I had to weigh up the rights and wrongs of any given situation. Urban had no such compunction.

Blue lights lit up the street. Urban, Sam, Pixie, Tyson and I exited through the front window as the scuffers knocked on the back door. By now I had entered the kids' mind-set and simply found it preferable to avoid the police if the option was available. Urban thought like one of those kids who live in the sewers in South America, too scared to come out because the police lock them up and make them disappear. He saw society's safety net as a fish sees the nets of a trawler.

Our little troop followed the warm orange glow of the bonfires and burning cars, avoiding as much as possible the eerie darkness. Soon we were back in the quiet zone, safe and sound. Pinky and Thieving Little Simpkins arrived almost as soon as we got settled, while Molly and Kara weren't far behind.

I sent Sam and Pixie home as they were still too young to stay over. Pixie terrified me. Young girls have vivid imaginations. In Ashtrayland, it didn't matter what was true or false, it mattered what people said. I was careful never to spend a second alone with Pixie under any circumstances. Girls over twelve and girls under twelve are two different kettles of fish in the eyes of the law: the former will get you several years on a protection wing; the latter will get you life. You have to worry about such things when you have other people's children in your house. I made it a strict rule that Pixie and Sam went home at nine. To their credit, they never complained that I was too strict with them, or that I treated them differently from the others. If anything, they appreciated the fact that I set them limits. Seemingly, there were none at home.

I allowed the rest of them to stay the night. I was probably feeling generous because it was Urban's birthday. Molly asked Urban out that night. I fell asleep on the settee and the two of them spent a frenzied night together in the spare room. Urban told me next morning that it was the best birthday present he'd ever had.

I was confused. I'd figured all along that Molly liked Urban, but didn't think Urban liked her. As I understood it, he considered her a slut of the highest order. 'I'm getting older, Chop,' he explained succinctly. 'Growing up. I'm a teenager. I'm getting hairs round my dick.'

'But she's a slag, Urban. You're always saying so.'

'I know, but she's my slag now.'

'I don't know, Urban. I just think you're all too young for this.'

Urban shrugged his shoulders. 'We're kids, Chop. We shag each other. That's what we do. Get used to it, because no one can stop us.'

Suddenly acutely aware that kids were having sex in my flat, I had to balance several moral and legal dilemmas. There wasn't much I could do about it: either they simply waited until I fell asleep, or they went somewhere else and did as they pleased. Should I have rejected them because of it, or should I accept that a great deal of water had already flowed under the bridge and work to change things slowly? I was able to rationalise it because of what I knew about the children's homes. The same thing happened there but the staff either chose to ignore it or pretended it wasn't happening. I preferred to face reality. The fact is that many underclass children lead full, active sex lives from the age of eleven or twelve. I told them about morals, pregnancy and disease, and left them to make their own decisions. I wasn't in charge of the world and I wasn't willing to take responsibility for everything that happened in it. That's not to say I washed my hands of the matter, but I didn't fall into a moral panic either. The Will to Life of the Unborn Child was strong in the Penthouse Posse. It would have taken a better man than me to stop them shagging each other, as Schopenhauer can confirm.

Not all the kids were the same. Pinky, for example, was a paragon of virtue. She came banging on the door the week after Bonfire Night. I opened it and there she was, sniffing and snorting, with tears rolling down her cheeks. 'I've had a row with my mum. Can I stop here for a while? I won't be any trouble, I promise.'

'Poor thing,' I said. 'Come here.'

We stood on the doorstep, hugging, and I was glad that none of the neighbours were about. 'There, there,' I said, looking down the landing over her shoulder. 'There, there.'

Had it been anyone else I'd have sent them to Greta's, but Pinky was different. I'm not sure why exactly. Maybe it was because she'd given me my first tattoo, something that would permanently remind me of her even as I lay in my coffin. Maybe it was because we were fellow artists, with similar world-views, both dedicated to the overthrow of capitalism. Maybe it was because she had morals and values. Maybe I just liked her as a person. Maybe it was a combination of all these things.

Pinky's arrival heralded a new tradition: Sunday night soon became girls' night. Pinky was sleeping in the spare room, along with Urban two or three nights a week and others on occasion. Thieving Little Simpkins was Pinky's best mate so she stayed over every weekend. Molly was going out with Urban so she went where he went. Kara was Molly's best mate so they stuck together. After a couple of weeks Trudi started turning up in case she was missing something. Even Greta and Spacey Tracy appeared on occasion. The no-tails had taken over the place before I knew it. It was my idea to limit them to Sunday to kind of free up the rest of the week.

What I didn't realise was that some of the girls were jealous of Pinky. Towards Christmas, Thieving Little Simpkins and I were in the kitchen cooking Sunday dinner.

'I can't believe you let Pinky stay here full-time. You treat Pinky and Urban different to the rest of us. They're your little favourites. Why don't you just admit it? You take Urbie to work with you ten times more than the rest of the lads and Pinky just turns up out of the blue and you let her move in. You wouldn't do it for anyone else. It's favouritism, Chop. Pass us that pan.'

She was chopping cabbage busily as she spoke. The comforting smell of roasting chicken filled the kitchen. I was doing the washing-up. I always found the kitchen a good place to talk to the kids one-to-one. They were often silly in groups, but if you got them alone you could talk to them like proper human beings. If you ever want to get any sense out of a teenager, do it in the kitchen.

'It's not that simple. I treat the lads different to the lasses, I admit. If Frank or Skeet turned up, I wouldn't let them stay more than a night. But they're fourteen-year-old lads. They're not that vulnerable. If anything, society's at risk from them. The difference is that Pinky's a girl and Urban's only thirteen. Why didn't you get him a present for his birthday, by the way?'

Thieving Little Simpkins swept the cabbage from the work-surface into the pan. 'Didn't know what to get him,' she said. 'What do you get the boy who has nothing?'

When the shed had closed, she had gone back to Bulwell House. Oddly enough, she hadn't been mentioned in the account of Urban's escape so she wasn't in trouble, although Sparky was. Social Services had since found her a place in a half-decent, long-term children's home and she was doing her best to make it work. She was attending school regularly, behaving herself, not running away, and doing everything that was expected. The weekends, however, were her own. I could have squashed a grape when she told me her latest news. She had spent the previous day (and night) with Skeeter and they were now an item. I wished them the best of luck. Skeeter could be volatile with other boys, but he was relaxed around girls and they responded to his strong, silent personality and rugged good looks.

By Christmas, girls' night was an established part of the social calendar. All the lads were banned, except Urban, Sam and me. Although Sam and Pixie couldn't stay over, both had the freedom to come and go as they pleased during the day. Urban and Sam were exempted because they were too young to pose a threat or put any sexual pressure on the girls. Molly thought she was training Urban up and so he didn't yet qualify as the real McCoy. She boasted that she'd had eighteen and a half men – Urban being the half. I was exempted, because it was my flat and they didn't have much choice. Perhaps they felt I was too old to pose a threat. Also, the girls liked to gather together to discuss their dealings with boys. Naturally enough, they didn't want boys overhearing and gossiping to the other boys.

The Sunday between Christmas and New Year stands out in my memory, because there were some startling revelations. Pinky and Thieving Little Simpkins had stayed the night before and were in the kitchen making spaghetti Bolognese for Sunday dinner. Urban, Sam and Pixie turned up mid-afternoon and were lying on the carpet playing Monopoly, taking up most of the floor space. I was on the settee, watching *Casablanca* on television. 'Sam,' I said, 'Urban's just put a five-hundred-pound note in his pocket. Urban, what's the point of playing if you're going to cheat?'

'You've got to cheat,' Urban replied. 'I bet he's got ten thousand quid in his back pocket.'

'Have I fuck,' Sam protested, getting to his feet and patting his pockets. 'Search me, Chop.'

'I'm trying to watch *Casablanca*. Argue among yourselves.'

'I'll search you,' Pixie said. 'I know what you're like.' There wasn't quite ten grand in his pocket. More like six and a half. In the end, I had to tape the rest of the film as the game couldn't continue without a secure bank. I got down on the dog-shelf with them and supervised their foray into the corrupting world of capitalism.

It was wonderful seeing the kids just being kids. They didn't get much chance to do that. Those little moments made it all worthwhile. I was proud to play some small part in improving their lives. The pleasure I gleaned in return proved that the law of karma was alive and well and living in Britain. I got back more than I gave.

Trudi arrived late afternoon, then Kara and Molly, the Eastie contingent. Dinner was served at six with a glass of red wine, which Kara had brought along. I'd picked up an extra settee on my rounds, so we now had extra seating capacity. The two settees formed an L-shape in the corner of the room by the window and the kids spread across them with plates on their knees. Thieving Little Simpkins and Molly sat at the table at the back of the room. I noticed that Trudi only had a minute portion, and even then she spent most of her time moving it round the plate rather than eating it. Molly, who I had also suspected of having an eating disorder, wolfed hers down like it was going out of fashion. Her thinness was due to starvation rather than anorexia. Only Pinky and I were bold enough to sprinkle on some Parmesan cheese. Urban and Sam preferred Heinz tomato sauce.

After dinner Pinky got out the weed. She was seeing a lot of her real dad. He gave her copious amounts of the finest West Indian skunk in an effort to make up for all the time he had missed with her. She accepted gratefully and shared it around, willy-nilly. I wouldn't have a bong in the house so she made spliff after spliff after spliff.

Why were spliffs allowed, but not bongs? This may seem inconsistent, but I was sticking to my principles. It was a question of poison and degree. Many of the kids were second-generation drug culture and understood that everyone had their own chosen poison: fags, booze, food, dope, smack, snailly, whatever. Smack was seen as a danger drug, especially if you injected it, but the rest were considered everyday commodities, like tea and sugar. There was no shock-horror thing attached to any of them. It was only a question of how much you took, how often and with whom. My father always advised me that if I was going to drink, I should drink beer, not spirits. 'Tha wain't nivver get addicted tut beer, son, but tha will tut spirits. They're stronger'n thee.' My mum confirmed this with her early death. I had passed on the same advice to Sparky, who was developing into a serious drinker. I advised the smokers to smoke the best West Indian weed in spliffs, not to sear their lungs with crappy solids in bongs. I advised Urban, who still had a sniffing problem, to sniff glue with a group of friends who could phone an ambulance if he got into trouble, not gas alone at the top of a disused mill imagining he could fly. It was all very well talking about drugs in theory, but I was faced with the practical realities. I saw nothing wrong in the odd spliff, the odd beer or the odd anything else, even for the kids, who would need to learn to handle these recreational commodities soon enough or go under. Addiction was the problem, whatever your poison. Bongs were getting heavy. I also had moral problems about letting the younger kids smoke weed, but I had to be realistic. They'd all smoked it already and it was preferable to glue or gas.

Trudi brought us up to date with everything that had been going on at Greta's. I still wanted to know why Yeah-yeah Ken had been beaten up, but the lads would never tell me the truth. They were pathological liars, who would lie to you even when they didn't have to. They were so used to lying that they couldn't help themselves.

Trudi finally solved the mystery. 'The lads kicked his face in because I shagged him.'

'Urrgh!' Pinky exclaimed, her voice full of disgust. 'You shagged Yeah-yeah Ken?'

Trudi combined her answer with an impersonation. 'Yeah, yeah. Oh, yeah. Yeah, yeah, yeah.'

'Why, though?' Pinky asked.

'Don't know,' she said. 'It didn't seem polite to refuse.'

'But he's twenty-odd.'

'I know, but the older ones shag better.'

'So would you shag Chop if he asked you?'

'Course,' she said. 'I'd shag Chop any time. He's lovely and cuddly.'

Pinky looked at me. 'Chop, would you shag Trudi?'

'Regrettably,' I said, 'there's a bit of an age difference. Besides, I wouldn't want to give the Babylon a reason to lock me up and throw away the key. They'll probably be here in the morning and I need to be able to look them in the eye.'

'Urbie, would you shag Trudi?'

'Already have done,' Urban replied.

Pinky was shocked. 'Never! When?'

'First night we stayed here.'

'Hear that, Simpkins? Trudi shagged Urbie.'

'She'd better not,' Thieving Little Simpkins replied from the back of the room. 'He's mine. I'm just waiting for him to ripen. He's my little baby.'

'Not any more, he's not,' Molly interjected.

'So, basically, you either have shagged or you would shag just about anyone in the world. Is that right, Trudi?'

'Yeah, yeah. Oh, yeah. Yeah, yeah, yeah.'

'Even Tyson's shagged her,' Urban added, bringing that particular conversation to a close.

There were more revelations later as the wine and the weed loosened people's tongues. I'd built something of a literary culture and the kids were in the habit of bringing their poems, drawings and essays on girls' night to show everyone. Sam brought a poem along called 'I Saw Him I Did', which he had written at home in his spare time. I'd been trying to get something out of him for ages, because he was intelligent and sharp. My theory was that the younger they started, the better they became. The poem was only ten lines long and the longest word in it had only five letters, but it was brilliant, with an internal rhythm all of its own:

I saw him I did
I know that I did
He said, 'It's a dream'
But that was no dream
And I know what I saw
If you know what I mean
Cos I know what I know
And I know what I mean
And I see what I see
If you see what I mean

You knew he'd seen something terrible, but you didn't know what. He read it out and it tickled all the older girls. They couldn't stop laughing and giggling for ages, as if it had touched a nerve.

I didn't find it funny, I found it frightening, and the more I didn't laugh the more everyone else did. 'Well, what's it about, Sam? We need to know to appreciate it.'

'Can't say,' he said, but he kept looking at Pixie, who had swapped places with Molly and was sitting at the table whispering to Thieving Little Simpkins. Molly came over and snuggled up to Urban on the settee.

'Well, everyone else seems to get it. Why can't you tell me? Don't you trust me or something?'

Sam studied the pattern on the carpet and bit at his thumbnail. 'It's not that, Chop. I just can't say.' He trusted me well enough, but he had greater loyalties.

I didn't want to turn a drama into a crisis but I was insanely curious. 'So you don't trust me, then. That's all I can assume.'

'Leave it, Chop,' Thieving Little Simpkins said. 'You don't want to know.'

'I do,' I insisted. 'I want to know.'

There was a long, strained silence, punctuated only by Trudi giggling to herself.

'It's about me,' Pixie said, at long last. 'Sam saw my uncle in my room, that's all.'

'Yes,' I said. 'And?'

And the silence was deafening.

FOURTEEN
LITTLE YARDIES

The rising sun you know will betimes fall,
Fall's first cloud presages winter snow,
Small children grow till standing strong and tall,
From little acorns mighty oak trees grow.

The stars come up and nightly doff their cap
As round and round and round the sun we go.
Anger, fear, resentment – and then ZAP!
From harmless children deadly Yardies grow.

Sparky
Buzzin' on an E in an Astra GTE

I noticed in the New Year that Sparky was taller than I was.
Not quite sixteen, he was the first of the crew to outgrow me. I
knew the kids were getting older, but I hadn't realised how
quickly. Kids grow up fast, these days, there's no disputing it.

Sparky was reading a lot and came round one frozen
Monday morning in February to borrow some books. He
missed Pinky by five minutes. She was spending more and
more time with her real dad and there was a possibility that
she might be able to live with him, a prospect that filled me
with joy. I genuinely preferred to live alone and having to
share my space was rewiring my brain. There was even talk of
her going to the West Indies to meet the rest of the family. She
was working hard to make the dream come true.

I was trying to get Sparky interested in history and the social sciences, but he only liked novels and poetry. I ran my finger along my politics bookshelf. 'What about Karl Marx and Friedrich Engels, *Selected Works*? You'll enjoy that, Sparky. It goes some way towards explaining why our lives are so fucked up at the moment.'

'Not for me thanks, Chop, lad.'

'How about *The Ragged-Trousered Philanthropists*? It's about the painting and decorating industry before trade unions. They're called ragged-trousered philanthropists because they work their balls off to make their bosses rich while they get a pittance. It's only a thousand pages long. Fancy it?'

He pointed his eyes towards the corner of the room and shook his head. 'Afraid not, Chop.'

'*The Decline of Working Class Politics*, Barry Hindess?'

'Nope.'

'Oh, well . . .' I sighed. 'Worth a try.' In the end, he took *A Clockwork Orange* and *Catch-22*. At least he was reading. *Clocky Orange* I considered a busman's holiday for Sparky, but it explained how we did our ultra-violence in the old days. I was a mad football hooligan at his age. At the Leeds–Munich European Cup Final of 1976, we wore cricket boxes, false eyelashes and bowler hats, and attempted to raze Paris to the ground after we lost. The French riot squad, of course, had other ideas and razed our heads to the ground instead.

Sparky had some new friends, a crowd of lanky, spotty, baseball-capped, Nintendo-playing, dope-smoking, beer-swilling, rave-loving, mad-driving, rap-talking party monsters. At least six of them were squatting in a two-up-two-down terraced house in Beeston, which was a rough neighbourhood south of the river. How he found the time or space to read, I'll never know.

'Come on,' I said. 'I'll give you a lift home.'

I didn't mind dropping him off because I had a friend, Madge, in Beeston who I didn't visit often enough. Beeston was an interesting place, cosmopolitan in its own way. Dangerous, but cosmopolitan. I'd guess the population was 40 per cent Asian, 30 per cent white and 30 per cent other races. It was the only place in Leeds where people from different backgrounds mixed without too much interracial strife. There was plenty of the usual kind of strife, of course. The natives called it Beirut.

For years, Madge and I had worked there together at 'the YM', a youth and community centre run by the YMCA. I knew more people in Beeston than I did in my own area. I knew all the kids from the youth club and most of their parents and younger siblings from the mums-and-tots group and the playschemes. The YM closed in 1990 in a round of spending cuts. Most of the kids I knew were now apprentice gangsters in their late teens and early twenties, but they remembered me and Madge well enough, because we had more or less brought them up while their parents were in the pub. I could have freeloaded drinks all day in Beeston on the strength of that.

Madge had this wooden plaque, a cross-section of a tree trunk, which she kept under a tree in her garden. The Groundwork Trust had presented it to the YM in 1988 to thank the volunteers who had helped with the landscape gardening. Six kids were mentioned. Two fared well: Colin had a job and a steady girlfriend, and Kelly was that girlfriend. Two were so-so: Danny was a smackhead, while Janice was a depressed single mum on the breadline. Two were dead: Dwaine had been a twocker who was killed in a car smash, while Jimmy jumped off a block of flats while he was drugged up to his eyeballs. You didn't have to be Sir Isaac Newton to work out the maths: one in three lives, one in three dies, and one in three we're not yet sure about.

I wondered if I could improve the odds for the Penthouse Posse. They weren't the first group of kids I'd known, or the YM lot before them. Multitudes were running through my head, a new crew every year, each one worse than the one before. I was like Mr Chips on smack.

Driving across town, Sparky asked about Pixie. 'Pinky says she's getting nonced up. We'll have to do something.'

'I can't get involved, Sparky. Best thing is to tell the law. It's not grassing with nonces. The scuffers hate them as much as we do. It's the one thing we've got in common.'

'No point, Chop. They won't do anything. Me and the lads'll deal with it. Just get us a name and address. You know what's what in East End Park.'

I promised to do my best.

'Coming in for a beer?' he asked, when we got to the squat.

'I don't drink and drive, Sparky. You know that.' I was more than happy to stick to laws I agreed with and that was one of them.

'A spliff, then? "Afore ye go"?'

That was different. 'Don't mind if I do.'

The squat was similar to Greta's house in Eastie but not as sophisticated. A worn settee faced a gas fire with broken elements. The only other furniture in the room was a portable television on a crate, which was connected to an old Nintendo games machine by a jungle of wires. Spurry and another lad were sitting on the settee with control pads in their hands. Their eyes were glued to the screen and their hands hit the buttons in a frenzied dance. As I watched, a young Chinese girl flew through the air and delivered a telling bicycle kick to a Sumo wrestler's head. He went down with a thud and the Chinese girl brought her heel down on his face with a banshee wail.

'Chop, Dale. Dale, Chop. You know Spurry.' The introductions over, Sparky went upstairs to get his weed.

'All right, lads? Who's winning?' I enquired, trying to make conversation. They ignored me. Indeed, they seemed offended that I was ruining their game with my inane prattle. Their fingers and thumbs moved around their pads quicker than the eye could follow. The Chinese girl delivered the *coup de grâce* and blood splattered across the screen as if a bomb had exploded.

'Up here, Chop,' Sparky called from upstairs.

Three single mattresses were scattered across the floor of the master bedroom. A young girl in a school uniform sat on one with a giant spliff in her hand. Half a dozen books were piled up at the side of the mattress with a clock and an ashtray resting on top. One was *The Complete Works of Shakespeare*, which seemed bizarrely out of place in such a seedy squat. All of the books were mine, of course, but I didn't mind. Books have a habit of going where they want to go.

Sparky introduced us in his usual fashion. 'Natasha, Chop. Chop, Natasha. Natasha's my new bird, Chop.'

She was fifteen or sixteen, but could easily have been mistaken for a twenty-three-year-old model. She was gorgeous. 'Hello, Chop,' she said. 'I've heard a lot about you.' She patted the mattress invitingly. 'Come and sit here with me.'

I sat on the edge of the mattress. Natasha was sitting with her back against the wall, her legs folded in front of her. Her school dress was skimpy, to say the least, and she couldn't help but display her credentials. Thankfully, Sparky plopped down between us and blocked my view.

'Tasha's family,' he informed me. She was one of us now, a new addition to the posse. Rule number six: 'Any friend of yours is a friend of mine.'

'Easy now,' I said, in our formal greeting.

'Easy now,' she replied, in the time-honoured tradition.

I had a couple of spliffs with them, but then Natasha got fruity. She had these long, lithe legs and they were all over Sparky like a rash. 'I'd better go,' I said. 'I've got some business to attend to.'

'So have we,' Natasha assured me, raising an eyebrow and giving me a sly wink. I was able to discern her facial gestures, even though she was flat on her back with her legs round Sparky's head.

Sparky brushed her off and saw me to the van. 'Soz about that, Chop. She gets a bit randy. She has to go home at teatime so her mum doesn't know she's bunking off school. I'll have to shag her all afternoon now.'

'Could be worse,' I said, inserting the key into the lock and twisting it firmly.

'Could be a lot worse,' he agreed. 'She's loaded as well. She gives me about a tenner a day. You'll have to come over and get blasted some time.'

'Not a problem,' I said, starting the engine and thrusting the van into gear. 'Give us a ring later in the week, you jammy little bastard.'

'Will do,' he said. 'If I'm feeling any better in myself. Go steady now.'

Sparky rang the next morning and invited me over for a little party the coming Friday. 'Natasha'll buy the pizzas and beer. That's the only night she's allowed out. Try and get Pinky and Thieving Little Simpkins to come. Tell Pinky to bring her sewing kit. Natasha wants the tattoo. Bring Urbie, if you like. I haven't seen him for ages.'

'I've got that address for you, by the way.' I'd asked around and a few people were worried about Pixie's uncle. 'He lives in one of those new houses at the top of the Drive.' I gave Sparky the address.

'Right. We'll soon sort that out.'

'What about Frank and Skeet?' I asked. 'Shall I get them to come over?'

'Fuck them,' he said. 'They've gone to Zombie Voodoo Land. They're just a couple of dirty smackheads. "No smackheads," that's rule number seven. Why do you think I moved out of there?'

I'd never heard Sparky talk about the other members of the posse like that. I decided I'd been remiss in my duties. I hadn't been to the mad house for a couple of weeks; neither had Skeeter nor Frank been to mine. Urban couldn't tell me much. If he stayed at the mad house once a week he was doing well. In an average week he stayed at my house a couple of nights, the Safe House a couple of nights and Molly's a couple of nights. He preferred to orbit the mad house rather than live there. Trudi still came to the odd girls' night on Sunday, but she didn't give much away. I realised I didn't know what was going on there and decided it was time to pay a visit.

I strolled down there in the afternoon. When I arrived the back door was locked. I banged for several minutes until a stranger eventually answered it, a spotty blonde girl, wearing glasses, aged about fourteen. She opened the door just wide enough to show her face. 'What, love?' she asked, looking me up and down. 'Are you wanting business?'

Oh, I thought. It's like that, is it?

I tried to push open the door, but she blocked my way. Her frail frame, however, was no match for my bulk. I shoved the door with all my might and sent her flying across the kitchen. 'Excuse me, love. I'm trying to get in. Where's Greta?'

She was terrified. She'd obviously had some bad experiences with men. She rushed out of the kitchen and up the stairs. I followed her into one of the bedrooms where I found Frank, Skeeter and Trudi sitting on the bed together tooting smack. I felt a horrid emptiness in my stomach. 'No,' I said, appalled. 'Not all three of you . . .'

I'd had an idea they were dabbling and experimenting, but I hadn't realised they were all bang at it. I couldn't believe how quickly they had gone downhill. Skeeter, who always tried to look good for ladies, was scruffy and dishevelled, as was

Trudi, who always tried to look good for the lads. The new girl looked like she'd been dragged through a hedge backwards while Frank had a style all of his own. It hurt to see them dossing there, gouching, eyes half closed, tinfoil everywhere . . . smackheads. Smack costs money and the only way they could get money was from thieving or prostitution. God alone knew what they were up to in their spare time.

Frank and Trudi were shamefaced and avoided my eyes. Skeeter defiantly put the tooter in his mouth and ran himself a line. The spotty girl edged over to the dressing-table and took a twelve-inch carving knife out of one of the drawers, then stood there brandishing it as if she were afraid for her life. 'Put it away,' Trudi told her. 'It's only Chop. He won't hurt nobody.' The new girl eyed me maliciously and twisted the knife ever so slightly in my direction. I didn't like the look of her one little bit. I knew trouble when I saw it.

Skeeter finished his line and removed the tooter from his mouth. 'He can't say much,' he croaked, still holding the fumes in. 'He does it himself. We're not thick, you know.'

I allowed my back to slide down the wall until I reached a sitting position. Resting my elbows on my knees, I bowed my head and pushed my fingers through my hair. Skeeter was right. There wasn't much I could say.

Clearly, I needed to re-evaluate my position on drugs. It dawned on me that the kids were behaving exactly as Greta and I behaved: taking drugs, being promiscuous and not giving a shit about anyone or anything, least of all themselves. I began to understand that we were their models, the only models they had. If we couldn't behave ourselves, how could we expect them to?

I hadn't thought about it before because it just wasn't part of my mind-set. I didn't worry about things like that because I was used to seeing myself as a free agent with no responsibilities. They weren't my kids. It wasn't my problem. Society could take the blame, not me. I was doing my bit by mopping up the blood. I now saw that many of the kids looked up to me and I should have been setting a better example. I'd known them six months and hadn't taken this on board. I assumed that because I could play about with heavy drugs and get away with it, everybody could. I binged on heroin for maybe two or three days, then left it for maybe two or three weeks. That way, I avoided addiction. They'd been taking it every day for a month.

I looked up, and said, 'Euston, we have a problem.'

Wednesday morning, two scuffers came tapping on my door. Tapping! Not banging or kicking! I didn't think it was scuffers, I thought it was the Jehovah's Witnesses or something, so I didn't even get Pinky into the priest-hole before I opened the door. Luckily, Urban was at Molly's. There were two of them, as always – smart young plain-clothes men in their late twenties or early thirties. The Babylonians were getting younger every day.

'Mind if we come in for a word?' Polite, as well as gentle with their fists and boots. What more could the public ask? They weren't the usual uniformed thugs. They were proper policemen, serious policemen, CID policemen.

I showed them into the living room. 'Take a seat, gentlemen. What seems to be the trouble? Would you care for a cup of tea?'

'No, thank you,' one said.

They looked alike to me. The only noticeable difference was that one wore a high-quality black leather jacket and the other was in casual blue corduroy.

They introduced themselves, then got down to business. The blue coat began: 'It's about a serious assault last night in East End Park. A gentleman beaten half to death by young thugs. Your name's been mentioned.'

'Has it?' I said, genuinely surprised. 'Who by, I wonder?'

'You were asking questions about the victim in the Slip Inn yesterday dinnertime. It seems an odd coincidence that he's badly beaten up that same evening.'

'It is a strange coincidence,' I agreed. 'Very strange indeed.'

'Too strange,' said the black coat.

'Well, it's nothing to do with me,' I said. 'Do I look like the sort of person who goes round beating people up?'

'Criminals often look much the same as normal people,' said the black coat.

There was a lull in the conversation. I, for one, couldn't think of anything to say.

'Look,' said the blue coat, 'this one could turn pear-shaped. If the victim dies, you're looking at conspiracy to murder. That's a life sentence. We know you didn't do it, but you probably know who did. Best you just tell us what you know right now.'

'But I don't know anything,' I protested. 'If I knew anything, I'd tell you.' I was a glib liar when I put my mind to it.

There was another strained silence. 'Then why were you asking about him in the Slip? Why did you want his address?'

I didn't have an answer for them.

'You'd better come with us,' said the black coat. 'Maybe we can clear this up at the station.'

They took a look round the flat before we left and found Pinky fast asleep in the spare room. 'Tut, tut, tut,' said the blue coat, shaking his head. 'Tut, tut, tut.'

My solicitor got me out bright and early Thursday morning. Initially, the scuffers thought I was involved in some kind of a paedophile ring with Pixie's uncle and they were hostile. After they had interviewed Pinky, their attitude softened. She persuaded them that, whatever else I was, I wasn't a nonce. They took her back to her mum and step-dad's, told them where she'd been staying and left it at that. They knew I'd had something to do with the assault, but I kept my mouth shut and they couldn't prove anything. Once I'd had the chance to think up a story, I told them I was asking about him because he wanted to buy my van. Until such time as he came out of his coma, they couldn't call me a liar. Even then it would be his word against mine. They didn't charge me with anything, but bailed me to come back in two weeks' time for further questioning. I wasn't going to grass on Sparky whatever happened and I knew Pinky wouldn't. We couldn't have helped them, even if we'd wanted to. We were bound by the Shed Crew rules. I'd have done time before I gave them a sausage.

It was all starting to get on top of me. I needed a day to myself. I locked up the flat and went round to see Madge in Beeston. I sometimes felt that I carried the world on my shoulders. She was the only person I could talk to sensibly about it, the only one who understood. 'It's doing my head in. They're all nuts. I wouldn't mind if there were only a few of them but there's a dozen to worry about. All nuts. Each and every one of them. I've been locked up all night because Sparky's nearly killed someone. The scuffers were talking about conspiracy to murder and life sentences. Why should I get locked up when I haven't done anything wrong?'

'You collude with them, Chop. I don't know if you mean to do it, but that's what you do in effect.' Even if I managed to deceive myself, I couldn't fool her. 'I don't think you realise how much influence you have over them. If you tell them something is wrong, they'll listen to you. You knew he was going to do it beforehand, didn't you?'

'Well, sort of.'

'Did you or didn't you?'

'Yes, I knew,' I admitted. 'I knew he was going to do it, but I didn't know how hard he was going to do it.'

'Then you collude with them, don't you?'

'Yes, in a roundabout sort of way.'

'No, not in a roundabout sort of way, you collude with them directly and knowingly,' she insisted.

'Okay, I collude with them. Is that your favourite word or something?'

'Just making the point, Chop. I care about you. If you don't get your act together soon, you could be in for a very large drop.'

I decided to behave myself at Sparky's on Friday night. I'd have a couple of beers, a couple of spliffs and that was all. I would set an example. Urban and Molly came over with me on the bus. Urban wanted to meet Natasha and he wanted to show Molly off to Sparky. Now that he was thirteen and had a steady girlfriend, he saw himself as a proper teenager.

I didn't know if Pinky would turn up. She knew about it, but I wasn't sure how much trouble she was in at home. I didn't dare ring her in case her mum and step-dad kicked off with me, but she and Thieving Little Simpkins were there when we arrived. Everyone was chilling out in the bedroom. Pinky had already told Sparky of our arrest.

'Thanks for not grassing, Chop,' Sparky said, handing me a spliff and slapping me on the back. 'Appreciated. I always knew you was a good 'un.'

Natasha threw her arms around me. 'Yeah, thanks, Chop. I don't know what I'd do without him any more.'

I peeled her arms off me. She was too forward for her own good. She made Trudi look demure. 'It's not over yet,' I said. 'You went overboard this time, Sparky. You can't just go round kicking people half to death. We don't have the right, even with nonces.'

To my astonishment, he looked me in the eye and quoted Shakespeare: ' "If you prick us, do we not bleed? If you tickle us, do we not laugh? If you poison us, do we not die? And if you wrong us, shall we not revenge?" '

It was difficult to argue with Shakespeare. 'Sparky,' I said, 'have you been reading *The Merchant of Venice*?'

'Yeah, I'm allowed to, aren't I?'

'I'm not saying you're doing anything wrong. What other plays have you read?'

'*The Tempest, The Merry Wives of Windsor, Measure For Measure, Comedy of Errors, Much Ado About Nothing, Love's Labour Lost* and *A Midsummer Night's Dream*. I'm going through 'em all one at a time.'

'In the order they're in the book?'

'Yeah, why not?'

If the comedies made him violent, I didn't want to be around when he got to the tragedies. 'And you like them, do you?'

'Fucking brilliant, man.'

'Have you ever seen the Bard on stage, live and direct?'

'No, never – and I don't know why you're asking me all these questions. I'm not queer or anything.'

'I'll get a couple of tickets for the Playhouse, Sparky. We'll go down and see something. Have a couple of beers afterwards. You'll have to take pot luck, like. I don't know what's on at the moment.'

'Sorted,' he said, then turned his attention to Urban without another thought. 'Come here, my son!' He grabbed Urban in a headlock and tried to choke him to death. Urban had to fight for dear life to extract himself. 'Getting stronger! Look at him! Little Urban! Going out with Molly! That's a man's job, Urbie. What's he like in the sack, Molly? Does he keep you satisfied?'

'He's getting the hang of it,' Molly said.

I sat next to Pinky on the mattress and handed her the spliff. 'What did your mum and dad have to say? I bet they're out for my blood, aren't they?'

'They aren't even bothered, Chop,' she said. 'In actual fact, they're really grateful that you looked after me. They were worried sick and they were really chuffed to hear that I'd kept out of trouble. I've told them loads of good stuff about you and they think you've sorted my head out. They'd like to meet you some time to say thanks. Mum says you can pop round any time you like. I've told them I've been seeing my real dad and that I might be going to Jamaica and everything. Everything's all right again now. Everything's sorted. I've never got on so well with them in my life.'

This was wonderful news after my disappointing week. I was upset with Sparky for going overboard on the nonce, but at the back of my mind somewhere I admired him for it. Zero tolerance was a concept I agreed with. If you stick something into a child's orifice, you destroy their lives there and then. They may never recover from it. It's the same as rape or murder. If you destroy innocence in that way, you deserve everything you get. It's unforgivable and you can expect no mercy. Sparky might have circumvented the due process of law, but his heart was in the right place.

We sent out for pizzas and chips, which Natasha insisted on paying for – good news for my wallet. We talked over supper. The general consensus was that it was my job to do something about Frank, Skeeter and Trudi taking drugs. 'You're the only one they'll listen to,' Thieving Little Simpkins insisted.

'You're kidding, aren't you?' I said. 'Trudi might, but Frank's in a world of his own and Skeeter hates my guts.'

'Skeet doesn't hate your guts,' Sparky said. 'He adores you. Are you thick or something?'

'Skeet does?'

'Course he does,' Molly said. 'We all do, you spastic.'

Saturday of that week I did a 'througher' with my mate Malcolm from the next block. A througher is where you drink all day until you can barely stagger home. Malc was my best drinking buddy, a fat, balding, fifty-year-old alcoholic with a speech impediment who had the shakes in the morning. He was an all-round disaster until you put a guitar in his hands, whereupon the shakes stopped, the lisp cleared, the fingers came alive and he had the bluesiest voice you ever heard. Always one for the karaoke and open-mike competitions in the local pubs, he had the power to move you if he was on form.

We normally started local, crawled our way into town, then went with the flow. I know I was supposed to be behaving myself and setting an example, but what the hell? I fancied a pint with a peer. My friends were important to my sanity. Malc was a good mate and I needed adult male company on occasion. Distrustful of young people, he was my own head-eating Mr Grimwig. 'Ya cart let kidsh in yer 'ouse theesh daysh, Chop. Ya musht be mad. The' not kidsh any more, the' crayshy, mad, fucking lunaticsh. The're all on drugsh, man. "Give ush twen'y quid, mishter, elsh am gunner tell t'police yu've nonshed ush up." Know what am shaying, Chop? Watch yershen.'

The kids met him, took one look at him and christened him Manx Kippers for reasons never divulged.

'Did you ever happen to mention that you liked Manx kippers, or that you came from the Isle of Man?' We were getting our first few down us in the Moon Under Water.

Malc gulped down half his pint and wiped his sleeve across his mouth. 'I don't like kippersh at all, too many bonesh, and I've never even been to the Isle of Man. I'm not even sure where it ish, unless it'sh up near Shcotland shomewhere.'

'Well, did you ever mention you had family in the Isle of Man?'

'No, becaush I haven't.'

I polished off my pint and licked my lips with relish. 'Have you ever been to the TT Races at all?'

'The what races at all?'

I picked up a couple of beer mats and pushed them round the table like little imaginary motorbikes. One aquaplaned on a puddle of beer and crashed into the ashtray with catastrophic results. Malc looked on, puzzled. 'Fuck it,' I said, firing the beer mats off in opposite directions. 'Who cares? Let's get more beer in. What'll it be?'

By Sunday, Urban had waited long enough for me to do something about Frank, Skeeter and Trudi. He was aware that I sometimes worked on a geological timescale. He hated the idea of his brother using smack and decided to take matters into his own hands. He went to the mad house and waited round the corner until everyone had gone out. He carried with him a copy of the *Radio Times*, a milk bottle and a box of matches. When he was sure the house was empty, he rolled up the magazine, inserted it into the letterbox and poured the contents of the milk bottle through this makeshift funnel. The milk bottle contained premium four-star petrol. His preparations completed, he looked up and down the street to check he wasn't being observed, then nonchalantly struck a match.

Do we have to shout and scream
To get across what we mean?
What do we have to do?
Encode our message to you?

We try hard to no avail
To paint a picture that is real,
You roam around your tiny minds,
Turn off the lights and close the blinds.

Wake yourselves! Be aware!
It's a nasty place out there!
You're the cause, you zombie ants,
Walking round in a trance.

Kara MacNamara
Playing up

Greta rang me Saturday afternoon. 'You're never gunner believe what's happened now! He's only gone and set the fucking house on fire! All the hallway's burnt out and there's smoke damage everywhere. It's lucky the whole street didn't burn down. Can he stay at yours for a week or two? Big Sink and his boys have put a contract out. Half the prossies in Leeds are after me. I'm gunner have to disappear for a while.'

I couldn't really refuse. Urban might not stay at home much, but he used the place as a base, somewhere to leave his clothes, bathe and eat. I couldn't see him on the streets again. 'Okay, I'll let him stay for a while. A couple of weeks at most.'

'Thanks, Chop. You're sorted.'

'Where will you be?'

'Can't tell you,' she said. 'It's on a need-to-know basis.'

Urban turned up at teatime with Sam and Tyson. They had Sam's games machine in a carrier-bag. 'All right to plug it in, Mr Chop?'

I said yes, but told Urban I wanted a word. We sat at the table while Sam rigged the machine to the television. 'Your mum's just rung me asking if you can stop here for a while.'

'And can I?' he asked excitedly.

'For a while,' I said, and he punched the air with glee. 'She hasn't got a house any more, Urban. That's why she asked if you could stay here.'

'No, I know,' he said. 'I torched it.'

'I know you torched it, Urban. That's what I'm trying to tell you. But why, Urban? What have you achieved?'

'Well, Frank wote be tooting smack there any more, will he?'

'I don't suppose he will, but what's to stop him going somewhere else?'

'Worry about that when we come to it. That it? I have to give Sam a good hiding.'

'No, that's not it. You can't just go round burning houses down, Urban. It's arson. Don't you understand how serious it is? You could have killed someone.'

'But I made sure no one was in,' he protested. 'I didn't kill anyone.'

'Urban, you don't *have* to kill anyone. Arson carries a life stretch in its own right. Do you want to spend the rest of your life in prison?'

'Chill out, Chop,' he said. 'You worry too much. No one's going to put me in prison. I'm too young.'

That was the problem. Some of the younger ones felt they

were immune to prosecution. They could do anything they wanted and get away with it. 'I'll only let you stay if you promise to behave. No arson, no twocking, no murder. Okay?'

'I can't promise about the twocking,' he said, trying to be honest. He was a man of his word. He wouldn't want to give his word and then break it.

'Arson and murder?'

'Promise,' he said.

That was good enough for me. 'Go on, then. Get on with your game.'

What else could I do?

Frank, Skeeter, Trudi and the new girl turned up not long after. Frank, Skeeter and Trudi came right in and made themselves at home. 'I can't put you all up,' I told them straight off. 'It's out of the question.'

'Relax,' Frank said. 'We're on our way to Stella's.' Stella was an old mate of Greta's who had helped the kids out more than once. 'Course, if you'd let us kick fuck out of that silly little bastard,' he continued, nodding towards Urban, 'we wun't have all this trouble in the first place.'

The new girl stayed out in the hallway by the front door. 'What's up with her?' I asked. 'Why doesn't she come in?'

'She thinks you mean her harm,' Skeeter informed me.

'Why? What is she? A paranoid schizophrenic, or something?'

'At the very minimum.' Skeeter had developed a rather likeable acerbic wit.

'Well, tell her to come in.'

'She won't.'

'Why?'

'She does crack. She thinks the insects are after her and there's hairs growing out of her fingers. You might be Chief Insect Lord for all she knows. She tries to burn 'em off sometimes – the hairs, that is, not the insects.'

'What does she do about the insects?'

'She's got, like, a big giant nit-comb.'

'Fucking hell,' I said. 'She's completely ape-shit, then?'

'Well . . . yeah . . . but she fucks like a rabbit, so I'm not complaining.'

'Weren't you going out with Simpkins five minutes ago?' I asked, confused.

He shrugged. 'Yeah, but I'm not any more.'

I looked at Trudi, because I knew she had a soft spot for him too. She raised her eyebrows and wiggled them, which told me precisely nothing. I couldn't keep up with their tangled relationships. With the exception of the younger ones, it was quite possible that every boy in the crew had been out with every girl, at one time or another.

'I'm worried about you lot, Skeeter. I'm really, seriously, genuinely concerned for your welfare. Do you know that?'

'Lend us a tenner, Chop. We need to get some grub.'

The new girl was called Moira – or Mucky Moira to her friends. Urban had told me what little he knew about her. She was fourteen, a smackhead, a crackhead and a prostitute. In his words: 'She goes down for brown and sucks cock for rock.' Word was that she had been sexually abused by her dad, who then kicked her into the gutter like a dog when she complained about it. She had ended up in Chapeltown selling her body to the highest bidder. Greta met her walking the streets one night and took her home for a meal. 'She's a sly one,' Urban cautioned. 'She doesn't say much, but she's always up to something. She's got Skeet tied round her little finger. Sparky says she can't join the crew because she does five Pakis a night. She's Tony.'

'*Tony*, Urban? *Tony*? Is that a nice word, son?' I asked.

Tony was a slang term for white girls who went with Asian boys, an abbreviation from Tony Whitemeat. Underclass kids could be frighteningly racist, especially towards those they labelled 'Pakis'. To this day, I can't figure out why 'Pakis', and

'Pakis' alone, provoked such hostility. The only thing I can think of is that they were perceived as sticking together among themselves. But there again, who could blame them when they faced such antipathy? It was a chicken-and-egg situation. I'd thought smackheads were the lowest of the low, but obviously Tony people ranked even lower. You learn something new every day. Urban simply wasn't aware of what happened when civilisations met. The thing that brought them together, usually after a couple of wars, was interbreeding. England had absorbed all creeds and cultures in this way over millennia and would continue to do so. I was more concerned about what Moira was doing, rather than who she was doing it with.

Frank, Skeeter and Trudi used the bathroom, one by one, while I washed and dried their clothes. Moira refused to use the facilities, but was eventually lured into the kitchen for a cup of tea. Had she known how many insects lurked under the appliances, she might have stayed by the door. All any of them owned was what they stood up in. I fed them and gave them a tenner to share to send them on their way. 'They'll only spend it on smack,' Urban warned, but you can only do what you think is right at the time. They could buy food with it if they wanted to. I wanted to help, but I couldn't stand guard over them twenty-four hours a day. I'd met Stella a couple of times and she was a decent woman. She had agreed to take them on and I, for one, wasn't going to stand in her way.

Not one of them said a single word directly to Urban or Sam the whole time they were there. I sensed that they were already growing into a distinctive sub-crew, with different goals and values from the rest of us.

Come May Day, Urban was still with me. We didn't see Greta for a couple of months until she turned up in Eastie again, living with a Joey. Lucky she came back when she did because I was getting all sorts of shit from the council over Tyson. He'd been worrying the neighbours. Greta agreed to look after him, so long as I agreed to look after Urban a bit longer. Urban promised to take Tyson for a walk every day.

May Day was memorable that year because it was the day of the 1997 general election, the Day We Were Liberated from Twenty Years of Tory Oppression. I'd been trying to behave myself, but that called for a celebration. One thing Mrs Thatcher had taught me was how to say, 'Fuck everyone else, today I'm going to do exactly what I want.' And what I wanted to do was get smashed out of my face and get laid. It all just got on top of me sometimes and I had to let off steam. Coincidentally, the May Day bank holiday fell on the day before Frank's fifteenth birthday and two days after Skeeter's, which also called for a celebration, so Stella was throwing a party!

By this stage I had reached the belated conclusion that, short of moving them in and working on them full-time, there was little I could do to change Frank, Skeeter and Trudi. So my new policy was to stop going on at them all the time and just accept them as they were. From my own experience, I knew that taking drugs was a process that took a long time to run its course. The three were in the early stages and there was little I could say or do to influence them. Sooner or later they would become addicted and the choice would have to be made: to be a mindless zombie ant shackled by drugs, or to fight it and free yourself. It didn't really matter what you were addicted to. Addiction was the problem. Both the fight and the resolution were internal; your self-respect, your inner strength, your self-awareness and your will all came into it. Some survived, some didn't, but once afoot the game must run its course. Most straight-heads don't understand what the drug culture is all about. In a way, it's a spiritual experience, a vast internal battle with oneself. Little can be done from the outside.

Frank and Skeeter told everyone not to bring presents to the party, just plenty of booze and drugs. Most people took them at their word, but I had a little trick up my sleeve. At the time I had a contract delivering sports and leisure equipment to various schools and youth clubs, and I often stored the stuff in my lock-up. I trundled up to Stella's mid-morning with a big, bouncy castle in the back of the van hoping that much fun would be had by all.

I rigged it up in the front garden and within seconds every kid in the street was bouncing about on it. Stella brought out a can of beer and put it into my hand. 'Oh, in't that nice? Are't you sweet? A bouncy castle for Skeet an' Frank. Ah . . . bless 'em.' Stella always spoke in the old tongue.

The Penthouse Posse arrived in dribs and drabs throughout the afternoon, as did many other guests, mostly mums and kids from the street. The party was in full swing by teatime. I got the impression that Sparky wasn't really into it, but he had to come whether he wanted to or not. Rule number eight was specific: 'Always be there.' He spent his time drinking from a can and smooching with Natasha in the kitchen.

I stumbled outside to see how the castle was getting on. Urban, Sam and Pixie had agreed to be stewards and were making themselves a small fortune in the process by means of extortion. The children seemed happy enough, although some were finding it rough. A group of the smaller ones had come off and were skipping beside it. Two girls turned the rope as fast as they could, while a third, in the middle, concentrated intently on her skipping. The rope-winders sang:

> *The big ship sails on the alley alley oh,*
> *Alley alley oh, alley alley oh,*
> *Oh, the big ship sails on the alley alley oh*
> *On the last day of September.*

They repeated the verse several times and I found it deeply moving, like an elegy to lost innocence or the end of all songs.

There was nothing else for it. I went back indoors and took a large cocktail of drugs.

Stella's fostering arrangements had the same legitimacy as mine. There was one small difference. Urban and I had separate rooms, while Stella dossed in with the kids. She had four of her own and there was simply nowhere else for the sub-crew to sleep. As far as I could tell, they all piled into a big double bed together. Stella was thirty-nine and had green hair, which told me everything I needed to know about her. The phrase 'mutton dressed as lamb' sprang to mind. Other than that, she was in good condition for her age.

The party was soon in full swing and the whiz and Es flowed like wine.

I'm not shy when the drugs are going round so I was buzzing my tits off and I wanted to shag Stella. I popped up to the offy for a bottle of brandy and got her into the bedroom, ostensibly to read my tarot. She was into discovering the mystical side of our nature and suchlike. She did a cross-spread on the bed, then looked alarmed. 'Oh, I dote like the looks of this,' she said. 'I dote like the looks of it at all.' You can guess which cards had come up: Judgement, Temperance, the Fool, the Devil and the Hanged Man.

I was just about to sweep the cards from the bed and make my move, when Sam came knocking on the door. 'Chop, you'd better come downstairs and have a word with Urban. He's going off it a bit.'

'Fuck off, Sam,' I told him. 'I'm busy.'

'Please yourself,' he said.

I should have listened to him. Seconds later, there came a tremendous series of bangs and smashes from outside, like the noise of a train crash. Stella and I shot to the window to see my van careering drunkenly down the road, smashing into the side of one parked car after another until every car in the street had been demolished.

'Fucking hell,' I whimpered. 'That's torn it. How come you didn't see that in the fucking cards?'

'I knew you'd say summat like that,' she said. 'You men are so predictable.'

Urban wasn't. Who could have foretold that he would steal my van?

We went downstairs to find the kitchen smashed up and the back door off its hinges. 'Urban's gone mad,' Frank said. 'He just lost it. I just said four little words to him. Then he went mad and twocked your van, Chop.'

Stella grabbed Frank's arms and shook him earnestly, just like they do in soap operas. 'What did ya say, Frank? What did ya say?'

Frank shrugged. 'I just said, "Mum's sold your dog." That's all I said.'

I punched the wall as hard as I could, busting a couple of knuckles in the process. 'Don't say that, Frank. She hasn't, has she?'

'Yeah. She's digging smack down there with that Joey. How do you think she pays for it? She'd sell me and Urb if we stood in one place long enough.'

The kitchen was knee-deep in children and their prattle meant that I couldn't think straight. 'Get out!' I screamed. 'Into the fucking garden, the lot of you!' They all ran out in a panic.

I needed fresh air. I followed the kids out into the garden where three big, bolshy, bouncer-type blokes immediately surrounded me. 'Is that your van? Whose van's that? Who's driving that van? Someone's getting killed round here, mate, and it's probably you.' I knew I was in for it whatever happened. My dad always told me that if I ever found myself outnumbered, I should go for the biggest or mouthiest of my opponents. Take him out and the others will leave you alone. I therefore pulled my shoulder back and cracked the talkative one right in the teeth as hard as I could. He went down, but came straight back up again with blood pouring out of his mouth, which was worrying, so I jumped up on to the bouncy castle and prepared to defend myself. I rolled and bounced and wobbled, out of control somewhat, but I was on my feet.

My new friend wiped the blood from his mouth and tried to join me on the castle. I booted him right under the chin and launched him into the air. I figured he was out of the equation for a while. The other two blokes did a pincer movement and managed to mount the castle, then bounced around me in a threatening, intimidating manner. When my friend got up off the floor rubbing his chin and joined them, I knew that my days as a removal man were over.

Luckily, the kids came to my rescue. Sparky and Pinky led the charge and soon the bouncy castle was inundated with children and young people of all shapes and sizes. The three hard nuts were savaged alive by a swarm of them. Pixie, the smallest, was trying to bite a bloke's ear off. Pinky was on top of one, repeatedly nutting him in the face. Kara had her thumbs in a bloke's eyes. The men were so helpless and distressed that I had time to bounce over to each of them in turn and punch their lights out. 'Which hurts most, bastard? Gnat bites or crocodile bites?' Bang! 'How do you like it when you're outnumbered, bastard? Eh?' Bang! Bang! 'Who's driving the fucking van, bastard? I'm driving the fucking van!' Bang! Bang! Bang!

While all this was going on, three police cars entered the street and a half a dozen scuffers joined the mêlée. I'd had a lot of whiz, I admit, and this might have affected my thinking processes. For some reason, I was convinced that I was the king of the castle and that they were dirty rascals. This blue foe were nothing more to me than fresh besiegers who had to be repelled and I laid into them with gay abandon. The kids were all over them too. Every time the scuffers tried to get on, we threw them off again, then threw the unconscious blokes' bodies at them for good measure. Eventually, they regrouped, broke through our ranks and sprayed us with CS gas, which put them in the ascendancy, as most of us couldn't see any more and our faces were blistering. The last thing I remember was a big, black stick swinging towards my head and then I remembered no more.

PART THREE
THE RAGGED-
TROUSERED
RECIDIVISTS

The law doth punish man or woman
That steals the goose from off the common,
But lets the greater felon loose
That steals the common from the goose.

    ANON
    On enclosures, 18th century

'Well, Urban, we started out in a sewer,
now here we are by a shallow grave.
What do you make of that?'

SIXTEEN
BOKONO WILL PROVIDE

Don't you know the damage you do
With your 'I Don't Give a Damn' attitude?
But you're all right Jack, take care of yourself,
You're an angry young man who's been left on the shelf.
Torching cars and breaking hearts.
There's nothing else for you to do.
You say: 'What you looking at? What you looking at, you?'

Mugging pensioners for a pittance or two,
'Do What I Like' is the creed you live to,
Steal, lie, cheat, break the law every day,
Till you go too far and they take you away.

You don't know the damage you do
And you can't change your selfish attitude.
Look at your life, reflect for a while,
You're a little charver scum getting on with his time.
Torching cars and breaking hearts.
There's nothing else for you to do.
You say: 'I don't give a damn. I don't give a damn, you.'

Manx Kippers
Feeling blue

The good times were over. When Urban had finished his day's
work the van was a write-off and without it we were penniless.
If that wasn't enough, I was fined £2600 on top, to be paid off

at ten pounds a week for the rest of eternity, for various offences including ABH, GBH, assaulting the police, obstructing the police, resisting arrest, road-tax avoidance, fraudulent display of a stolen tax disc, receiving stolen property (said tax disc), no insurance, no MOT, possession of Class-A drugs, drunk and disorderly, causing a public nuisance, embezzlement of a bouncy castle and affray.

Most of the crew were also arrested at the party. All but Sparky and Skeeter got out quickly on bail, charged with minor public-order offences. Sparky was wanted on a dozen other counts, including assaults, twocks and, now that the DNA tests were complete, GBH on Pixie's uncle. The bad news was that Pixie's uncle was out of his coma; the good news was that he wouldn't be walking too well for a while. Sparky was remanded in custody and sent to Doncatraz Young Offenders Institution for the criminally insane. Skeeter, a year younger, was remanded to detention centre on several counts of twock. Frank, who I'd expected to go down with Sparky and Skeeter, was given 120 hours community service and avoided incarceration.

As usual, Urban got away with everything. Some kind of divine force seemed to be protecting him. He damaged twelve cars before he slammed the van into a bus shelter. Luckily, he'd learned his lesson on the Aberdeen job and this time had worn his seatbelt. He staggered away from the wreck and took sanctuary at the Church of England Safe House for a much-needed period of rest and recuperation.

The police had a deal with the Safe House and didn't arrest kids there, no matter what. Runaways under sixteen were in a rather beautiful catch-22 situation. They had no legal right to leave home, couldn't access benefits, couldn't work and couldn't enter into a legal contract to obtain independent living accommodation. In short, apart from crime and prostitution, they had no legitimate means of supporting themselves. Furthermore, anyone (like me) who helped them was guilty of 'harbouring' under the 1989 Children's Act and liable to be imprisoned. When the police caught runaway kids, they often had little choice but to hand them back to the very people who were abusing them. The Safe Houses were given special exemption from the harbouring laws and the Children's Society was doing its best to keep its finger in the dam.

Urban stayed with them for three weeks, and by the time he came home, the scuffers had more or less forgotten his one-man demolition derby. I hadn't. At first, I was mad with him for killing Elsie, but then I realised it didn't really matter. I was sick of shifting junk in any case. He'd probably done me a favour. A woman called Maggie came round from the Safe House and asked if I'd be willing to take him back. Greta had disappeared off the face of the earth again and, frankly, they didn't know what else to do with him. They were good people at the Safe House. Maggie was the first decent social worker I'd ever met. She was a bit posh for my taste, but she was straight and honest and she accepted that our rules, values and morals were different from hers. I told her straight about my history, about my many and various problems and about my criminal record. 'Frankly,' I said, 'now that I understand what's involved, I'm not sure I'm capable of looking after him.'

Maggie said I was about the most remarkable person she'd ever met. To take in someone else's kid, under such circumstances, in such a climate, was fantastically amazing in her opinion and she didn't care who knew it. Two males who obviously cared for each other and weren't afraid to show it. Two males! Of all people! She couldn't think of anyone in the world more qualified to care for Urban. 'It's amazing,' she said. 'Fantastic.'

I'd never thought about it like that. Was it Mark Twain who

233

said that he could live for a month on a good compliment? With care and frugality, I might be able to eke this one out for years. Indeed, I might have to because there was nothing in the fridge.

'Was she blagging my head or was she serious?' I asked Urban, when she'd gone.

'I think she was serious,' he said. 'But she might've been blagging your head. Soz about the van, Chop. Tyson's gone. I've searched high and low, but I can't find him anywhere, or Mum. I'm fucked. I don't know what to do. I bet you hate me now an' all.'

'Don't be silly,' I said. 'I'd forgive you anything. Forgiveness is what it's all about, Urban. Remember that when you're the World Teacher. It's quite important. Elsie was just scrap metal. I'm more concerned about you and Tyson.'

That old bottom lip of his started wobbling and for the first time since I'd met him he broke down and sobbed his heart out. I hugged his head and looked out of the window until the storm abated. The cloud factories were still hard at it.

Next morning I signed on the dole, but I soon found that my benefits were nowhere near enough for the two of us to live on. They weren't enough for one person to live on, never mind two. Naturally, I declared Urban as a dependant and attempted to claim child benefit and single-parent allowance, which in our new situation was the difference between life and death. Nothing doing. They didn't believe I was looking after him. I took him in the next day, sat him down and pointed to him. 'There he is,' I said. 'Right there in front of your eyes.' They still didn't believe me, so I got a letter from the Safe House confirming my story. They still didn't believe me. I asked Social Services to confirm the facts, but as far as they knew Urban was back with his mother. The dole, meanwhile, contacted Greta and asked her what was going on. They sent her regular supplies of cash so they were probably the only people in the universe who knew where she was. Urban was living at home with her, she said. I was nothing but a nonce, she said, and she had put the matter into the hands of the police. Meanwhile, she frittered all the benefits away on drugs and booze. She didn't mind me looking after Urban, but no way was she giving up her rightful entitlements as a mother.

I took serious umbrage with her after this little trick. It was my opinion that 95 per cent of the people in the underclass were clinically insane. Previously, I had merely considered her to be one of the many. Now I saw her as nasty and malicious. Selling Tyson was bad enough, but selling Urban and me would take a long time to forgive. It left us on the verge of starvation and destitution.

I desperately needed a new scam. My meagre savings had dried up and we were in real trouble. 'Gerrajob then, sither,' my dad said, when I went round to try to borrow money from him. My dad was coming up for seventy, bent and withered from a lifetime's slavery in the pits. Still, he would brook no nonsense.

'Class traitor,' I said. 'What kind of thing is that to say to your own son? What do you take me for? Do you think I'm Joeying about for them bastards? I went though a year-long strike with you and that's the thanks I get.'

'Aye, sither, un that wut nearest thy ever come to doin' a day's wuk.' My dad lived in Eastie, but came from Methley originally, which was a little pit village between Leeds and Castleford where they spoke broad Yorkshire. 'An' tell them barns o' thine to stop nickin' all t'cars. Tha's'll get nowt frum me till tha sorts thissen art, sither.'

I picked up the framed picture of Mum and Dad in their wedding regalia. It was fading with age, slowly becoming sepia. Next to it was a small china plate with a gilded edge, Mum's favourite ornament when she was alive. It showed an ancient sailing ship being tossed about in a stormy sea. The waves were vast and threatened to overwhelm the struggling vessel. Below the picture, it read, 'May fair winds attend you on your voyage through life.'

'Dad,' I said, 'the mining communities were self-policing. That's not the case any more – the strike ended that. It's not my fault there's no law and order. Why should I take the blame for everything? Lend us a fucking tenner!'

'No, sling thy hook. Does tha think A'm fuckin' med a money?'

'Bollocks, then.'

It's hard on the breadline. Families fall out over nothing. My dad was surly and awkward, but I loved him dearly. He had nothing himself, so he couldn't be expected to sub Urban and me. He was there for me when I was young, which was all that mattered. He taught me independence and survival, so I had the tools I needed if only I could put them to use. He also gave me my love of poetry, which he considered the nearest thing we had to philosophy. When I was a kid he was always quoting silly little rhymes and ditties that contained infinite wisdom. One popped into my head as I left the house:

> *That money talks I can't deny,*
> *I heard it once, it said goodbye.*

'Money's nowt,' Urban said, as we tucked into our supper. I'd bought cheap frozen vegetables from the market and made them into a vegetable curry, but it hadn't turned out according to plan. Urban tilted his spoon and allowed the unappetising gruel to splosh back into the bowl. 'We don't need money, Chop. Bokono will provide.'

'Urban,' I said, 'have you been sniffing again?' I knew he was still sneaking off down the canal for the odd sniff, but I could never quite catch him. He couldn't fool me, though. Whenever his breath smelt of industrial peppermint, I had my suspicions. 'Talk sense, lad. You're not making any sense. Who or what is Bokono?'

'The Great God Bokono,' he said, taking the lid off the pepper pot, only to discover that we were out of pepper. 'The Bringer of Fishcakes.'

'Fishcakes sound good,' I acknowledged. 'Tell me more.'

Bokono was the god worshipped by the canal children of Leeds. It was an all-seeing, all-knowing, all-compassionate god, and it was always there for you, even when everyone else had deserted you. Urban couldn't say what it looked or sounded like, because he had never seen or heard it. Bokono was beyond all human comprehension and knowledge, so there was no point messing your head up even thinking about it. Bokono was an *it*, rather than a *he*. It wasn't male or female, black or white, it wasn't even human. Best not to try to picture it in case you had a bad trip and blew out your fuses.

'If you've never seen it, or heard it, how do you know it's there?' Schrödinger's cat again.

Urban pushed away his bowl. 'I know because the High Lord Zombulglast told me when I was glued up and the High Lord Zombulglast knows his shit.' Bokono, apparently, was so unknowable that it could only be contacted through an intermediary. 'We can eat well for fuck all, Chop. Why don't I show you? I've lived on nowt all my life because Bokono looks after me.'

' "Consider the lilies", Urban. Is that what you're saying?' He didn't know what I meant, so I got out the King James Bible, which was my mother's only bequest to me when she died. ' "Behold the fowls of the air: for they sow not, neither do they reap, nor gather into barns; yet your heavenly Father feedeth them. Are ye not much better than they?" Matthew six: twenty-six.'

'That's it,' he said enthusiastically, relieved that he'd finally found someone who knew what he was talking about. 'Spot on, that's how it is, except it's Bokono what does it.'

'I think we should make Bokononism the official religion of Ashtrayland, don't you, Urban? You really could be the World Teacher, you know. You might have just invented a new earth-shattering religion. We may change the world yet.'

Convinced, I converted to Bokononism and started work the next morning. We warmed up in Morrison's in the town centre, where I bought bread and milk and stole two hundred pounds' worth of razor blades. It wasn't that I took a lot of razor blades; it was just that razor blades were phenomenally expensive. I'd always hated paying for them. Now I had a year's supply. At lunchtime, the Prêt à Manger sandwich shop was crowded with suits and ties from the offices, making it a simple matter to purloin half a dozen of their delicious sandwiches, two cream cakes for afters and lashings of fresh orange juice to swill it down. We picnicked on a bench in City Square and, fittingly, I thought, fed the pigeons with the leftovers. After lunch, I got Urban a nice pair of Levi's from the Army & Navy Store and a nice leather belt for myself from Marks & Spencer. We finished the day's reaping by going back to Morrison's for a nice joint of minted lamb for our tea.

'Not bad for a beginner,' I mused, as I tucked into the best meal I'd had since Elsie's demise. 'You were right, Urban. Bokono will provide.'

My appearance helped me greatly in my new career. I was chubby, wore glasses, had short hair and, with my newly acquired razor blades, was now clean-shaven. In my best clothes, you'd be forgiven if you mistook me for the Chancellor of the Exchequer. Most shoplifters are stupid. They go in looking like they've just got out of bed, which in most cases they have, and are surprised when the store detectives follow them around. I wore a shirt and tie and developed a wonderfully insouciant technique whereby I followed the store detectives around until they nicked someone. Then, while they were preoccupied, I cleaned up.

I did have some moral reservations, but they were overridden by my survival instinct. Basically, I was putting a penny on everyone else's bread, which was nothing like what Mr Morrison was putting on, but nevertheless it was there. I didn't think I was setting a bad example to Urban, because he'd already been the biggest thief on the planet before I met him. Furthermore, after my initial training period I wouldn't let him come with me when I was grafting. I took all the risks myself and he was well fed and clothed because of it. I couldn't get any benefits for him, nor could I find a job. Despite my political objections, I looked for a job out of necessity, but was debarred because of my criminal record and my anti-capitalist views. Fair enough. If that was how they wanted it, that was how they would get it. I didn't mind relieving capitalist multinationals of junk, but I often thought, What a waste. I was a capable and resourceful man. If society couldn't use me, let's see if they could catch me. I enjoyed being a shoplifter. I loved every second of it. It was my peaceful, non-violent way of avenging myself upon my society. And, of course, it helped me to pay off the fines.

The trick to successful shoplifting is not to be greedy. Greed is death to the grafter. I only took what we needed to survive, and maybe a little extra to swap for tobacco and dope. Bartering was back in vogue and it was easy to exchange a nice piece of stolen meat for a nice fifty-gram pack of bootlegged tobacco, or a nice pair of stolen jeans for a nice lump of prohibited dope. I worked mainly at lunchtime when the shops were crowded, toiled for maybe an hour, then went for a couple of pints in Big Lil's to exchange information and goods with my fellow criminals.

'Stay out of Boots, Chop, man. Know what A'm saying? Bang on top, charver. Give it a miss.'

Martin was my new business associate who spoke in the croaky voice common to all smackheads. He was a smackhead, but he didn't look like one. Indeed, he looked like a professional footballer with the designer gear, which he stole, the miniature mobile phone, which he taxed, and the Rolex, which he carjacked. He was in his mid-twenties and wasn't too far down the road. His complexion was still good and his eyes still fresh. I worked best on my own, but some jobs needed a second pair of hands. On my rounds, I noticed a flaw in Lillywhite's security arrangements. They sold top-class designer sports gear, which Urban loved to wear and which bartered well, and I wanted to get my hands on some. Security was heavy, unfortunately, and the only plan I could devise required two participants. I asked Martin if he'd care to work with me and he agreed. The shop was open-plan and too close to the exit doors of the shopping centre. It was a simple matter to walk round, gather up half a dozen items looking as though you fully intended to pay for them, drop them over a handrail to your mate who was waiting outside the shop and then nash off down to Big Lil's, detag them in the toilet and sell or barter them in a matter of seconds. This was my cash crop. Other than that, I mainly reaped at a subsistence level.

Urban and I lived from day to day. If the fridge was full, we dossed around doing nothing. We had lots of spare time so I carried on with his education. He got quite interested in some of the characters from the Bible, especially that Jesus O'Nazareth bloke, so I read it to him quite a lot. Also, he listened in on novels that I happened to be reading myself. I just read aloud instead of in my head. I tried my best to teach him to read, but met with unexpected difficulties. He had mastered the alphabet fairly quickly and could handle words of two or three letters, but I couldn't get him past the cat-sat-on-the-mat stage. Longer words seemed to jumble up on him and turn themselves around until they made no sense. The only conclusion I could draw was that he was dyslexic. Also, he had difficulty concentrating on anything for more than a few minutes at a time. After an early burst, I was aware that I was making no progress with him whatsoever. As if we didn't have enough problems, he needed specialist teaching of some description.

Despite this, life was good. Life is always good when you don't have to worry about money. We didn't have a penny to our name, but we didn't need it. My dole just about paid the household bills, so we had a roof over our heads whatever happened. Anything else we required, we simply plucked from the trees.

Through the summer of '97, Urban and I filled our time with Away Days and Weekend Breaks. Urban had shown me how to live for nothing, now he showed me how to travel for nothing. Put the two together and you had the perfect holiday. The first and last trips were the best, the first because it was all new to us, the last because it began our slow reintegration into society.

Late June, we decided that we needed a change of scenery. I was worn out from shoplifting three times a week and Urban was exhausted from doing nothing all day. The rest of the crew were generally leaving us to our own devices. Sparky and Skeeter were inside, Frank and Trudi were getting deeper into Zombie Voodoo Land, Pinky was planning her trip to the West Indies, and Thieving Little Simpkins was working hard at school, hoping to get some GCSEs. The only people we saw regularly were the Eastie contingent: Molly, who was still going out with Urban, Kara, Pixie and Sam. Urban and Molly weren't getting on so well. Urban told me in confidence that he didn't love Molly any more because he'd met someone else at the Safe House. 'Teezer, they call her, but don't tell Molly. I'll tell her in my own way.' Young people are so fickle in their relationships.

It was Friday morning, Urban and I were bored and we had twenty pounds to our name. 'Let's go to the lake,' he suggested, out of the blue.

'Mmmm?' I said. I was studying form, and the favourite in the two thirty at Wetherby had caught my eye.

'The lake. Let's go to the lake.'

I looked up from the racing pages. 'What lake?'

'The lake where Mum took us before we got put in care. There was trouble one time and she took us up this big lake to hide out for a while. I was only little so I can't remember much, just this big fuck-off lake.'

'How big?'

'Massive. You couldn't walk to the end of it. The biggest lake in England.'

'Windermere, I reckon. What about it?'

'Let's go there. It's summat to do.'

It was a nice idea, but we couldn't afford it. With our new-found survival skills we could live for very little once we got there, but the cost of travel was prohibitive. 'We can travel for nothing,' Urban insisted. 'Bokono will provide.'

He was right, of course. You could travel for nothing. You could do anything you wanted to do. He used some kind of a Nietzschean device, the Will to Holiday, something like that. He just made it happen. The journey of a thousand miles begins with a single step. We simply packed the camping gear into two rucksacks, caught a bus into town and stood atop the M621 with our thumbs out. Within ten minutes, we had a lift off a nutty guy driving a minibus who took us over the Pennines and dropped us at the junction of the M61, just north of Salford. The police took us to the next services as we were making their motorway look untidy. A travelling saleswoman who asked a lot of questions dropped us on the M6 within marching distance of Kendal, the Gateway to the Lakes. We jumped the train from there to Windermere, paid our fares on the open-top bus to Ambleside, stashed our bags in a bush, and the next thing you know we were stood on Loughrigg Fell looking down across Lake Windermere.

'You were right,' I said. 'It is possible to travel for nothing. I love Bokono, don't you?'

'Bokono *is* love,' Urban said. 'Remember that when you're John the Baptist. It's quite important.'

We stayed in the woods a couple of nights, then rode home on two tasty mountain bikes provided by Bokono, a yellow fat-framed Raleigh for Urban and a red Muddy Fox with suspension for me. They were hanging on the back of an Audi A6, weighing it down. We felt sorry for the car and relieved it of its burden. It was a simple matter to cut the straps and we were soon riding the Dales Way back to Yorkshire. I had planned to sell the bikes on our return, but Urban wouldn't hear of it. It was the first quality item he'd ever owned, so I let him keep his and flogged mine to fund further expeditions.

We closed the summer with our last trip, to the big Smoke. Urban was thirteen and three-quarters so for him it would be the last summer of childhood. I was therefore determined to send him out with a bang. Coincidentally, Diana, Princess of Wales went out with a bang in a car smash at the end of August that year and Urban wanted to go to her funeral. He was convinced the Babylon had killed her and he wanted to get to the bottom of it. Twockers were used to being driven off the roads by the scuffers and he wondered if the same thing had happened to her. It was rare that events outside east Leeds impinged on our world, but Lady Di was one of us, a fellow sufferer, even if she was profoundly wealthy, and we needed to say goodbye. I contacted a mate of mine in London who agreed to put us up, which meant that we could travel light and didn't need the camping gear. We set off early doors

Thursday, hitched as far as St Albans, jumped a train and were in Trafalgar Square by teatime.

Thursday night, we stayed with my mate Jim in Twickenham. I got him his job down there, so he owed me a couple of favours. His apartment was worth £250,000, which to me was ridiculous money – it would keep me going for about two thousand years – but it was smaller than my flat and we had to sleep in the living room. Jim's bird didn't like us, because we were common northern scum and she couldn't understand what we said. We borrowed their bikes Friday morning and rode into London along the river. London was just as I remembered it: despicably ugly, disgustingly filthy, and the people were diabolically rude and ignorant. What was more, it got worse the further you were from Twickenham.

En route we visited the Houses of Parliament, where we met a bloke who was running a one-man campaign for English independence. He had dozens of St George's flags draped across the railings at the side of the road. Passers-by were avoiding him like the plague, naturally assuming that he was a neo-Fascist, a football hooligan or both. Urban went straight over and talked to him. 'The Welsh, the Scots and the Irish all have their own parliaments,' the lobbyist complained. 'Why shouldn't we, the English? What's wrong with us, eh?'

I explained to Urban that we were standing in front of the British Parliament, not the English one.

Urban looked confused. 'So have I got this right?' he asked. 'Everyone in the empire gets a say apart from us.'

'Bang on, son,' said the lobbyist. 'Sign here.'

Having joined the English Parliamentary Party, we rode on down the Embankment to the Tower of London. We couldn't afford to go in, and the walls were too high to scale, so we chained the bikes and bunked on the Docklands railway to Canary Wharf instead. Urban was astonished because the train had no driver. I was astonished too and felt uncomfortable on a driverless train. Perhaps for the first time I realised that technology was outpacing my ability to cope with it.

We climbed the dome of St Paul's in the afternoon and we were in the West End by teatime, where we stole our supper and thank-you presents for our hosts. Urban spent several hours in SEGA Land, Leicester Square, while I sneaked off for a couple of pints of southern dishwater and a look round the mucky-book shops. Then, of course, I couldn't find him again and ended up at the police station complaining that the nonces had him. I waited by the bikes until he finally returned around eleven p.m., saying he'd been exploring. 'This is probably the shittiest place on earth,' he said, summarising his research. I didn't have time to worry about that. My feet were aching and the incessant crowds and the traffic noise were driving me to distraction.

Our natural route home took us along Piccadilly, then Kensington Road, past Kensington Gardens. I wanted to show Urban the sea of flowers that had been left for Lady Di, but we weren't prepared for what we saw. It was an ocean of flowers, almost two metres deep in places and covering half an acre of land before the gates of the palace. Just looking at it made you want to cry. What was more, there were hundreds of mourners dotted around the park, most of them equipped for an all-night vigil. Groups of children were sitting cross-legged in candle-lit circles, singing and praying. Urban and I were moved to tears and sat there till five o'clock in the morning, soaking up the atmosphere and talking to the other mourners, who had come not just from all corners of Britain but from all corners of the world. There was no need to go to the funeral in the morning. We had paid our respects and for the first time in a long, long while we felt we were part of something greater than the Shed Crew.

SEVENTEEN

EXPERTS, CONSULTANTS AND SUCH

Why are people such bastards?
You're asking, but I don't know why.
Unfathomable freaks with outrageous cheek,
It's enough to make you fucking cry.

Why are people such bastards?
Experts, consultants and such.
Getting paid for fuck all so give them a call,
And they won't charge you overly much.

Why are people such bastards?
Salesmen and pushers of pens.
Talking shit with a grin and raking it in;
Don't trust them, they're all double-bent.

Why are people such bastards?
Why do they all charge too much?
Even men of the cloth are ripping us off,
So let's go get completely fucked.

Chop
Disaffected

Summer drew to a close and it was becoming clear, even to me, that Greta had no intention of ever coming for Urban. By default, I was therefore responsible for his long-term care and well-being.

Urban didn't mind in the least. He had come to detest his mother and habitually referred to her as 'the Dog Killer'. Since taking up residence, he had single-handedly redecorated the spare room and made it his own. The walls he painted a garish green and plastered with Ordnance Survey maps and posters. He had his own stereo, Walkman, TV and games machine, as well as a warm, comfortable bed. A warning sign on his door read, 'Smack-free Zone', and a skull and crossbones indicated the dangers lying in wait for anyone foolish enough to ignore it. He loved having his own safe space and I had never seen him happier.

I was content, rather than happy. Happiness was something I aspired to, but never expected to achieve. I was, however, gradually getting used to the idea that I now had a permanent or semi-permanent responsibility. It was time to grow up. I'd avoided responsibilities all my life. I'd always seen myself as a deep-cover agent in the war against capitalism and it wouldn't have been fair to burden myself with them. Urban changed all that and I cared very deeply about him. To me, he embodied everything that was wrong with the world. I felt that Bokono had sent him to me as a kind of test, one that I was determined to pass.

He'd been with me nine months all told, and a new school year was upon us. I knew that if I didn't act soon another year would pass him by without education, health care or help for his dyslexia, all the things that other children took for granted. Having spent the best part of a year hiding him from the authorities, I now realised I needed their help. Without official sanction, there would be no possibility of accessing schools, benefits, doctors, dentists or other essential services. He had no inoculation marks, which left him wide open to polio, TB and the High Lord Zombulglast alone knew what else. Also, his teeth were in terrible shape and needed urgent treatment. I had little option but to approach Social Services cap in hand.

They weren't interested at first, but I went up to their offices and blocked the reception for three-quarters of an hour until they agreed to send someone round. Today was the big day and I was nervous. The flat was a tip. Urban and I spent all morning scrubbing and cleaning until it was something like presentable. Finally, we sat down in the kitchen for coffee and bacon sandwiches. 'I tolm you not to trust my mum,' Urban said, poking an escaped bit of sandwich back into his gob. 'I tolm you the firss time I mem you. Why ditm't you lissem? You never lissem to a worm anyone sayshem. Dit um know that about umself, Chop? Mmm?'

'Shut up,' I said. 'Don't talk with your mouth full. And straighten your baseball cap.'

Mr Ko was an immigrant from Hong Kong who had made good in this country and become a social worker. 'Ah, Misser Choppah, you say Herbal Grimshaw no your responsibility. Why you say this?'

'Why do I say it?'

'Yes, why you say?'

'I don't know,' I said. 'Why does anyone say anything?' Such metaphysical questions were beyond my jurisdiction. 'I'm with you, Mr Ko. "All words not in praise of Bokono are wasted words." Is that what you're saying?'

Mr Ko looked confused and consulted his case notes. 'Ah, Herbal Grimshaw from Rotherham?'

'Eh?' I said. 'No, he's not from Rotherham. He's from Leeds. Why do you say that?'

'Say wha', ah, Misses Choppah?'

'Say that he's from Rotherham.'

'Ah, Misser Choppah, why anyone say anything?'

'I don't know.' I said. 'You tell me. You're the fucking social worker.'

We eventually got a meeting at Social Services with a Mizz Williamson, Mr Ko's supervisor. She said I was racist and threatened to close down the meeting. 'I'm not racist,' I told her. 'I'm merely saying that I can't communicate with Mr Ko. We inhabit two different universes. That's all I'm saying. How does that make me racist? I expect you'll be calling me sexist in a minute, you fat ugly dyke.'

We got short shrift from Social Services.

Next, I tried to get Urban into a school. They said he was a PPRVU, whatever that was, and that he would have to be referred to the Pupil Referral Unit. That's what they said, but I think they had a colour bar: the school was 90 per cent Asian and they didn't want any poor white trash. I tried to refer him to the Pupil Referral Unit, as advised, but they weren't accepting referrals.

Next, I tried to sign him up with a doctor. The middle-aged quack looked him in the eye and spoke slowly, as if he were talking to a mindless zombie ant. 'Where . . . are . . . your . . . medical . . . records . . . young . . . man?'

Urban returned his gaze. 'I . . . don't . . . know,' he replied. 'I'm . . . not . . . the . . . fucking . . . doctor . . . around . . . here.'

Urban had moved around so much that it was impossible to find his records. Without records, you didn't exist and they refused to register him. Luckily, we lived close to Jimmy's A and E, which we used in lieu of a GP. A six-hour wait was better than nothing.

It was a similar story at the dentist's. Urban had strong teeth, which seemed to be immune from rot, but a front one was missing and the rest were all over the place. He urgently needed a brace, or corrective surgery of some description. He was very conscious of his 'gammy' teeth as he thought they made him look ugly. Shakespeare, as always, came to our rescue: 'There is no great beauty which hath not some strange-ness in the proportion,' I told him. You might not have been able to get a dentist in England, but they couldn't take

Shakespeare away from us, although you sensed that they probably would if they thought they could get away with it.

Even the scuffers had lost interest in him. Urban and I talked it over and agreed that he should give himself up over the van business and Burner Brown's head. If I could get him in front of a juvenile court, I might be able to get some help. Unfortunately, Sparky had already confessed to the crimes. Sparky was up for so many offences that it was no burden for him to have extra charges 'taken into consideration'. I told the scuffers he was lying – which wasn't grassing, if you think about it – but they didn't care. They were more interested in their clear-up rate than in abstract concepts such as truth and justice. As far as they were concerned, the case was closed.

In short, no one gave a shit about Urban Grimshaw and I was left to cope with him as best I could. I was appalled by this state of affairs. I was, by my own confession, a man who lived alone. I wasn't sure that I was suitable to be looking after children. I certainly wouldn't want any child of mine to be cared for by someone like me. It always makes the headlines when a child disappears off the streets, but many more are lost because they fall through society's safety net in this way. All society's agencies had washed their hands of Urban. We had no choice but to muddle through as best we could. At least we had each other. I tried not to show it to Urban, but I was becoming increasingly embittered. It was virtually impossible to communicate with anyone from officialdom. They were on a completely different wavelength. What really riled me was that we now had a Labour government so we couldn't even blame the Tories for our woes.

Labour wasn't Labour any more. It was already apparent that they planned to do precisely nothing about anything, except maybe make sure the economy was okay by the IMF. They were more right wing than the Tories. They were sell-outs. I could see that at a glance. Life for the underclass in

Britain towards the end of the twentieth century was like a cross between Orwell's *1984* and Kafka's *The Trial* – bizarre and surreal in ways unimaginable.

In early October Skeeter got out of jail. They released him in the morning and he was knocking on my door by dinnertime. He had to report to the Probation Service and he needed to borrow money for a Day Rider ticket.

'You mean to say they let you out without a release grant or anything? How do they expect you to get about or find somewhere to live?'

'Cunts,' he said succinctly.

He was heading back to Stella's, but he had a meal with us first and washed and dried his clothes. I noticed a big change in him. Quiet at the best of times, he now communicated exclusively by means of grunts, tuts, hums, facial expressions, body language and words of one syllable. He was like most teenagers, then, in that respect, only more so. The detention centre had had a profound effect on him and he was now immune to all forms of human contact. A door had slammed shut in his soul and no one would ever reach him again.

I rang the Probation Service on his behalf, explained his circumstances and asked if it would be all right for him to report tomorrow. 'No,' they said. 'If he doesn't report by five o'clock, he'll be in breach and the only place he'll go tomorrow is back to jail.'

'Thanks for your understanding,' I said. 'You're wonderful human beings. Who came out on top in the care versus control debate, by the way?'

Having removed the stench of prison, Skeeter headed off around four thirty to do his duty to the state. Urban took the opportunity to tag along to probation and head up to Stella's afterwards, as he hadn't seen Frank for some weeks. I watched them walk across the estate from the living-room window. A couple of the local boys were standing on the corner. One said something to Skeeter, who stopped dead in his tracks. I opened the window intending to shout down and warn the kid: 'Don't even think about it, son! You're stepping out of your division!' Too late. Skeeter launched into him without further ado, punching him down to the ground, kicking him half to death and stomping on his head for good measure. It was like me playing chess with the Yardies. No competition. The kid's mate ran away, leaving Urban to pull Skeeter off. By the time I got down there, Skeeter and Urban were gone. Playing the concerned passer-by, I got the kid to his feet and escorted him to Jimmy's to have his face stitched up and his head bandaged.

Skeeter was a lost boy, beyond my help.

Trudi was a lost girl. She landed on my doorstep in the bleak mid-November, four or five months pregnant. 'No,' I wailed. 'No, no, no, don't tell me that. You're still a kid yourself. Why, Trudi? Why? I've told you about the pill and johnnies and everything. Why don't you listen?'

'Chop,' she said, in matter-of-fact tones, 'I'm nearly sixteen, and then I'm allowed to have a flat. You know how it works. The only way I'll get a flat is if I've got a kid. Then there's the child ben' o' course . . . mustn't overlook that.'

'Fucking hell, Trudi,' I moaned. 'Whose is it?'

'Could be Frank's, could be Skeeter's, could be Urban's, as a matter of fact, could be a lot of people's. How the fuck should I know?'

'No, Trudi, no, no, no. We've got enough fucking mouths to feed! Haven't you ever heard of Malthus, you stupid, ignorant tart?'

It was no good losing my temper. There was another human life inside Trudi so she was now exempt from all the normal rules and regulations. Rule number three: 'Pregnant women are temporarily exempted from the argy-bargy.' The only thing that mattered was to bring this bright new human consciousness to fruition. Urban was happy to share his bed with her, bearing in mind that it might be his kid, and I gave her a key to the door. It took us a week to wean her off smack, but she refused point-blank to give up cigarettes and she didn't care what the doctors said. Meanwhile, as a kind of birthday present to the child, I was trying to devise a means to break the cycle of deprivation that blighted our country. Thus far without success, I might add.

Trudi brought even more bad news. Frank and Skeeter were injecting. 'I don't mind tooting, but no way am I digging, 'specially not now I'm pregnant. Now, neither of them's interested in me. They don't want to know. It's like talking to a couple of zombies.' She let her jaw drop, so that she looked like a mindless imbecile and did her zombie impression. '"Er . . . wha' . . . car't talk to you now, Trude . . . got to get some zombie juice . . ." That's all they care about now, their fucking gear – and some old slut down the road noncing 'em both up. Just wait till I tell Greta.'

Urban didn't seem concerned about his brother's sexual activities. You could look at it that Frank was being sexually abused, or you could look at it that he was gaining sexual experience courtesy of an older woman. He was, however, appalled to hear that Frank was injecting. 'To lose a mother, Master Grimshaw, may be regarded as misfortune, but to lose a brother too looks like carelessness,' I quipped, misquoting Oscar Wilde.

Urban wasn't amused. It was all I could do to keep him away from Stella's with his trusty milk bottle and matches, but he kept his promise to me not to commit arson or murder.

Trudi stayed with us until early December when I managed to reconcile her with her mother. Janice was the salt of the earth, but a drunk whose idea of a good time was to have cider for breakfast, then to drink more cider until she got lewd and disgusting in the afternoon and collapsed in a heap by early evening. She was the same age as me, but looked a decade older. Trudi introduced me to her family as 'Chop-He's-Not-A-Nonce' and called her mum a slut to her face.

The first time I had visited a riot broke out. 'Trudi, love, go tut shops for Mummy.'

'Mummy, love, fuck off. Go yourself. What do you think I am? Get off your fat, stinking arse, you waste of fucking space.'

'Trudi, love, don't talk to Mummy like that, else Mummy'll have to smash you in the face wi' t' tin bucket she normally pisses in.'

'Try it, love. Just fucking try it.' Mummy used to knock Trudi about a lot when she was little, but Trudi had toughened up during her time with the Shed Crew and wasn't going to take it any more.

Then, indeed, Mummy went for Trudi with gusto and the two of them thrashed around the room demolishing everything that hadn't already been demolished in previous fights. Trudi's mum didn't seem to be aware of rule number three. She was barely aware of the day, month or year. There were countless brothers, sisters, uncles, aunties, nephews, nieces, step-relatives and in-laws who came and went at random times throughout the day. The whole family enthralled me.

Things got really bad in the run-up to Christmas. I got nicked for grafting in Marks and Sparks and received another £250 fine. I only nicked a tray of porterhouse steak, but I also happened to have a pair of £80 jeans in my possession and no receipt. A sign behind the custody desk in the police station proclaimed: 'Only 12 more shoplifting days to Christmas.' It remains one of the few pieces of evidence I've ever seen that the Babylonians have a sense of humour. They went steady on me in court, because I wasn't a known shoplifter. Another offence in quick succession, however, would mean that I was a known shoplifter. I could then expect the maximum punishment that the law would allow – and draconian was not the word. I had to lay off it for a while and, in short, the money dried up. In mid-December, in the middle of winter, in an all-electric flat, the electric company unceremoniously cut off the electricity.

Christmas was pretty shit that year, although the candles were atmospheric.

'Did you get anything nice from the fat, unshaven, mythical mince pie eater invented by Coca-Cola?' Sparky wrote in the New Year. 'Let's hope 98 is better than 97, eh? I think they pawned us off with a used year last year instead of a new one. Not much happening this end. Don't suppose my case will ever come to court. I wouldn't mind so much if I knew what my sentence was, then I could get my head down and do it. It's the not knowing. Tasha's all that keeps me going. Don't know what I'd do without her.'

His case had been dragging on interminably. He'd been away eight months and in court a dozen times, but still the Crown Prosecution Service hadn't been able to get all his papers together. Sparky, previously so full of life, was getting more and more depressed by it all. The lawyers and barristers didn't seem to mind, though. Some of them were claiming eighty pounds an hour from the Legal Aid system and charging forty for every letter they sent out. They were even bigger robbers than the banks. 'This letter is to remind you that we haven't written to you for some time. Please contact us if you have any new thoughts. Find us at Chez Truffles most nights of the week after work.' Sparky thought that the courts, the police and the lawyers were all on the same side. 'They all piss in the same pot,' he wrote.

I was on talking terms with one of the lawyers. At some point I must have decided to attend if one of the kids was in court, which meant, of course, that I was attending court several times a week. Nearly all the kids were with the same law firm, which specialised in juvenile offenders. They had one young lawyer who was pretty damn good at his job and that's something I admire in a person. His name was Adrian Perriwinkle. He stuck up for the kids and worked hard on their behalf. He did such good work that he was mentioned in official Ashtrayland dispatches and was awarded the title of consultant shit-talker to the crew. He nudged me one time, and said, 'Do you know you're the only person in Leeds who's in juvenile court more than I am?' I quite liked the guy, even if he was one of them. Thus are bridges built between nations.

Pinky and Thieving Little Simpkins were both excluded from school early in '98, Pinky for knocking someone out and Thieving Little Simpkins for saying something to one of the teachers. After that, they went into some kind of mad phase, the likes of which I have seldom seen before or since. Pinky went mad for the white stuff and Thieving Little Simpkins went mad for the brown stuff. It wasn't long before Pinky had a new set of friends who were all party animals, while Thieving Little Simpkins had a new set of friends who were just animals, plain and simple. The Whiteheads and Brownheads are the two distinct and easily recognisable sub-groups of modern youth culture. Both are mutually exclusive. Nevertheless, Pinky and Thieving Little Simpkins stayed friends because some things are more important than others.

As I saw it, the situation with drugs was akin to the prohibition of alcohol in 1920s America. Prohibition caused the problems, not the booze. Gangsters were standing on the running-boards of cars in Detroit with machine-guns before anyone knew what had hit them. The prohibition of drugs in England at the end of the twentieth century was having a similar effect. It was never wise to ban people from doing as they pleased. In modern times, it wasn't even possible. It was a simple matter to buy drugs on the Internet, in the pub, outside the playground, or next door but one. Booze, drugs, fags, whatever, you have to choose for yourself whether or not to use them. Nicotine is ten times more addictive than heroin yet cigarettes are legal. Prohibition of drugs only puts the trade into the hands of hardened criminals, who cut them to maximise the profit so that they become little better than poison. Why not regulate the trade, tax it and use the profit to educate people and help those who trip over the edge into addiction? Why can't pigs fly?

The Eastie contingent were plodding along as always. Molly and Urban split early in the new year. Molly wasn't happy about Urban sharing his bed with Trudi and, generally, they had grown apart. The divorce was amicable and happened almost without anyone noticing. Molly was now going out with Colin Parker from East Park Mount and couldn't have been happier.

Urban had been two-timing Molly for quite a while with Teezer. He brought her up one Sunday to meet the girls and she soon became part of the family. She was shy and retiring at first, but you knew she was putting it on. She had a suppressed smile going on that gave the game away. She'd been in care since she was three and had survived well. Long-term kids with stable placements can prosper. She'd met Urban once or twice over the years, but always thought him a bit of a div. Then he'd jumped into bed with her one night at the Safe House, surprised her with his fervour and she'd loved him ever since. She communicated mostly by means of combined movements of the eyes and eyebrows, an effective form of communication that was easy to understand. She was half English and half West Indian with a beautiful dark olive skin. Slimmer than the slimmest of supermodels, she was tall and perfectly proportioned with fashionably spiky hair and all the latest gadgetry and accoutrements, like a real live Barbie doll. Even at thirteen she was a stunner. She and Urban were happy and they were staying out of trouble, so I gave them the usual lectures and let them get on with it.

Kara, on the other hand, was a lone outlaw on the run. The Education Welfare was on her case and she was fighting a valiant battle to defeat them. Her EW officer was taking her to school every morning and she was devising ever more ingenious ways to escape. Observe her school at nine fifteen in the morning and you might see her shimmying down drainpipes, scurrying along passageways or back-crabbing against walls to avoid the cameras. She wouldn't stay in school and that was that. I let her doss at the flat the odd afternoon and we got quite chatty. She was really getting into her poetry and was turning out some excellent stuff.

Sam and Pixie, meanwhile, were just beginning their criminal careers. East End Park had deteriorated into nothing short of a war zone, with twockers having wacky races up and down the streets at night, and children sniffing glue and having orgies in the midden yards. The police didn't even bother to turn up any more. Half the estates in Britain were the same and the Babylonians were snowed under. Sam and Pixie had come to the attention of the juvenile-delinquency industry, so I left them to it. They still terrified me and I was glad to see that someone else had picked up the hot potato.

Stella's branch of the family was the biggest worry. They were on gear, gear was expensive and that made them grafters. Grafters are like robotic crime-machines. They get up in the morning needing gear. Gear costs fifteen pounds, so they need fifteen pounds and they need it quick. Anything that came within their range of vision was fair game. Your car window wasn't safe, whole shelves were cleared at supermarkets, workmen up ladders came down to find their tools gone, kids were accosted in the street for their phones and trainers, and your garden gnomes were abducted while you slept.

So some of the kids were doing all right and some of them were doing shit, but each and every one of them was surviving. They were all still alive. That was the main thing. That was the level we were at.

EIGHTEEN
TOWER BLOCK BLUES

It kicked off again last night at half past eight:
All screaming and shouting, voices so full of hate,
Kids running riot smashing up the block.
I rang the cops but I could have been talking to a rock.
No way to avoid it, there was nothing I could do,
But suffer in silence these tower block blues.

See the walls are so thin here you can hear every sound
And as for a refuge, there's not one around.
It was the weekend and the drop-in was closed;
Didn't have any coin so the pub was no go.
No way to avoid it, there was nothing I could do,
But try to blot out these tower block blues.

Well I awoke this morning my whole body on fire
And getting a shotgun was my fervent desire.
Act out a movie, call it Death Wish 12 –
Blow away the dead-heads that make my life hell.
No way to avoid it; there was nothing I could do.
I was sick of living these tower block blues.

Manx Kippers
Oh yeah

As the New Year got into its stride, a couple of things started
going our way. It seemed that way, but you never could tell.
Sometimes what appeared to be good news turned out to be

quite the opposite, and vice versa. I'd settled into a kind of siege mentality. Yes, it was hard. Yes, the enemy was strong. And yes, there were even more dark days ahead, but together we would see it through to the end. I just focused on each task and dealt with one thing at a time. The most important thing was that I was able to get Urban some education. Bits of new money were coming into the inner cities for small-scale experimental projects, but that was better than nothing. I read in the paper that the Mandela Centre in Chapeltown had received funding for an unorthodox education project, aimed at kids who were excluded from mainstream schools. I rang them immediately and tried to refer the boy. I didn't hold out much hope, but it was always worth trying your luck.

Urban wasn't really eligible to attend, to tell the truth, but careless talk costs lives. Theoretically, the project was for people living in the Chapeltown geographical area, but when I rang them the person I spoke to said they couldn't take Urban 'because he's white'. I had them and they knew it. I threatened to kick up such a storm and fuss over their institutionalised racism that they wouldn't know what hit them. I promised to picket the project every day, to bombard the media with letters and petitions and go to the European Court of Human Rights if necessary. In the end I think they gave him a place to shut me up. Okay, he was the only white kid there, but that bothered neither him nor me. Qualified teachers were teaching him and that was all that mattered.

In such circumstances a lesser white boy might have been bullied. Whites had oppressed blacks for centuries, and now that the tide had turned, some of the meaner kids were keen to get their own back, but Urban was strong both physically and mentally and gave as good as he got. Several factors contributed to him gaining the acceptance of his peers. He had been seen around when his mum lived in Chapeltown: his face was known on the streets, he was safe. Also, he was going out with Teezer, who was originally from the area and who all the boys fancied. Teezer's real dad was a prominent West Indian bad boy. Her mum, although white, had had several relationships with black men and was as fierce as any Zulu warrior. No one messed with her. Teezer had inherited many of her mother's qualities and stuck up for her man at every opportunity. The only thing that caused Urban any real trouble was the fact that his trainers weren't up to scratch. An investment of seventy-five pounds in a new pair of Nike's soon gave him the required foot-credibility and he settled down to his studies.

After a couple of weeks, I rang to check how he was doing. I thought they might take it out on him because I'd been such an obnoxious bastard. In the event, they loved him. The bloke whose life I had previously made a misery I now knew to be Mr Jackson, a respected and honoured teacher of the youth. 'It's amazing,' he said. 'Urban uses metaphor in everyday speech. I asked him what it was like not to be able to read and write. He said, "I feel like a blind man without a white stick." He comes out with words that the other kids have never heard of. Don't you think that's amazing?'

'It is,' I agreed. 'So he's doing all right, then?'

'Yeah,' Mr Jackson said. 'It's a tragedy he's missed so much schooling. He's as sharp as a knife.'

'He is,' I said. 'You don't know what this means to us. Keep up the good work, Mr Jackson, and let me know if you have any problems with him, will you?'

'Will do,' he said.

And that was that. Urban was in a school of sorts and he was doing well. Miracles never ceased.

Things weren't going quite so well at home. I'd had several run-ins with Urban over his behaviour and attitude. When he first came to stay with me, he wet the bed almost every night. I didn't make a fuss as it seemed understandable, given his previously unsettled lifestyle. It had eased off and eventually stopped as he became more comfortable and confident that our relationship was long-term. He had a relapse at this time, however, which I put down to the stress of starting a new school. In fact, it was down to his continuing sniffing problem. He rolled in one Saturday night glued up out of his eyeballs. He even came up in the lift with his glue-bag in hand and frightened the neighbours. He wet the bed that night and I realised that the pattern was related to his sniffing, not schooling. I felt I had to do something so I grounded him for a week.

I felt a grim satisfaction at grounding him, I must admit. He thought I was joking, but I was perfectly serious. I was finally taking my responsibilities as a foster-parent seriously.

He served half his sentence voluntarily, then ran off to the Safe House in protest at my cruelty. The issue developed into a minor battle of wills between us. He hadn't done much wrong, relatively speaking, but having handed out my first ever punishment I felt it important that he accepted my 'parental' authority. If I didn't stick to my guns, I could never hope to control him in the future. He stayed at the Safe House for a week. Then they rang to ask if he could come home. I said he could come home only if and when he agreed to complete his punishment. They were getting him to school every morning and Mr Jackson assured me that he was continuing to progress, so I let the game play itself out. Another week passed, then Urban finally agreed to let me have my own way. He came home and we carried on as if nothing had happened. He served the rest of his sentence without complaint. I'd won the battle if not the war.

Kids need limits. They'll kick against them until they're blue in the face, but secretly they quite like them. Children aren't so disruptive and unruly, so nervous, so frightened, when they know someone has things under control and is looking out for their interests. A similar relationship probably exists between a citizen and his or her government.

My finances were also improving. Madge's boyfriend was called Daz. In many ways he was a typical Beestonite – a drinker, a smoker, a gambler and a brawler. He was completely the opposite of Madge in every respect. The two were like chalk and cheese. Nevertheless, he had a heart of gold. He admired what I was doing with Urban and took me under his wing. He worked at the Barnbow weapons factory in Cross Gates where they made Chieftain tanks. He had two kids, an ex-wife and the Child Support Agency were fleecing him. Angry at the injustice of it all, he had devised a little sideline at work to earn himself extra beer tokens. He operated the same philosophy as me: they screw us so we screw them back at every opportunity. Every time he left the factory, he took a rucksack full of metal with him. Sometimes they sent him out in the van, in which case he took a van full of metal with him. None of us knew what the metal was called. We only knew you got five quid a kilo for it at the scrappers. It was some kind of fancy alloy. It might have been nuclear-tipped uranium for all I knew. I didn't care. Beggars can't be choosers. I called it Bokonium in honour of the Great God Bokono and left it at that. It was my job to take it down to be weighed when we had a good load. Daz couldn't do it in case he was seen. It would have cost him his job and his reputation. He knew that, if collared, I wouldn't grass. The operation earned me fifty to a hundred pounds a week. Okay, it wasn't strictly legal and I knew I was storing up trouble for the future, but it solved the immediate crisis and put food on the table. Honesty is for rich people. The poor can't afford it.

Daz also donated a stolen ex-Ministry of Defence computer to the cause, which got us on to the Internet, or t'Internet as we called it locally. The first thing I did was type in 'dyslexia' – only to find that it was a little understood condition and, even when recognised, there were no readily accessible public resources available to do anything about it. To get help, you had to be lucky or rich. The website did mention that Richard Branson was dyslexic, which, I suspect, was meant to give you hope. Richard Branson didn't need to read and write. He had Joeys to do it for him.

The second thing I did was type in 'Bokono' – only to find, to my very great astonishment, that there really was a Great God Bokono. Bokono was a fully recognised voodoo god in the West African Republic of Benin, formerly known as Dahomey. This was a revelation to me. It was one of those incredible facts of nature that occur against such odds and only after such a wild combination of events and coincidences that it's impossible to believe them.

Urban couldn't have known about Bokono and Bokono couldn't have existed purely by coincidence. Something was going on. This had been my theory all along and here was my proof. With this convoluted logic, I convinced myself that it was Urban's and my mission to start a new religion. Ashtray-land was dying because there were no religious or spiritual values in the underclass any more. Christianity had shot its bolt. Islam was too confrontational and too hard on the living flesh. The Indo-Chinese religions were too vague. Judaism was too exclusive. Communism, my native religion from birth, was a discredited failure, probably for the very reason that it lacked a spiritual component. The only solution was to start something new, something original, something suitable for the coming new age.

Bokononism was the obvious solution. Britain was in a unique position in the world. Because of our empire and our history, we had gathered together in our small islands a representative cross-section of all the peoples of the world. It was time to take the best bits from them all and build something delicious: the spirituality of the Hindus, the community spirit and family ties of the Muslims, the ancient wisdom of the Chinese, the love of freedom and equality of the Afro-Caribbeans, the work ethic of the Jews, the bloody-mindedness and wry humour of the Australians, the blarney of the Irish, the passion of the Scots, the unorthodoxy of the Welsh, combined with our own English love of justice, fair play and democracy. Put them all together and you had a vision for the future, a direction, which Bokononism could exploit.

Our first prophet would be Burnam Burnam, who landed at Dover in 1988, the year of Australia's bicentenary, planted the Aborigine flag under the White Cliffs and claimed these islands for the Aboriginal peoples of Australia, declaring, 'We wish no harm to England's native people. We are here to bring you good manners, refinement and an opportunity to make a *koompartoo*, a fresh start.' That was what we needed. A fresh start.

I wasn't sure if I really believed in Bokono or not and I wasn't sure that it mattered either way. Any religion is 90 per cent bullshit, 10 per cent compassion, common sense and basic human decency. Bokononism at least recognised itself as bullshit. I therefore found it preferable to any other religion and it was a genuine comfort to me in my everyday life. I felt that I had resolved my mother's Christianity with my father's socialism. The Tories had become Compassionate Conservatives while we had become Caring Communists. Maybe there was hope, after all. Also, Bokononism was something Urban and I could share. We had a little proverb for every occasion: 'Bokono knows best', 'Bokono will provide', 'Bokono, him say, man with hand in pocket feel cocky all day.' We had invented our own particular brand of Bokononism together and it brought us much fun and many a good laugh over the years.

I did make one small strategic error around this time.

During my researches into the Great God Bokono, I discovered that there already was an organised Bokononist religion. I typed 'Bokononist' into the net instead of 'Bokono' and found that it was the religion on the fictitious West Indian island of San Lorenzo. A real-life cult following had since developed. Clearly, Urban and I had merely been tapping into the mass consciousness. There was a new kid on the block as far as gods were concerned and soon the world would have to sit up and take notice. The error I made was to get too involved with Bokononist customs and culture.

The whole thing was based on a cult science fiction book, *Cat's Cradle*, by Kurt Vonnegut. In Bokononism everyone belongs to a *karass*, which is like the group you belong to. A *granfaloon* is a false *karass* – say, like nation or religion. A *wampeter* is the pivot of a *karass* – say, like Urban. I related to all this, because it explained my relationship to Urban and the crew. My *granfaloon* was my left-wing politics. Bokono, him say, politics irrelevant. There are certain Bokononist practices that the islanders of San Lorenzo indulge in, among them the rite of *Boko-maru*. Bokononists believe that it's impossible not to love someone once you have touched the soles of your feet together. My error was playing *Boko-maru* with Natasha.

Boko-maru really does work and Natasha and I became over-familiar. Lying on the settee, facing one another, watching telly, I massaged her feet while my foot rested on her inner thigh. Harmless enough, I thought. We had developed such a warm, cosy, family atmosphere in the flat that everyone lazed around all the time like contented cats. There were others in the room and there was nothing sexual about it, but it was inappropriate touching all the same, and Sparky wasn't going to like it when he heard about it.

My new-found wealth, courtesy of Daz and the MoD, meant that I could get out and about a bit more while Urban was at school. I hadn't been to Stella's for a while, largely because I was still working hard to straighten up my act. Urban and I wanted to change the world. We had decided that the only way to change the world was to change ourselves. If everyone did this then the world, by definition, would change of its own accord. I was trying to cut out some of the drugs, even at the cost of enjoying myself, while Urban had agreed to stop sniffing, even at the cost of losing direct communication with the High Lord Zombulglast. While no one ever said that changing the world was going to be easy, I was only human. Like the ship on my mother's plate, I was buffeted and tossed around in a stormy ocean of insanity. I did my best, but sometimes my resolve weakened and I needed the occasional day off. I felt I'd earned one, so I headed for Stella's with a clear conscience.

I took large quantities of drugs and finally managed to get Stella into bed, which relieved much of the tension I'd been feeling. As I massaged her back, she brought me up to date with events. The sub-crew were no longer with her. 'The' nicked forty quid out o' me draw' so I hoofed 'em out. That wa' tight as fuck after all I've done for 'em, little bastards. They're bad on t'gear now, Chop. Worse than I ever wa'. They get through half a dozen bags a day between 'em. Rocks an' all. Not just smack. One of each, ev'ry time. Them rocks is worst thing ever invented. They're out ev'ry day grafting. The' dote give a fuck no more. Mucky Moira's on t'batter, Skeet's doin' muggin's an' street robberies, an' Frank's shoplifting. They're just plain crazy now, Chop. I cun't handle 'em no more, I'll be honest.'

'Bad news,' I said. 'Where are they staying?'

'Dote know. Down your way, last I heard. Lincoln Green somewhere wi' someone called Lucy. Lucy Screwloose, Moira calls her.'

'Bad news,' I said. 'Very bad news indeed.'

Finding them was harder than I'd imagined it would be. I'd

thought I inhabited the very lowest social stratum, but I was wrong. I was merely the lowest of the low; the sub-crew were subterranean. They had descended so low that they were out of my reach. I kept hearing rumours that they were in Lincoln Green, but they were only rumours. There were about twenty blocks of flats on the estate, scattered liberally between mine (the posh end of Lincoln Green) and the town centre. They looked similar to the municipal blocks in Chechnya that you saw on the news. Many of the flats were empty, the windows boarded up or broken, the lifts smashed and inoperative. The estate had a reputation as a dumping ground for the dregs of society. I had little doubt that the sub-crew were down there somewhere, but finding them was another matter. Many of the residents were heavily armed and they didn't take kindly to people who asked too many questions.

Urban would blend in better than I, so I sent him down to see what he could find out. He came back in a right old state. A 'foreign-looking bloke' had offered to help him. He helped by inviting Urban into his flat, locking the door and then pro-positioning him for gay sex. Urban put the television through the window and escaped only by climbing down from the third-floor balcony. 'There's that many rent-boys and prossies down there, they must think everyone's at it,' he complained. We didn't report the incident to the police. It was the kind of everyday occurrence that they couldn't be bothered with. No point troubling them with trivialities.

There was still no sign of them by February. Girls' night had gone out of fashion, but I held a special one as it seemed the best way to get everyone together. I figured that someone must know something. The Eastie contingent turned up, along with Thieving Little Simpkins, Natasha and Trudi. Thieving Little Simpkins had lost weight and was showing the first signs of heroin use. I asked her about it, but she denied everything. There wasn't much I could do, so I let sleeping dogs lie. Pinky didn't show at all as she had a better *soirée* to go to. The crew were growing up and growing apart.

The Eastie contingent didn't know anything about the sub-crew. They were clinging desperately to what remnants of community spirit existed in East End Park. This was their only chance and they knew it. Trudi was quiet and the bump was showing in her belly. Thieving Little Simpkins wasn't particularly interested in anything. She had a plan and she was sticking to it. 'I plan to survive,' she told me. 'We've lost Greta, Sparky, Tyson, Skeet and Frank so far. Who's next? Not me, I'll tell you that much. I got fucked up young so I know what it's like out there. It's evil, Chop. Desperate. All you can do is survive. Nothing more. That's the plan. You look after Urbie, Chop. I'll look after me. How does that sound?'

'Sounds about right to me,' I agreed. 'What about you, Natasha?' Natasha got on quite well with Skeeter, so I hoped she might know something.

'What about me?' she asked defensively.

'Do you know anything?'

'About what?'

'About Skeet and Frank? The sub-crew? What do you think we're talking about?'

'Oh,' she said. 'No, nothing.' She didn't seem her normal self.

'Anything the matter?' I asked.

'Nowt, really. It's just that Sparky might be getting out. I can't stop thinking about it.' She told us that Sparky had written to her. He was in court soon. His papers were in such disarray that Mr Perriwinkle thought they would have to let him go. Natasha ran on the spot sitting down to show her excitement and anticipation at the prospect.

I finally tracked down the sub-crew in early March. They were living in a block of flats just along the road from Lucifer Towers. Trudi had known their whereabouts all along, but had kept it to herself. Loyalty was her middle name. The sub-crew didn't want to be found, and if the sub-crew didn't want to be found, finding them was no simple matter.

Trudi was approaching full-term and had come to ask a favour. Would I be with her at the birth? This was such a rare honour, such a vast mark of respect, that I was moved. It almost made all the years of hardship and torment worth-while. 'Why, Trudi,' I said, wiping a tear from my eye, 'I'd be honoured, but I really think you ought to ask a member of your family.'

'No,' she said. 'I want you.'

How could I refuse? While we were being lovey-dovey, I asked her for a favour in return. I asked her where the sub-crew were and she told me. 'Down Chechnya,' she said. 'With Lucy Screwloose. I'll take you down there if you like.'

I'd seen some hovels in my time, I'd even lived in a few, but I'd never seen anything quite like Philadelphia Heights. Neither of the lifts was working, so Trudi and I had to walk up six flights of stairs. The stairwell was carpeted with human excrement, vomit and untold rubbish. The walls were papered with obscene graffiti. It made you ashamed to be a *Homo sapiens*. In Philadelphia Heights, as in the country as a whole, there was no sense of ownership, no sense of belonging, no sense of community. A shrivelled old lady tutted and shook her head as she passed us on the stairs. I couldn't help but agree with her. I nodded and pursed my lips in reply. No words were necessary. I knew what she was thinking. She'd worked hard, paid her taxes and fought off the Nazis to earn this ignoble end to her life. She felt sorry for today's young people. They were ignorant and uncivilised and they knew no better. No one cared about anything any more. The change from a low-wage-low-price economy to a high-wage-high-price economy had not suited her, or me for that matter. We both belonged to another age, an age that would die with us. Mine was the last generation. A new age was coming, for better or worse. I had no doubt about that. And the death throes of the old age would not be pretty.

On the sixth floor, we approached the flat along a narrow balcony overlooking the Kremlin, the Government's ominous DSS headquarters, which overlooked our estate. The carpet in the hall there had cost fifty grand and all the jobs went to Cockneys, which was good for the local economy in that the prostitutes prospered, but other than that there was no communication with our estate whatsoever. They lazed about in Turkish baths while we languished in abject poverty. The sense of oppression was heavy. The kitchen and bathroom windows of the flat faced on to the balcony. Both were boarded up. The door looked like it had been kicked in and repaired on several occasions. Trudi knocked and a sallow-faced Frank answered. He was no longer plump but thin as a rake. His voice was croaky. 'Aw right, Chop? How's it looking? What you been up to? What's happening?'

Good questions all.

If anything, the inside of the flat was worse than the outside. There was no excrement or vomit but there were cups full of spit, ghastly stains on the carpets and furniture, needles and burnt spoons all over the place, and lice big enough to be seen by the naked eye, no microscope necessary. I hesitate to call the carpets and furniture 'carpets' and 'furniture'. 'Dross' would be a better word. The whole place was so outstandingly filthy and disgusting, such a disgrace to humanity, that it awakened some sleeping race memory deep within me. It must have been how we as a species had lived before the Stone Age.

'Wow!' I said, looking around, trying to take it all in. '*Chic*. Bohemian. Pre-Jurassic. I like it. I like it a lot. Mind if I take a look round?'

'Feel free,' Frank said. 'Want a cuppa?'

'Erm, no, no, thank you. I'm all right, Frank, thanks all the same.' If I was going to catch Aids or hepatitis B, I at least wanted the sexual satisfaction beforehand. A cup full of spit is no Holy Grail.

Frank waved a demonic striped cup at Trudi. 'What about you, Trude?'

'Four sugars, please,' she replied.

'We haven't got no sugar.'

'Stick it up your arse, then, you nonce.'

'Well, fuck you, you slut.'

'Fuck off, knobhead.'

'Shut up, trollop.' With Frank and Trudi, the more things changed the more they stayed the same.

I took a look round while they were arguing. Tracey Emin had nothing on this place, or Damien Hirst. The whole flat was a work of art. I opened the kitchen door, half expecting to see a cow pickled in formaldehyde, but it was even more startling in its bareness: no cooker, no fridge, no washer, no plates, no food, just a kettle, a Breville toasted-sandwich machine, a bag of acetic acid, a candle, another burnt spoon and lots and lots of filth. The bathroom was equally barren, the most interesting feature being the torn bits of newspaper hung up beside the cistern, something I hadn't seen since childhood. Another race memory was evoked, of cold nights in the midden yard, shrivelled testicles and arse-wipe – as my dad called it – like sandpaper. I found Skeeter in the master bedroom, hemmed in between Mucky Moira and an andro-gynous creature with whiteman dreadlocks and multiple pier-cings of the face who I took to be Lucy Screwloose, all three dead to the world even though it was four o'clock in the afternoon. The walls told how Lucy Screwloose had earned her nickname. 'Oblivion' was plastered large and small over every spare inch of wall space. *Oblivion. Oblivion. Oblivion.* That was all it said. Over and over again. Everywhere. I found it immensely disturbing.

Oblivion. That was what it was all about. That was what everyone was seeking. In that moment I knew with complete certainty that one day I would die, as would all mankind. We were not immortal. We were merely a transitory and temporary phenomenon, no more than a trick of the light.

I made another mistake that night. I had my first dig with the sub-crew. I no longer cared about the rights and wrongs of the situation. I just wanted to know what it was like, what the attraction was. My dad always said, 'Try everything once. If tha dun't like it, tha dun't have to do it agen, does tha?' Tried it. Didn't like it. I had often trodden around the edges of oblivion. I had never been right down there inside the black hole. All I remember is the fear. A bottomless, hopeless pit of fear and despair. It frightened the life out of me. I will never go there again.

NINETEEN
CHILDHOOD'S END

Smoking crack?
You'll be back.
Think I'm joking?
Keep on smoking.

Mucky Moira
Open 4 biz

A series of life-changing events struck around Easter '98. I'm not sure what was going on. Maybe the planets were aligning, or the Age of Bokono was upon us, or it was the time that the Aztecs called *Apachakuti* – the world turned upside-down. Everyone in the Shed Crew, the neighbourhood and probably the world at large was affected by the seismic events that followed. Had I been religious in the traditional sense, I might have mistaken Easter '98 for Armageddon. As the century neared its close, all manner of nutcases and fruitcakes were prophesying the end of the world. My money was on a meteor hitting us from space, although I wasn't convinced that the bookies would be around to pay out afterwards if I won.

It's hard to recall the exact sequence of events. Blow followed blow, one after the other, like gigantic hailstones raining down on our heads. I had no sooner recovered from one before the next hit, leaving me dizzy and anaesthetised. I must therefore relate the events as they have been etched into my subconscious, as I can't guarantee to get everything in precisely the right order. Basically the kids had been storing up trouble for years and it was time to pay the piper.

Sparky kind of summed it all up. He got out of jail towards the end of March and he was back inside again by early May. He got away with the GBH, because the police and the Crown Prosecution Service had cocked up his papers. The judge got fed up and threw the case out of court, which was jolly nice of the old boy. This was one of the rare occasions when the incompetence of our public servants worked in our favour, so no one was complaining. There was even the suspicion that the scuffers had messed up on purpose, because secretly they thought that Sparky had done right.

Sparky went straight back to his old ways, enjoying himself and doing what came naturally: twocking, drinking, fighting and fucking, glad to be alive and free – aware that he was alive and free! He and Natasha were in a kind of love-hate relation-ship, which was up and down like a yo-yo but they seemed happy enough. He did have a bone to pick with me, though, and it was a matter of what I thought I'd been doing with Natasha on the settee that time. 'Eh?'

That 'eh?' always worried me. I tried to explain, but I'd broken one of the unwritten rules and we both knew it. 'Fucking hell, Sparky. Give me a break. There's Trudi and Molly and even Moira if I was desperate. So I pick Tash to nonce up, do I, knowing you're right behind her with a car full of lads with baseball bats? Am I really that thick?' I often had to explain to friends, family and neighbours what the kids were doing in my life. Conversely, they had to explain to friends, family and interested officials what *I* was doing in *their* lives. If I looked like a nonce, they looked like fools. I had to be above suspicion. Sparky had put a great deal of his faith and trust in me and I had let him down.

'Know something?' he asked. 'You're the hardest bloke in the world to hit. That's my bird, Chop. My fucking bird!'

'I know, but—'

Bang!

He gave me one in the eye, quick-time, before I could talk him round. He stormed off, but came back a few days later with his mate Spurry. I thought they'd come to do me over properly this time, but they took me out to the pub instead and violently ripped the piss out of me all night long. 'Foot-fucking perverted silly nonce. We'll have to get him a proper lay, Spurry. All the frustration must be getting to him,' etc., etc. I sported a smashing black eye for a couple of weeks and we left it at that. Sparky and I agreed that the punishment had fitted the crime and the matter was closed.

Sparky was no longer a boy. He had filled out nicely in prison and looked healthier than I'd ever seen him. At seventeen he was taller and stronger than I was, and he had much more money than I did. His mates had progressed from twocking cars to hijacking lorries and were into some serious crime. It was no longer appropriate for me to ask what they were up to. It was on a need-to-know basis. He told me that he and Natasha were trying for a baby and that was why he didn't need any doubts about who else she was messing with. I felt honoured that he considered me a threat. Unfortunately, he got thrown back into jail after a job went wrong and someone got their head stoved in. Sparky was a proud recidivist who boasted that they couldn't 'break' him. He did get Natasha pregnant before rejoining Her Majesty on remand, so life-changing events were becoming almost an everyday thing. I wasn't sure how long he was looking at, but I was laying seven to four that the baby would have been born before he got out. 'That's just how these love-hate relationships with criminals go,' Natasha told me, as they escorted Sparky from the dock.

The foot business had changed things a bit. My halo had slipped. I wasn't perfect, after all. This subtly altered the way the kids behaved with me. They were slightly worse, but no more than that. Possibly they were exactly the same, but were less worried about showing me their worst excesses because I was now officially as bad as they were. For my own part, I took it on board that no one is perfect, least of all me.

I think the Moira implosion came next. The Chief Insect Lord turned his full fury on her and she lost it completely. She was last seen running down Spencer Place in the heart of the red-light district in only her knickers and bra, screaming and waving her arms about, hair streaming in the wind. The police thought she'd been raped and arrested her for her own protection. The tale was that she grabbed the copper's hand and thrust it down her knickers. 'Get it out! Get it out! It's gone down there! A big black cockroach-type thing! Aaarrrgh!' They took her away in the little green van to the white room with padded walls and that was the last any of us ever saw of her. Poor Moira. She never had a chance. She had a first-class case of crack psychosis and was a clear example to the other kids of where that road led. Crack is dangerous. Instantly addictive, moreish on a cosmic scale, physically and psychologically damaging, dangerous even to acquire and an insane way to burn money, it's one drug that needs leaving well alone. Smack pales into insignificance beside it.

Having said that, the smackheads were also being called upon to pay their tab. Skeeter and Frank both caught the tail-lash of events. Both were collared for nasty little crimes, just when the Government was clamping down on exactly that sort of unruly behaviour by young thugs. Frank had avoided prison thus far because he wasn't violent. He was an amiable buffoon, a shoplifter, a beggar and a general all-round nuisance, but in no way a danger to anyone. Then, to get money to pay for drugs, he snatched an elderly lady's handbag outside a post office. She'd been in the war so she held on tenaciously. Frank pulled her along the pavement for a few yards. That was violence and the term 'aggravated' was added to his charge sheet. Even then, they might have gone easy on him had he owned up and shown remorse. He did no such thing. He pleaded not guilty, made them call all the witnesses, dragged the case on for days and probably cost them the price of a small home in court costs. He was given three years' custody for his trouble. Skeeter, on the other hand, guilty of a savage attack on an Asian's face with a brick, owned up and showed remorse, kept it cheap and got away with eighteen months. There was no such thing as justice, just luck.

Thieving Little Simpkins also copped it. She'd been taking one of each with a different crowd, 'one of each' being 'an item' of whisky and 'an item' of brandy, or a white and a brown, or a bag of crack and a bag of smack. Crack users nearly always end up on heroin as it's the only thing that can bring them down from the crack. Conversely, smack-users nearly always end up on crack, because the two things always go together. Thieving Little Simpkins was trapped in this vicious circle and it was getting her into trouble. She was racking up shoplifting offences like they were going out of fashion, until eventually the judge cried, 'Enough!' She got to spend a year with a crowd of murderous lesbians for her endeavours – life-changing by anyone's standards.

Only Pinky seemed immune to the dangers of drugs. Like me, she used drugs to examine the other side of her nature but never allowed them to dominate her psyche. She selected them like a child selects sweets. She was a Giro-junkie, who went mad when she had money, but managed to cope the rest of the time without drugs or money until the next Giro popped through the door. She had brains and she was doing all right. She was living in Wortley with two other girls and they raved, raved, raved, shagged, shagged, shagged, and party, party, partied all the time. I'll say one thing for the rave culture – they certainly know how to enjoy themselves. Pinky and I had become great friends, so we kept in touch, but she had grown apart from the rest of the crew. She was much the same as the other kids, but lacked their self-destructive instinct. She was intelligent, intuitive and had a more solid family background than the rest. I felt that she would negotiate the rapids, come fair weather or foul.

Next, I was rocked by a bitter personal blow. I lost my friend Cooch to a brain haemorrhage. She just dropped dead in the street as she was walking along. She was thirty-seven. With the foot thing and Stella and everything, I had decided that it was time to find a steady girlfriend and Cooch was at the top of my list. I'd known her for most of my adult life. We met when she was going out with a mate of mine from the chess club. I was going out with someone else, but we often met as couples. I always liked Cooch and she liked me. We'd been friends ever since and often socialised. I just loved her. She was the funniest, most alive person I ever knew, but she drank quite a lot and landed herself in a string of violent and abusive relationships. When she died, we all wondered how much they had contributed to her death.

Cooch was drink culture through and through, but the drink and drug culture was becoming a nightmare, destroying families, health, job prospects and relationships in our decimated communities. I was probably typical of the area. I talked a lot about quitting drink and drugs and sometimes I made an effort to do it, but my resolve seldom lasted more than a few days. It was hard to change. I'd been drinking heavily since my teens and I lived in the middle of a culture where everyone was the same. The only place I saw my dad regularly was in the working-men's club, where he more or less lived. If I wanted to get out of the house the only place to go was the pub. Manx Kippers, my best mate, was a chronic alcoholic, so I'd have a pint or three with him every day almost in passing. Even the chess club met on licensed premises. The Free Plasterers Social Club stayed open while anyone was drinking, which was pretty much all the time. The teetotal straight-heads went home at ten o'clock, but the seasoned veterans played – and drank – into the night. Drunken brawls in the early hours weren't unknown and the Doctor once needed five stitches after I hit him over the head with one of the big wooden match boards. There was no escape from the drink culture, but finding a way to change was becoming vital.

Cooch left two boys, Cormack, nineteen, and Joe, fifteen. Dad wasn't around much so both had long since looked to me as their adult male figure. I haven't mentioned them before as they were never part of the Shed Crew or the Penthouse Posse. Nevertheless, they were an important part of my circle of family and friends and henceforth they would be needing more of my time. Joe was at my flat the night his mother died. He met Urban through me and they had become friends. I got the call at four a.m. It was Cooch's sister. 'Chop, can you bring Joe over the hospital? His mum's in a bad way.' Some instinct told me that Cooch would not survive the night and guiding Joe through the grief process became my primary concern. Cormack would have to wait. He was in Doncatraz at the time, serving five years for armed robbery with a toy gun. Add all this together and the whole world, for me, had suddenly become a much more melancholy place.

Then something happened on the estate that changed things for ever, something so bad that it made the front pages of the newspapers and *News At Ten* and brought us into the national spotlight. It was nothing to do with the Penthouse Posse, but the similarities were so glaringly obvious that they couldn't be ignored. It was no longer enough to talk about change. Change had become a necessity. We were made to feel ashamed of ourselves. It was no longer possible to get up in the morning and look the world in the eye.

It began with a small article in the evening paper, a plea from a mother to her eighteen-year-old daughter, missing from the previous Wednesday. Molly and Kara brought the paper round and pointed it out to me. Molly, previously a frail waif and stray, had developed into a buxom teenager of fifteen; Kara, too, had become more shapely and feminine. Both were in the final year at school, which hardly seemed to matter as neither of them ever went. Molly was still getting drunk and shagging about in the park and Kara was increasingly strange, if not deranged, but on the whole they were doing all right.

Kara was becoming quite the radical feminist, refusing to be used as meat by the boys. 'Molly's like a kid in a sweet shop,' she told me. 'She thinks that because she can have any boy she wants she's got sexual freedom. Really, the boys have never had it so good. They're happy. They're charging around like bulls in a china shop.'

'Take no notice,' Molly responded. 'She doesn't say that when she's got half a dozen Es down her. She's worse than I am.'

The two of them took a keen interest in mispers, sensing perhaps that they might be next. On this occasion they were especially interested because they knew the missing girl. Her name was Angela Pearce and she came from East End Park. She was known to be not-quite-the-full-shilling, so most people let her be. It was understood that she was a neutral in the civil war that was going on, a non-combatant, an innocent civilian in what was slowly but surely becoming an armed conflict. The general consensus was that she had probably found herself a boyfriend and was sowing her wild oats. At worst, some nonce had her and was taking advantage of her naïvety.

I didn't take much notice at first. Missing girls were ten a penny in East End Park. The Penthouse Posse were only the tip of the iceberg. I didn't think anything of it.

Two days later, the girls spotted a more urgent headline: 'Police Step Up Search For Missing Girl'. The first article had been inaccurate. This one said that Angela had been missing for fifteen days. Her mum was worried sick. Her sister was frantic. Slim, five-foot-three, blonde Angela was said to have mental problems. She was on medication and could become 'incoherent, aggressive and unreasonable'. A perfectly normal Eastie Girl, by all accounts. She was fucked in the head, like us.

Molly didn't like it. 'I don't know,' she said. 'I don't know about this one. The sensible plan is to give yourself up when you get this sort of publicity. Why hasn't she come in?'

The following Monday we found out. Angela was dead. Her body had been discovered in a shallow grave. She'd taken a sustained beating for up to twenty-four hours. The police were appealing for anyone who knew anything to come forward.

Kara handed out the coffees as I flicked through the paper. 'Kara, would you say anything if you knew who it was? Say your boyfriend did it?'

'Fucking hell, yeah,' she said. 'Course I would. The no-grassers rule doesn't apply to murderers or sex monsters. If my boyfriend done it? Are you mad? Who do you think he'd be doing it to next? I'd be down the Bridewell quicker than you could microwave a fish.'

'A fish?' I queried.

'Yes, a fish,' she insisted.

On the Wednesday, we discovered that whatever it was that the world was coming to, it was coming to it right on our doorstep. The papers revealed that Angela had been savagely murdered in one of the blocks of flats in Lincoln Green and buried on the old rec down by the Kremlin. The girls sat on the floor in stunned silence as I read out the catalogue of atrocities. Angela had been abducted, robbed, imprisoned, locked in a cupboard, hit in the face with an iron and beaten with a pool cue; cigarettes were stubbed out on her face, her hair was set on fire and she was made to drink disinfectant. Finally, she'd had a plastic bag put over her head, then been strangled and buried.

If that wasn't bad enough, this wickedness hadn't been perpetrated by a lone individual, a crazed lunatic, but by a group of kids very much like the Shed Crew. Five young people had been arrested for Angela's murder, three girls and two boys, ranging in age from sixteen to twenty-two. The twenty-two-year-old male was getting most of the fingers pointed at him, but Kara thought she knew better. 'There's two girls,' she said. 'Sisters. Two is better than one. It makes you ten times stronger. They're the gaffers.'

We were reading between the lines. None of us knew the murderers. One had been given a flat on the estate, but no one had helped her establish her tenancy, no one had helped her make her slum habitable, no one had helped her with the money-eating electricity meter. She had therefore moved a little crew in to help her survive. They had no work, no prospects; they were on their own, outside the law, outside normal society. They were blaggers like us; but, unlike us, no one had taught them it was wrong to kill. It was clear to us that they'd taken Angela for a muppet or a Joey. But, in our vocabulary, this meant a victim, a dupe, a greenhorn, a touch, a mug, a sucker, a target, a quarry, not a kill.

They had got her in the net, planning to tax her, but something went wrong. They had gone overboard. Maybe jealousies or passions were involved. Maybe they were high on booze or drugs or glue. Maybe they'd got off on the power. Who knows? I'd seen the conditions they were living in and I knew what kind of kids they were. They were abandoned kids, and abandoned kids are capable of anything.

Finally, I understood that my time with the Shed Crew had not been wasted. Okay, they were all in jail, or in the mad house, or pregnant, but at least they knew where to draw the line. Sparky had battered Pixie's uncle half to death, but only half to death. Neither he nor Skeeter had crossed that final bridge. By being loyal and sticking with them through thick and thin, I had perhaps shown them that not everyone was the same. If only one person cares, it can make all the difference to an abandoned child.

I knew that, although there were similarities between the two groups, the Shed Crew could never have done such a thing. If anything even remotely like it was going on, half a dozen voices would have been raised in protest. If that didn't work, they'd pick up the nearest heavy item and whack the perpetrator over the head with it. They might have committed the odd manslaughter between them – accidents happen, after all – but never murder. When it came to the important things, the Shed Crew knew the difference between right and wrong. Some people didn't. It was as simple as that.

As individuals, we had to take some of the blame on ourselves. As someone outside the system, I saw the insiders taking me for a fool and a Joey, ripping me off, taking me to the cleaners. If that was the way the system worked, you were sometimes left with little choice but to rip someone else off who was weaker than you. Give these people a name, like muppet or Joey, and you had someone even lower down the social and evolutionary ladder than you – and you suddenly didn't feel quite so shit about yourself. We had developed a dog-eat-dog society, where it was every man for himself. No wonder kids were killing kids for kicks.

After almost two years with the Shed Crew, I managed to get my first legislation on to the statute book. I talked to them about it one by one. Rule number ten had previously read, 'No rapists or killers.' It was a simple matter to amend rule number two to read, 'No nonces, rapists or killers,' thus leaving the tenth spot free. Rule number ten then became: 'No keeping Joeys, slaves or muppets.' This, I believe, was Ashtrayland's greatest contribution to world culture, although I don't suppose the Americans or the capitalists will ever deign to sign up to it.

Sally's death affected us all, one way or another. It made us look at ourselves and see ourselves as we really were. We were a mess. A disgrace. Me, the Shed Crew, the neighbourhood, the nation. We couldn't even claim to be third world. We had degenerated into savages and Philistines. The civilisation created by the Greeks and Romans had ended with us, the British.

Fortunately, in the midst of all this chaos and disaster Urban continued to thrive. He was now fourteen and had grown more than a foot in the time I'd known him. He was in a school of sorts, he could read and write after a fashion, his sniffing was all but under control, he had a stable home life, or about as stable as it got in our neck of the woods, and he had a girlfriend who adored him. His mum rang occasionally and he made the effort to meet her, but he seldom stayed with her for more than an afternoon or an evening. She and I weren't seeing eye to eye and I wouldn't have her at the flat. He also had some contact with his eldest sister and his grandmother. All in all, he was becoming a proper little teenager. Like most of them, he only came home to get changed, have a bath, cadge money and empty the fridge. He seemed happy to be leading something approaching a normal life and it was evident that his only ambition was to enjoy it while it lasted. He'd missed out on so much that other people took for granted and he clawed it back whenever and wherever he could. He was even becoming educated in his own way, complaining that people were thick because they'd never heard of Enlightenment or Bokono. A fair improvement on the homeless urchin I had taken under my wing. He was confident, healthy and happy within himself. I was pleased with his progress but he had benefited from twenty-four-hour, round-the-clock social-work attention and surveillance, which I simply wasn't able to give them all.

Easter is normally associated with a death, but I remember Easter '98 for a birth. My godchild was born on 26 April, weighing in at a frail five pounds. Trudi had been sneaking off for the odd toot on the sly and the baby was a smackhead. The surgeon was an Asian woman, an artist who inspired awe in me. I watched as she cut the infant from Trudi's belly. I almost fainted, but Trudi squeezed my hand and reassured me that everything would be all right. The baby didn't cry. She rattled. They rushed her into the corner, gave her her first fix and then she was fine. Once she'd calmed down, I looked into her eyes as she gripped my finger. So much faith and trust and love in the eyes of one so new to the world – and we'd already betrayed her. That was when I changed for good. I knew I had a duty to do something to make the world a better place for her and others like her. It was time to end the war I'd been fighting for so many years, a war largely with myself, and get on with something useful.

Despite everything, I was quite enjoying life. Respect. That was Secret Ingredient 256. I'd never managed to glean much respect in my life, neither self-respect nor the respect of others, but suddenly I was getting respect everywhere I went, from the pub, to the Safe House, to the Chapeltown Exclusion Project. People who had previously whispered behind my back that I was a fat, stinking bastard were now whispering that I was a top bloke, a good'un, one of the best – and all because of Urban Grimshaw and the Shed Crew. Word had gone round. The word was that I was a decent human being who put others before himself. I was amazed at how much respect this got me, even in the underclass. Because of it, my many and various failings were overlooked, even forgiven, by friend and enemy alike.

I figured I was on to something. Here was a way through the

gathering storm. I couldn't control everything that happened in the world or be held responsible for it. All I could do was my best. People of good will I treated with good will. People of bad will I also treated with good will. In so doing, I grew in good will. No matter what happened, I resolved to treat my fellow creatures with decency and respect and to put my trust in Bokono. That was all I could do. Then, even if the world collapsed around me, and it showed every sign of doing exactly that, I would be able to hold my head high.

That was the plan. You had to have a plan. I'd learned that much from Thieving Little Simpkins.

TWENTY

THIS LAND OF
SUCH DEAR SOULS

This land of such dear souls, this dear dear land,
Dear for her reputation through the world,
Is now leased out – I die pronouncing it–
Like to a tenement or pelting farm.
England, bound in with the triumphant sea,
Whose rocky shore beats back the envious siege
Of wat'ry Neptune, is now bound in with shame,
With inky blots and rotten parchment bonds;
That England that was wont to conquer others,
Hath made a shameful conquest of itself.
Ah, would the scandal vanish with my life,
How happy then were my ensuing death!

William Shakespeare
The Immortal Bard

In the summer holidays, I found Urban a dentist. A seedy, back-street dentist, admittedly, but a dentist none the less. A dentist who didn't mind taking people on without paper-work, even though, strictly speaking, it wasn't legal. 'These teeth are a mess,' he said. 'We'll have to take about four out, knock the others back into shape with a mallet, lash them up with barbed wire and clamps for a year or two, and even then they won't be perfect because, quite frankly, they're already beyond repair. Are you sure you want to go through so much agony? You might be best off leaving them be.'

I looked into Urban's eyes. It had to be his decision. He pursed his lips and nodded. He would bear up under the strain. 'Yes,' I said to the dentist. 'Something has to be done to put things right.'

'Very well. See the receptionist, make an appointment and we'll get started ASAP. We'll have plenty of time to sort out the bureaucracy and red tape in due course.'

'You're a good man,' I said. 'The Order of the Golden Tooth will henceforth be our highest honour.'

The dentist looked baffled and checked that all the laughing-gas canisters were where they should be. 'Jolly good, then. Hope to see you soon.'

We were also making progress in other areas. Urban had had a relapse with his sniffing problem and was picked up by the law for walking around the town centre, glue bag in hand, shouting at people. He went up to a suit and tie with Teezer on one arm and Pixie on the other. 'Hey! You! You think you're fucking summat, don't you? You're fuck all, right? You might have a job and a car and a stripy suit, you bastard, but you haven't got two little spunkers like these to fuck every night, have you, you bastard, eh? That's why you're always going with prostitutes, innit, you dirty fucked-up nonce?' He kicked the bloke in the knackers and twocked his mobile phone.

Without going into the rights and wrongs of the situation, suffice to say that it got us into a juvenile court, where I was able to explain to the magistrate some of the difficulties we were facing. The magistrate was kind enough to put Urban on a two-year supervision order, which forced Social Services to take a hand. They sent Mr Ko back to us, because they couldn't have people like me deciding who was a good social worker and who wasn't, and we made up our differences. With his help, I was able to get benefits for Urban, if not a fostering allowance, which could only be given to good, normal, decent people who didn't take drugs and therefore didn't have criminal records. The Social Services' records, such as they were, enabled us to pinpoint some of the hundreds of places where Greta had lived, and after a protracted search we tracked down Urban's medical records. I was then able to register him with the local quack and get him the inoculations he should have had when he was five. There wasn't a school in the land that would touch him with a bargepole, but the Pupil Referral Unit were happy to accept a referral from Mr Ko, provided I promised not to go anywhere near the place and not to ring them up making abusive phone calls. This was a step up from the Chapeltown Exclusion Project, one step closer to normality, so I agreed to behave myself. They assured me that they would either get him back into mainstream education, or train him up to do some menial job in the future. He was due to start in the new school year. His reading and writing were already much improved, I'd given him a good background education verbally as best I could, and hopefully we were moving in the right direction. Slowly but surely we were reintegrating with society.

Obviously, the rest of the crew had not fared quite so well. I felt a real sense of guilt at this, constantly asking myself if I could have done more, but I was only one man and I could only do so much. I dreamed of winning the lottery and opening a Safe House in the country, with a budget and staff and suchlike. I would call it The Margaret Thatcher Memorial Home for Sardonic Children. There, I would teach kids about consciousness and enlightenment, about Bokono and the High Lord Zombulglast, about the coming of the World Teacher and the new age, and about the enemy, the Great Satan, the Chief Insect Lord and his BMX-riding minions, the Babylonians and the evil capitalists who were destroying the world. I would teach kids the difference between right and wrong and I would teach them to fight their corner. No more than that. I didn't know it at the time but a man called Osama bin Laden was having similar ideas in another part of the world. Furthermore, he had the money to go out and do it. Unfortunately, he didn't share my non-violent approach.

Meanwhile Urban was my main concern. 'What's that say?' I asked, pointing, as we walked home from the dentist's.

'Bus stop,' he said confidently. '4, 4C, 49, 50 and 88.'

'Correct,' I said. 'And that?'

'No parking.'

'Yep. That?'

'Benson and . . .'

'Hedges,' I said. 'Soft g. A g can be hard or soft. A soft g is more like a j. Hedges. See?'

'Hedges,' he said.

'Hedges,' I confirmed. 'That's what killed my mother, by the way – Benson and Hedges and barley wine. Leave them both well alone, Urban. That's my advice.'

'You were lucky,' he said. 'Smack's killing mine. Come on.'

A CCTV camera on a pole followed our progress as we cut through the Kremlin car park. 'I hate this building,' I complained. 'It's too vast, too massive, too oppressive. The fucking Ministry of Truth.'

I had 1984 on video, so he knew what I meant. 'Double-plus bad,' he agreed.

There was a gigantic golden architectural feature stuck on top of the building like a sore thumb. 'One day, when I win the lottery, I'm gunner hire a big crane and nick that fucking pile of shit off the top of there and take it away on a big lorry. Then I'll dismantle the crane before anyone gets up in the morning and everyone will wonder where the ugliness has gone.'

'Good idea,' he said, 'I like it, but I wish that fucking camera wouldn't keep following us everywhere.'

'Get used to it,' I said. 'Big Brother is watching you.'

A slim concrete footbridge arched over the Inner Ring Road into Lincoln Green. Urban and I stood at the highest point and watched the traffic roll by. 'What's that say?' I asked, pointing to the back of a forty-tonne lorry that had just rumbled underneath.

'Don't know,' he said. 'I can't quite . . .'

' "Musschenbröek, Jacobsen and Grünewald, International Haulage Contractors, Rotterdam, Copenhagen and Stockholm." Fucking hell, Urban. That's an easy one. You're letting me down here, boy. I don't think you're really trying.'

Playfully, he punched me in the arm. 'Shut up, knobhead.'

I grabbed him round the neck and knuckled the top of his head in response.

'Gerroff me, you silly fat bastard,' he cried, wrestling himself free and running off down the bridge on to our side of the tracks. 'Come on, Chop! We haven't got all day.'

'We have,' I said, following. 'That's exactly what we have got. We're the leisured classes, don't you know?'

On the other side of the bridge we ran into a camera crew filming the old rec, which sloped down the hill to the Duke of Mabgate pub at the bottom, a real-ale pub, one of my favourite drinking haunts. There were half a dozen people in the crew and about a dozen spectators looking on. Urban recognised old George, who lived in our flats, and asked what was happening.

'They're filming,' he said.

'Filming what?'

'Haven't got the foggiest,' old George replied.

A blonde woman seemed to be in charge of proceedings. She had a clipboard, so she must have been important. 'Ask her,' I said.

Urban tapped her arm. 'What's going on, love? This is our patch.'

She smiled sweetly. 'We're making a programme for the

BBC.' She spoke as though she had a reproduction of the Elgin Marbles in her mouth.

'What kind of programme?'

'It's for a series called *Forgotten Britain* with Fergal Keane.'

'Who?'

'Fergal Keane,' she said. 'He's the special correspondent for the BBC.'

'Is he?' Urban said.

'Yes,' she said.

'Oh,' he said. 'What's so special about him?'

Urban had never heard of him, but I'd read one of his books about the genocide in Rwanda. The BBC always sent him to the worst trouble spots in the world. Now here he was in Ashtrayland. I could hardly believe it. Maybe someone did give a shit after all. Maybe we weren't alone. Maybe they knew how bad things were. *Forgotten Britain*. A good title.

Pretty soon the cameraman had seen enough. The soundman hoisted his furry stick over his shoulder and the crew ambled down the narrow ginnel leading into the estate, the curious spectators following them at a respectful distance. If only they'd known they'd just missed their chance to speak to the World Teacher in his formative years.

Urban and I stayed put. We weren't followers. We went where we wanted to go. We parked our bums on the bench looking down across the rec and I got out my tobacco tin. 'Want one, Urban?'

'Please, Chop. What they want to film the rec for? There's nothing here.'

'There is,' I said, fluffing up the tobacco in my tin. 'Look at the rubbish everywhere.' There was the usual collection of wrappers, carrier-bags, cans, broken glass and cider bottles. 'That's the first impression you get when you walk into the estate. See that bloke down there walking his dog? He's at one with the universe. See the crows there picking at the ground?

They're eating worms. See the town-hall clock in the distance? That tells you what time it is. See the sky? It's very blue today. See the line of trees down the right-hand side there? That's where Angela Pearce's body was dumped. It shouldn't have happened, Urban. It's too bad and we all need to be ashamed of ourselves. That's probably what's brought them here. They probably want to find out why we've all turned into animals. There's all sorts of shit going on all over this rec, if you only look. A camera sometimes helps you see what's right in front of your eyes. Be like the camera, Urban. Don't judge.'

'You're very philosophical today, Chop.'

His vocabulary was improving nicely. 'And you're very eloquent, my lad. Have I ever told you that I'm very proud of you, Urban? Look at you, reading signs and using big words. You've overcome impossible odds and you constantly try to better yourself. That's all anyone can do.'

'I couldn't have done owt without you, Chop.'

We interlocked our little fingers and performed the secret Bokononist handshake. 'Come on,' I said. 'We're turning into a mutual-admiration society. Let's go pay our respects to Angela.'

We strolled down the hill into the cover of the trees. In the long grass, we found a small white wooden cross sticking out of the ground at an obscure angle. A rectangle of disturbed earth was clearly visible. Three gorgeous bunches of flowers wrapped in Cellophane and numerous individual flowers had been left by the grave. Angela's body had been taken away, but this unhappy, shaded spot would for ever remain a shrine to we Ashtraylanders.

Urban and I stood together by the grave, silent, embarrassed to be human beings.

'Well, Urban,' I said, my innate cynicism perhaps showing through, 'we started out in a sewer, now here we are by a shallow grave. What do you make of that?'

He knew a rhetorical question when he heard one. 'Remember Lady Di's funeral?' he said. 'The sea of flowers?'

I nodded. 'Quite a contrast, isn't it?'

'Yep.'

He picked up a handwritten card and examined it minutely.

'What's it say?' I enquired.

'It says, "Love you all . . . ways from Kim."'

'Nice,' I said.

Urban removed his gold cross and chain and laid it on the grave. 'All right by you, Chop?' It was an heirloom from my nan. I'd given it to him on his fourteenth birthday. It was all right by me. The next person to stroll past would take it, but it didn't seem to matter. Material possessions no longer had any meaning for us and there was little else to be done, given the circumstances of the situation.

Leaving Angela to rest in peace, we headed back into the estate. We walked in silence a while, past the endless blocks of flats, the rent office, the Youth Base and the Health For All project to the Lincoln Green shops. The film crew was already busy in the post office.

'Want to go see Trudi and Hope?' I asked. Trudi had been given one of the ramshackle old maisonettes over the road from the shops. Hope, her daughter, father uncertain, already six weeks old, was a new addition to the Shed Crew. Indeed, Trudi had put 'S. Crew' down as the father on the birth certificate, as any one of the boys might have been responsible for her conception.

'Are you listening to me, Urban?' I said. 'Do you want to go see Trudi and Hope?' He wasn't listening: he seemed distracted, in a world of his own. 'Hello?'

He stopped walking, bit his lower lip and looked me in the eye. Reticently, he said, 'Come and sit over here, Chop. There's something I've been meaning to have a word with you about. Kind of . . . man to man.'

'Here it comes,' I said.

The shops formed a U-shape off Lincoln Green Road. Built in the sixties, they were becoming increasingly dishevelled. At one time, not so long back, there were benches and trees in the square, but they'd all been taken away: the benches because drunks and rowdy kids sat on them, the trees to improve the view for the CCTV cameras. We sat on the wall of the flowerbed, which had once contained flowers but was now bare earth.

'Teezer's pregnant, Chop. She's carrying my daughter.'

The camera crew came out of the post office and entered the St Mary's Church Centre. I hoped they'd pick up on the fact that we didn't have a Church of England church on the patch. The last one was pulled down in the seventies. A shop giving benefits advice and free cups of tea wasn't quite the same thing. No one was interested in dogma any more, but a man needed somewhere to meditate and think things through. It might also be argued that some people on the estate lacked moral guidance.

'I had a sneaky feeling you were going to say something like that, Urban. I must be getting telepathic in my old age. How do you know it's a girl?'

'Teez went for a scan last week.'

'Why didn't you tell me at the time?'

'Thought you'd go mad,' he said. 'Thought I'd best wait for the right moment. We'd like you to be kind of honorary granddad, if you're willing. You've been like a dad to me and, well, you know . . . it's gunner be hard.'

I didn't know whether to laugh or cry. What difference would it make either way? It wouldn't change anything. Trudi had one, Natasha had one on the way, now Teezer. They were like breeding machines. Babies were obviously the latest fashion accessory. The Spice Girls had a lot to answer for.

'Oh, well . . .' I said, ruffling my fingers through his hair. 'What the fuck? Congratulations, son! Well done! That's my boy! Course I'll be honorary granddad. It's an honour to be asked. If you were a bit older I'd take you for a pint. As it is, I'll just remind you that any muppet can have a baby, but being a father takes a real man. Remember that when you're the World Teacher, it's quite important.'

Loss of innocence was the price the Shed Crew paid for the Thatcher years. Modern childhood was short and sweet at the best of times; theirs had been almost non-existent. This, to my mind, was a crime against humanity. Thatcher would never be brought to justice, people like her never were, but she would be reviled throughout history by the likes of me. Our communities, the only strength we had, had been decimated. Now, Urban was to be a father at fourteen. What was in store for his kids, I wondered. The experience of each new generation seemed worse than that of the last. The spiral of deprivation, once spinning, was hard to stop. It gathered a momentum all of its own. I knew that it would continue apace and there was nothing I could do about it.

And yet there was hope. We'd survived. We'd invented bizarre new support networks that Social Services, the police and other government agencies couldn't even recognise. We were a community again – the underclass. I had nothing but respect for Urban Grimshaw and the Shed Crew. I'd never known anyone like them and I was proud to be their friend. Hardship and adversity had bred qualities and strengths in them that the straight-heads could barely imagine. They were strong and tough, resilient, hard, almost a new species. *Homo superior.*

This was what the Government – yes, New Labour, America's little Joeys – didn't seem to understand. We couldn't be controlled any more. We'd broken our conditioning. We could do anything we pleased and no one could stop us. If they wanted any sense out of us in the future, they would have to open a dialogue and treat us like equals.

'There's summat else,' Urban said. 'I'm getting a bit sick of all this World Teacher and King Arthur shit. My head's fucked up enough as it is with me mum and our Frank and everything without having to worry about being the World fucking Teacher as well. I just want to go to school, learn to read and write and lead a normal life. I can't do all your weird shit for you, Chop. I'm Urban Grimshaw. Nobody else.'

He was growing up, developing his own sense of identity, getting more and more into his own world, his own universe, becoming his own man. I couldn't believe how tall he was getting. He was almost as tall as me, which made me insanely proud of him for reasons I didn't quite understand. I'd grown too. I had been an alky, druggie, nihilist depressive when I met him. With his help I had my addictions under control, had replaced a desperate nihilist philosophy with a positive, optimistic and happy brand of Bokononism, while my depression had deepened and matured into a full-bodied, ripe and fruity melancholy. I attributed all these advances directly to him. 'But you've taught me so much, Urban. You could just as easily teach everybody else, you know. You really could change the world if you put your mind to it.'

'Maybe,' he said, 'but I don't want to. It's not my job. I just want to be normal, like everybody else. You don't, Chop. You like being different. Maybe you need the attention. Maybe you've got attention-deficiency syndrome, like me mum. Maybe your whole generation's got it.'

'See? You're teaching me about myself right now, as we speak. You're a natural. You can't just pack the job in. I'll need a month's notice, at least.'

'Okay,' he said. 'This is me giving my notice. I quit. I've had it. It's a shit job in any case. You don't even get the national minimum wage. I liked it better as a removal man.'

I was just about to say, 'Look! You're still doing it! You can't help yourself!' when someone beeped a car horn at us. I looked up to see a little red Metro pull up beside the flower-bed. Sam was driving, his head barely above the steering-wheel, with Pixie in the passenger seat.

Sam wound down the window. 'Yow! Urbie! Mr Chop! What's happening? Just been up the penthouse, but no one's in.'

'That's cos we're down here, Sam,' Urban said. 'I've been to the dentist's. I've got to wear a brace.'

I slapped Urban on the back. 'Come on. I've got an idea.' I would allow myself a small self-indulgence before settling down to become a completely boring straight-head for the rest of my life. 'If you're seriously quitting, we'll have to get rid of Excalibur. That will make you normal again. Are you sure it's what you want?'

'Definitely.'

'You two,' I said to Sam and Pixie, 'what are you doing for the next couple of days? Think your so-called parents will let you do a nash for a while?'

'We can do what we like,' Pixie assured me. 'No one cares about us.'

'Come on, then. Move over, Sam. I'm driving.' That way, there was less chance of killing anyone or being pulled by the Babylon. 'Just got to nip back to the flat, kids, then we're off for a little ride.'

We got to Waterhead on Lake Windermere as the sun was setting. I parked by the lake and we watched the sun go down over the Furness Fells, the mountains silhouetted against a blood-red sky, the waters aflame.

It all had to be done right. Everything had to be perfect. Once the sun had set, we scouted around a while, got the lie of the land and made our plans, then unpacked the car and began to walk. Houses clung to the hill as it rose up steeply from the road. We climbed a narrow, rocky footpath until the land flattened out, then over a stile built into a dry stone wall, crossed a field full of sheep and finally came to the tree line as the land began to rise once more. In the woods, we found a sleepy, shaded hollow, which seemed to have good voodoo, and there we made camp. We selected the location with care. We wanted to light a fire later on and not be seen. Pixie and I pitched the tents and laid out the sleeping-bags, while the boys collected wood and camouflaged the tents with twigs and branches. Finally, we smeared mud on our faces and we were ready for action.

It was a quarter to midnight as we returned to the lake. A thick mist rolled across the surface of the water like dry ice. There was no moon. We had only the stars to guide us. We wore gloves and balaclavas. We were fully equipped and determined. Urban carried Excalibur, I carried a pair of bolt-croppers, Sam carried a screwdriver, Pixie carried a gallon of petrol, a rag and a box of matches. None of us spoke. We all knew what we had to do.

Sam and Pixie jumped into the car. Sam started it with the screwdriver and drove it to a slight rise a hundred yards up the road. Pixie emptied the petrol over the seats, lit the rag and threw it into the vehicle. There was a *whoosh* and a *voom*, the quayside lit up and the two young friends came running back towards us as fast as their legs would carry them. Urban and I, meanwhile, were arranging the getaway. A line of rowing-boats floated and bobbed against the side of the quay, prevented from floating away by a long chain that held them all together and bound them to the shore. Urban held the chain, while I smoothly snipped the padlock with the bolt-croppers. We were planting the oars in the rowlocks as Sam and Pixie jumped aboard, then we rowed out towards the middle of the lake as fast as we could.

The blazing car was our beacon, our message to the world, but even before we got to the middle of the lake a fire engine arrived from Ambleside, blue lights flashing and siren blaring. We were safe, though. It was pitch black on the water. We could see them, but they couldn't see us. 'Quick, Urban!' I cried. 'Throw Excalibur into the lake while the flame still burns.'

Urban stood up, causing the ship to wobble dangerously in the water. Sam and Pixie steadied him as he sent Excalibur spinning high into the air. I felt a strange sense of longing and heartbreak as I watched the noble sword disappear into the mist.

We rode home on four tasty mountain bikes provided by Bokono. On our previous trips, Urban and I had plotted a safe route from Ambleside to Dent, high in the Yorkshire Dales, which had the highest railway station in Britain. From there we usually took the train back to Leeds in style and comfort. Dent was on the old Settle to Carlisle route, so trains were infrequent and we faced a four-hour wait. The view was impressive and didn't disappoint throughout that time. Dent station was on top of a high moor looking down over Dent village snuggling into its leafy dale. A beautiful and restful scene, a reminder of how things used to be and still were for the lucky few.

I must have looked wistful. 'What's up, Chop?' Urban enquired, coming over and kicking my foot. 'You look pissed off.'

Pixie and Sam had wandered down to the end of the platform and were rooting about in a large wooden toolbox. A distant clank confirmed that they had found something interesting. We were the only people on the tiny station so I turned a blind eye. They weren't hurting anyone. Urban and I were sitting on a bench looking down across the valley. 'I don't know,' I said. 'I was hoping you'd change the world for me, or that King Arthur was coming back, or that something dramatic was going to happen.'

'Chop, man, that's your job. You're the only one who can read and write properly. You have to tell it for us. You're the teacher, not me. Look what you've taught all us lot.'

'What? Like how to play chess and take drugs and get locked up and get pregnant and get dragged off to the nuthouse kicking and screaming? Stuff like that?'

'No. Like how to be friends and be decent with one another and chill out and not be fucking lunatics all the time. Stuff like that.'

'Maybe,' I said.

'You should get in touch with that Fergal Keane bloke and let him know what's really been going on round our patch. He won't find out at the post office.'

'Maybe I will,' I said. 'Maybe I'll write him a letter. Come to think of it, maybe I'll write him a whole fucking book.'

EPILOGUE
WHERE ARE THEY NOW?

Everything that happens happens as it should, and if you
observe carefully, you will find this to be so.
  Emperor Marcus Aurelius Antoninus
  Meditations

Urban is now twenty-one and has four children – one to Teezer, two to another girl, and one to yet another – but has had trouble holding down a steady relationship. He has worked in a slaughterhouse, as a demolition man and as a stagehand in a local theatre, but has had trouble holding down a steady job. He likes a spliff and a beer, but won't touch heroin. He has been to prison several times, mostly for twocking, and has recently moved into his own flat. His reading and writing still aren't great, but he has the basics. On the whole, he's happy and enjoying life. On his twenty-first, I asked him if he would like me to adopt him as my son and he said he would.

Tyson is gone, but not forgotten.

Sparky has been to prison several times. He's built like a brick shithouse and is finally exploiting his leadership potential. He works as a ganger on a building site, which means that he has a crew of lads under his direct control. He and Natasha had two children, then split up in their early twenties. He now lives in Rotherham with his new girlfriend and their three-year-old daughter. He likes a drink, but doesn't touch drugs. He's popular, well off, knows everyone in his area, but recently got into trouble again for enforcing Sarah's Law in his neighbourhood by beating up a convicted paedophile.

Skeeter and Frank are still friends and were recently padded up together in the same jail. Both have been to prison dozens of times and both still struggle with heroin. The pattern has been that they come out of prison clean and fresh, but then idleness and boredom send them back to the dealers. Both promise that they will be making renewed efforts any day now to get off the gear. Skeeter has a son he doesn't see.

Sam is currently serving time for aggravated vehicle-taking and violence.

Greta recently had most of the veins in her arm removed after a dig went wrong. She still moves from home to home and still shows signs of mental illness. She still has problems with alcohol, but has recently joined a methadone programme to tackle her heroin addiction. Her children have mostly forgiven her her faults and now generally feel sorry for her. In her own way, she tried to be a good mum, who was there for her kids in body if not in mind.

Pinky is a single mum, living on a council estate with her six-year-old son. She has had several relationships, but so far has not found Mr Right. She has never been to prison and has avoided the snare of addiction. She keeps fit and likes to go out at the weekend. She is attending college and has recently gained a vocational qualification in the sports and leisure industry.

Thieving Little Simpkins is also a single mum, living in Ilkley with her four-year-old son. She went to prison a couple of times before she gave birth. Since then, she has kept out of trouble and joined a drug rehabilitation programme. She is currently down to a hundred milligrams of methadone a day.

Trudi had two daughters. Both were taken from her by Social Services and given over for permanent adoption without her permission. She is now the only person in the world who hates social workers more than Greta and I do. She currently works as a prostitute and is addicted to heroin and crack cocaine. I have offered to do anything I can for her on numerous occasions, but she refuses all help. When I asked her why she wouldn't make any effort to help herself, she said simply, 'Because I've lost so much.'

Kara is in a steady relationship and has a steady job. Her boyfriend also has a steady job and that makes them DINKYs with money coming out of their ears. They have just taken out their first car loan and will soon be looking at buying a house. Kara does kick-boxing in her spare time to get the aggression out of her system.

Molly has lost touch with the rest of the crew, but when last heard of had two kids.

Pixie is back with her mum, who has now been released from the care of Her Majesty.

I'm a writer.